DEATH ROW

Concept
Glenn Hare

Art
Kathy Bergmann

Technical
Russ Yanda

Copyright © 1989 Glenn Hare Publications
A Division of Dyna Corporation
6300 Yarrow Drive
Carlsbad CA 92009

All rights reserved. No part of this book may be reproduced in any manner whatsoever without the express written consent of the publisher.

ISBN 0-9624857-0-5

WE NEED FURTHER DEATH ROW INFORMATION

We believe this publication to be the most complete single-source of information regarding death row inmates available. It is a useful reference for many law enforcement agencies, legal professionals, and journalists.

It is our intent to continue to provide a compendium of this important information on a regular basis in the future. We need your help.

Any writing, photographs, or original drawings regarding death row inmates will help us in our effort to chronicle capital punishment. Please write, or call, to give us details on any materials you may have that would be meaningful in future Death Row publications.

Death Row Editor
Hare Publications
6300 Yarrow Drive
Carlsbad, CA 92009
Phone: (619) 438-2511

DEATH ROW

Volume 1, No. 1   1989

Standards of Decency

Steven J. Casey

The dust and the gunsmoke had hardly cleared from Beijing's Tiananmen Square when the Chinese government went looking for the leaders of 1989's most dramatic pro-democracy rally.

Soldiers roamed through the city, alternately keeping and violating the peace. Pictures of the government's suspects were exhibited in public and seen on television news in the United States. One by one, we were told, several of them had been rounded up and taken to trial.

They were convicted and executed following expiration of China's statutory period permitting appeals. That period is three days.

Assuming the executions followed Chinese law, the condemned protesters had their hands tied behind their backs, were forced to kneel down by soldiers or police officers, and then were shot in the back of the head.

According to Amnesty International, an activist group foursquare for the world-wide abolition of capital punishment, China has executed more than 500 people between 1985 and 1988 for crimes including murder, robbery, rape, theft, embezzlement, drug trafficking, assault and battery, kidnapping and trafficking of women, showing pornographic material, using poison or explosives, and organizing reactionary societies. The trials and executions are often marked by public humiliation of the condemned, Amnesty International reports.

Iran, which showed the world the power of a fired-up literary critic when it ordered a holy hit on "Satanic Verses" author Salman Rushdie, has executed half again as many people as China. Capital offenses there include murder, drug trafficking, adultery, prostitution, suppressing the struggle of the people of Iran, and the ever popular "being at enmity with God."

Around the world, 100 countries impose the death penalty as punishment for such crimes as murder. Approximately 27 countries and territories still carry a death penalty statute on the books, but have not executed anyone for at least 10 years and are therefore regarded as having, as a practical matter, abolished the death penalty. Another 18 countries impose capital punishment only for exceptional crimes such as those found under military law or committed in wartime.

In those nations using a death penalty, the procedures of trial and appeal are as different as the cultures of the countries themselves; the range of offenses subjecting an offender to death are as different as the methods by which that death is administered. The days of crucifixions, of drawing and quartering, of boiling the condemned like lobsters are over. Governments around the world execute their criminals by hanging, shooting, beheading, stoning, electrocuting, gassing and injecting them. Some add flourishes to the execution, as Iran does when it flogs a condemned prisoner before hanging him.

The United States provides for every form of execution practiced internationally but two: beheading and stoning. Saudi Arabia provides only for beheading and stoning. The United States is the only nation in the world to permit execution by electrocution, gas or administration of a lethal injection.

Throughout recorded history, mankind has been generous in setting out offenses punishable by death, and imaginative in devising the form of the punishment. Religious crimes have often led to death: false prophesy, gathering sticks on the Sabbath, witchcraft. Iran today punishes membership in "atheistic and hypocritical mini-groups" by

Governments around the world execute their criminals by hanging, shooting, beheading, stoning, electrocuting, gassing and injecting them.

Some acts springing from personal predilection or weakness have been defined not only as crimes, but as capital crimes: adultery, incest, sodomy, prostitution, gluttony.

death. Some acts springing from personal predilection or weakness have been defined not only as crimes, but as capital crimes: adultery, incest, sodomy, prostitution, gluttony. Ordinary crimes which have led to death for offenders include murder, theft and the use and trafficking of illicit drugs. Albania today provides for execution of those citizens who try to leave.

In the United States, in those states permitting capital punishment, we are concerned with procedural regularity, with fairness, with an absence of cruelty. We have written rules protecting a panoply of cherished rights, governing the introduction of evidence, and providing for thorough—indeed, exhaustive—review of any death sentence. Still, by the lights of Amnesty International, the United States is one of 16 countries to impose the death penalty "contrary to minimum international standards," and thus is held by zealots to be no better than Equatorial Guinea, Turkey, Libya—and Iran.

Abolitionist ardor aside, the death penalty is an issue that continues to inflame public debate. But that fire has not burned so long in the American conscience as might be thought.

Although challenges to specific sentences of death were not uncommon, until well into the decade of the 1960s little argument reached the United States Supreme Court that capital punishment should be struck down in its entirety.

In the mid-1960s, that changed. Attorneys for the NAACP Legal Defense and Education Fund began a sustained challenge to the constitutionality of the death penalty. That effort was largely responsible for bringing before the Supreme Court for the first time a number of issues specific to the death penalty.

The court also had a doctrine before it that had emerged in 1958 in a case having nothing to do with the death penalty, but which would have a profound impact on the debate over the constitutionality of capital punishment and the court's role in deciding that issue. That case was Trop vs. Dulles, in which forfeiture of citizenship was held to violate the eighth amendment. In that case, Chief Justice Earl Warren wrote that the eighth amendment "draw[s] its meaning from

the evolving standards of decency that mark the progress of a maturing society." That doctrine was to be adopted as a benchmark by both sides in the court's debate over capital punishment, and arguments for and against abolition would be measured by that Warren standard.

With the Trop doctrine established, in 1963 Justice Arthur J. Goldberg embarked upon a highly unusual course, circulating to each justice a memorandum on six capital cases in which application for review had been made to—but not granted by—the high court. Dealing at length with cases not even set for argument was unusual enough, but what made the memorandum even more unusual was its subject: the constitutionality of the death penalty under the eighth amendment's prohibition of "cruel and unusual punishments." That was then an issue that had not yet begun to capture serious public or court attention. None of the six cases in question even raised that issue, making the Goldberg memo yet more remarkable.

Goldberg's memorandum discussed current standards of morality and ethics, coming as it did from the philosophical viewpoint that in order to decide whether a punishment is cruel and unusual, it is necessary to examine the standards of contemporary society.

The court denied review in all six cases, although Justices Goldberg, William O. Douglas and William J. Brennan, Jr. dissented in one of them, writing that the court should have taken it up to decide whether the death penalty was unconstitutional for a rapist "who has neither taken nor endangered human life." That dissent brought an echo of the Warren "evolving standards of decency" doctrine that has framed the eighth amendment debate ever since.

In 1968, one of the issues dealing squarely with the death penalty was before the court, in part as a consequence of the NAACP's legal battle. In that case, Witherspoon vs. Illinois, the Supreme Court held that "death qualifying" juries by excluding potential jurors with a bias against the death penalty was unconstitutional. That stricken practice had been used in almost every state then having a death penalty. With history's hindsight, Witherspoon can be seen as a visible manifestation of the high court's edging up on capital punishment, preparing to strike it down. (Witherspoon, however, was later modified.)

The steps toward abolition continued over the next three years, although they were at times tentative. In 1969, a case called Boykin vs. Alabama challenged the constitutionality of capital punishment for robbery, but the court decided the case on other grounds and did not have to face the eighth amendment issue. A case argued before the court on the same day as Boykin, a case called Maxwell vs. Bishop, did not offer the frontal challenge to the death penalty Boykin did, but wound up contributing more to the capital punishment debate in the court. Maxwell provided the court the opportunity to do some serious wrestling with two tough issues. First, the constitutionality of a unitary trial—one in which the question of guilt or innocence is determined at the same time as (if guilt is the verdict) the question of whether the defendant should be executed or imprisoned for life. The issue here was whether the defendant under this unitary scheme is placed in a catch-22, having to choose between remaining silent and limiting his evidence during trial (to protect his innocence, and not let his own testimony convict him) or presenting evidence to mitigate his punishment—evidence which would likely constitute an admission of guilt. Second, Maxwell dealt with whether letting a jury decide the question of life or death, in its absolute discretion and without specific standards to guide its deliberations, violated the accused's constitutional right to due process.

After intense private discussion and debate among the justices, debate which necessitated a rehearing of the case by the court and reportedly involved repetitive changes of mind on the part of at least one justice, those issues ultimately were left unaddressed in the short opinion which decided Maxwell on other grounds. What the case did though, was forcefully focus the court's attention on these issues. The following court term, 1970, that debate contributed to the opinion in McGautha vs. California, in which the court upheld unitary capital trials, and standardless jury sentencing.

McGautha, although a due process and not an eighth amendment case, nonetheless edged the court ever closer to taking on the underlying issue in all death penalty cases: Is capital punishment cruel and unusual, and therefore impermissible? That constitutional question has been described by Justice Brennan as "lurking" in McGautha, and in Maxwell and Witherspoon as well. It would not long lurk.

By the time McGautha was decided, the court had an impressive backlog of death penalty cases seeking review. Decisions on whether to hear those cases had been suspended, pending the McGautha resolution. In a private conference in June 1971, the justices discussed how to handle those backlogged cases which raised direct eighth amendment challenges to the death penalty. Justice Brennan would later write that he was dispirited because he alone believed that capital punishment was, under all circumstances, unconstitutional, and suggested the court simply deny review of all those cases. The rest of the court decided to take on the eighth amendment issue directly, however, and Brennan and Justice Potter Stewart were assigned to find what the court regards as "clean cases" to decide.

They found four, and all were set for argument on the same day in the fall term. It was mid-1971, and the court went into summer recess.

Before 1972, no state or federal court had stricken the death penalty as violative of the eighth amendment. The death penalty was about to fall. Temporarily.

It would fall first in California.

On February 18, 1972, the California Supreme Court invalidated the state's death penalty law, holding that it violated the cruel or unusual provision of the state constitution. The death penalty, the court said, offended contemporary standards of society and was no longer practiced by civilized societies.

The cast was all assembled and the stage was set for the U.S. Supreme Court to follow California's lead when, at 10:09 a.m. on Monday, January 17, 1972, argument commenced on the first of the four "clean" cases carefully selected by Justices Brennan and Stewart. The argument in that case, Aikens vs. California, framed much of the issue that would be heard repeatedly that day: Did the

The appellate process in death penalty cases only infrequently turns on any claim of innocence.

court have the right, indeed the responsibility, to review state legislative decisions to impose death, as the petitioner argued; or was the question not whether the death penalty struck the federal high court as moral or immoral, but whether there was a constitutional prohibition of what the state had sanctioned?

Argument by attorneys to justices of the United States Supreme Court is not at all like argument to a lay jury. Lawyers' arguments to trial juries can, and frequently do, continue for hours virtually uninterrupted. In the Supreme Court, each side is strictly limited to 30 minutes, and much of that is taken up with questions from individual justices, a colloquy which puts the justices' particular concerns in sharp focus as surely as it destroys the continuity of any legal sales pitch by counsel.

What emerged from that day's sometimes-disjointed arguments was a picture of a court grappling with concrete interpretation of the perhaps deliberately broad prohibition on "cruel and unusual punishments." That grappling continued well after the argument, ultimately resulting in each justice filing a separate opinion in the case that was to become the landmark, Furman vs. Georqia. The opinions totalled more than 50,000 words: 12,500 words for each contained in that grand phrase of illusive meaning, "cruel and unusual punishments."

Furman invalidated Georgia's capital punishment statute because the court found that, providing no standards, it imposed the death penalty "freakishly." The court's decision had the effect of striking down all state death penalty laws then in effect, although there was no commitment by the court that the death penalty, per se, was under all circumstances unconstitutional under the eighth amendment. Only Justices Brennan and Thurgood Marshall took that absolute a view. For the first time, the United States did not have a death penalty. Sentences of approximately 600 condemned prisoners around the country were commuted, and state legislatures began the scramble to enact death penalty statutes that would survive constitutional challenge. That scramble was made difficult by one case producing 10 separate opinions, one from the court reversing the penalty and one in concurrence or dissent from each justice. Lawmakers attempted to divine what would survive challenge before the Supreme Court, and some guessed wrong. California, for instance, guessed that Furman meant an acceptable death penalty law must provide for mandatory death sentences in certain cases, thus removing the objectionable unbridled discretion from the jury and judge.

Four years after Furman, the eighth amendment issue was again squarely before the Supreme Court, fittingly in another case from Georgia. The post-Furman Georgia capital punishment statute had become a model for several other states and, once again, the death penalty nationally rested upon the strength of a Georgia law.

That law required a bifurcated trial—a trial first on the issue of guilt and, if that was resolved with a guilty verdict, a separate proceeding on the issue of sentence. The Georgia law required also that if the state wished to impose death, the jury had to find one or more "aggravating circumstances," specifically set out in the law and proven to the jury by the prosecutor's evidence, and required as well that the jury consider mitigating evidence in making its life or death decision. The jury was permitted to consider only those aggravating factors set out in the statute, but was obliged to consider any mitigating evidence offered. That mitigating evidence might include the youth or lack of criminal sophistication of the defendant, his cooperation with the police, his emotional state at the time of the crime. It was this legislative scheme that the United States Supreme Court upheld in Greqq vs. Georqia. The court thereby sanctioned capital punishment as then constituted in Georgia and, more important from a national perspective, in the states which had followed Georgia's careful legislative lead. Since Furman, 37 state legislatures enacted capital punishment statutes, and several federal criminal statutes authorize imposition of a death penalty. Across the country, juries wrestling with the facts of their cases, with their emotions and with the rules of law continue to award death sentences—to the point that more than 2,000 condemned inmates are now on death row, crowding facilities and wreaking havoc upon state and federal appellate systems. With certain refinements, adding protections to the accused and more sharply defining permitted applicability of death penalty statutes, Gregg is still the law today.

In one significant development, the court in 1987 put to rest a "proportionality" argument that challenged the death penalty on the broad claim that some statistics show killers of white victims more likely to receive the death penalty than killers of blacks. That cut the ground out from a number of death row inmates—including whites who had killed white victims—whose cases were awaiting resolution of that issue.

Two of the most emotionally if not numerically significant of the court's post-Gregg refinements deal with whether execution of mentally retarded murderers is constitutionally proscribed, and the minimum age at which killers can be put to death. Those issues were decided in three cases in 1988 and 1989.

Justice Sandra Day O'Connor has emerged as a pivotal vote in a variety of cases, death penalty matters among them, to all appearances inheriting the swing position from retired Justice Lewis F. Powell. In a case decided in 1988, she cast the deciding vote when she refused to countenance the death penalty for an Oklahoma killer who was 15 when he committed his crime. The following year, she came down on the other side of the issue, upholding a death sentence for two killers from Missouri and Kentucky who were 16 and 17 when they committed grisly murders. Those 1989 eighth amendment decisions immediately affected 25 of the inmates on death rows around the country at the time of the rulings. The court's upholding the legality of teenage executions saddened death penalty opponents, who had hoped the court would at least limit Gregg by exempting minors.

The Missouri case involved Heath Wilkins, a lad with a history of abuse as a child and abuse of drugs, and with a criminal history dating back to age seven when he took up the practice of burglary. The Kentucky case centered on Kevin Stanford, whose entry into crime was delayed until age nine, and who had a lengthy criminal record as well as a long history as a drug abuser by age 17 when he raped and murdered a gas station attendant.

In July, 1985, Wilkins and Pat Stevens robbed Linda's Liquors and Deli in Avondale, Missouri, while two others waited for them nearby. Nancy Allen, a 26-year-old convenience store clerk, had the misfortune of working in the store at the time of the robbery, and spent her last shift in terror and death. Stevens grabbed her, and Wilkins stabbed her in the back and chest. The mother of two pleaded for mercy, her plea answered by Wilkins who stabbed her in the throat.

This pair of robbers received $450, cigarettes, wine, and peppermint schnapps.

In January, 1981, Kevin Stanford and two acquaintances decided to rob the service station next to Stanford's apartment. The major contribution of 15-year-old Troy Johnson to this criminal enterprise was to hide in the bathroom while Stanford and 18-year-old David Buchanan sexually abused and otherwise terrorized the sole attendant at the station, 20-year-old Baerbel Poore. Stanford then put his victim in a car, drove her out into the woods and gave her a last cigarette — before he shot the terrorized woman twice in the head. Buchanan and Johnson followed in another car.

Their take: $143 in cash, 300 cartons of cigarettes, two gallons of gasoline. And the life of a frightened young woman.

In writing to uphold the lethal injection execution of Wilkins and the electrocution of Stanford, Justice Antonin Scalia confronted the argument that since 18 is the minimum age most states set for determining majority and its adult rights and responsibilities, it is the minimum age at which executions are permissible. That doesn't follow, said Scalia.

"It is, to begin with, absurd to think that one must be mature enough to drive carefully, to drink responsibly or to vote intelligently in order to be mature enough to understand that murdering another human being is profoundly wrong, and to conform one's conduct to the most minimal of all civilized standards," he wrote.

Justice Brennan disagreed. "There are strong indications that the execution of juvenile offenders violates the contemporary stan-

The significance of the thumbscrew or the torture rack...is that they treat human beings as non-humans This...is the link between clear acts of barbarism and modern American capital punishment.

Below: This human head mounted on a power pole in an unidentified Chinese city is a warning to citizens to keep within the law.

Above: A public hanging of the last of Hadji Sami's gang, which tried to blow up the private train of Mustapha Kemal, President of Turkey.

Below: The death of a Thousand Cuts. This death is taken most seriously among the Chinese.

PHOTOS • THE BETTMANN ARCHIVE

Left: A black man is lynched for the assumed rape of a white woman.

Above: Engineer Luis Segura Vilchis facing the firing squad in Mexico City, for the plot against Obregon.

Below: Depiction of the guillotine, a form of capital punishment popular in 18th century France.

Right: The gas chamber in San Quentin Prison in California.

"It is, to begin with, absurd to think that one must be mature enough to drive carefully, to drink responsibly or to vote intelligently to understand that murdering another human being is profoundly wrong."

dards of decency," he wrote. But Brennan, it should be remembered, finds compelling indications that the execution of any offender "violates the contemporary standards of decency."

On the same June day of 1989 that the court found no constitutional impediment to the execution of 16- and 17-year-old killers, it also declined to find an absolute constitutional bar to the execution of mentally deficient murderers. That opinion revolved around the ordered execution of a 22-year-old Texan with a mental age of six. Justice O'Connor sided with the court's liberals— Justices Brennan, Marshall, John Paul Stevens and Harry Blackmun—voting to spare Johnny Paul Penry, at least temporarily. It did not necessarily remove the threat of death from an estimated 200 to 400 other mentally deficient death row residents around the country. Justice O'Connor expressed the view that Penry's jury should have been allowed to consider his retardation in determining the sentence, but she did not join the liberals' call for a blanket prohibition on executions of mentally retarded killers on eighth amendment grounds.

The mental retardation case was handed down almost 10 years after Penry, a recent parolee after serving time for an earlier rape, brutally raped and beat Pamela Carpenter, sister of former National Football League player Mark Moseley, then stabbed her in the chest with a pair of scissors. At home in Livingston, Texas, Carpenter was using the scissors that would become her murder weapon to make Halloween decorations when Penry began his assault. Although prosecutors said Penry killed his victim so she could not identify him, she managed to give police a description of her assailant before she died.

In the Texas courts, evidence showed that Penry has an IQ between 50 and 63, has organic brain damage, a mental age of 6-1/2 and the social maturity of a 9 year old. Although the court's decision spared Penry—at least until after another jury is able to consider the appropriate sentence, taking into account his retardation—it does make clear that there is no categorical prohibition against execution of retarded killers; no minimum number of IQ points a defendant must have in order to qualify for a death row apartment.

While many Americans understand that the status of capital punishment—or any other area of law—is not immutable, the entire appellate process by which cases are heard and decided and the law evolves is more than a little baffling. And that which is misunderstood is often mistrusted.

To most people, the notion of an "appeal" after a criminal conviction suggests a defendant desperately asserting his factual innocence to a higher court, asking that an awful injustice be overturned and an innocent man set free. Such is the stuff of fiction but rarely, if ever, of reality.

The appellate process in death penalty cases only infrequently turns on any claim of innocence. Often, it involves what the lay public calls "technicalities"—highly-refined legal debates that to many people seem so arcane as to be insultingly irrelevant. At times, the issues on appeal at least touch on innocence, involving questions of sufficiency of evidence, adequacy of identification, accuracy of judicial instructions.

The appellate process in these cases involves, first, "direct review," which is a defendant's statutory right to have his conviction reviewed by appellate courts to ensure that he was not convicted unlawfully or in violation of court rules. On direct appeal, what the court may consider is limited by the record at trial. Every defendant is legally entitled to one direct review of his conviction, including review by the U.S. Supreme Court if that court determines to take up the case.

Because a defendant is entitled to but one bite of the direct review apple, death penalty appeals involve, mostly, something called "collateral review."

Often, application for that review will reach well outside the trial record and ask the court to grant relief on any of a number of grounds, including for instance, incompetence of counsel, newly uncovered evidence or recent court decisions that have put the case in a different posture. Collateral review is discretionary with the courts, and many courts allow convicted defendants to keep coming back again and again, presenting a seemingly never-ending string of new allegations of "error" in the handling of their cases—"error" requiring appellate relief in the form of reversal or rehearing by a lower court.

It is this lack of finality to death penalty litigation, and the burden repetitive appeals put on the courts and their ability to dispense justice, that has caused frustration at the highest levels of the judiciary. This causes public frustration as well, especially in states where valid death penalty statutes are on the books but executions remain bottled up by decade-long legal conflict. Death penalty defense attorneys see that collateral review process not as a source of frustration, but as the single best avenue by which the client can avoid the executioner.

The appellate process begins after a bifurcated trial. In the first part of that trial, sometimes called the "guilt phase," the defendant is tried for a capital murder. Assuming the jury returns a verdict of guilt, the second portion, or "penalty phase" commences. Evidence is presented as to both aggravating and mitigating factors, and the jury deliberates the appropriate punishment in light of those factors and the crime itself.

Assuming the jury returns a verdict of death, the trial judge has an independent, constitutional duty to review that verdict. In some states, his discretion is only to let it stand or reduce a death verdict to life in prison, in other states the judge may actually order death when the jury has decided upon life. That review over, the defendant's direct appeal commences—going to the state's highest court, immediately or through an intermediary state appellate court. Once the state's high court approves the conviction and the sentence, the defendant may file a petition for certiorari—review—by the U.S. Supreme Court. That is where direct appeal rights end, for the U.S. Supreme Court need not take up the case of every litigant—even death penalty defendants—who seek its protection.

If certiorari is denied, as it usually is, the defendant can seek a writ of habeas corpus from his state courts. Usually, the state habeas action is undertaken a considerable period of time after the U.S. Supreme Court has declined to give the defendant relief. When that is denied, the condemned killer is back at the door of the U.S. Supreme Court, again seeking review of the state's adverse decision. If he doesn't get favorable action there, he's off to the federal district court with a request for habeas review of errors he says the state courts made on constitutional questions. If the district court denies his request, he can usually get a "certificate of probable cause" and request a stay of execution from the U.S. Court of Appeals in whatever circuit covers his state.

All this can take years, and the process is far from over. The defendant, barring relief from the Court of Appeals, makes another trip to the U.S. Supreme Court, requesting a stay of execution and Supreme Court review of the denial of his habeas relief. By the time that is denied, the case may have been reviewed eight times or more by state and federal courts. Is that the end? No.

One by one, additional constitutional "errors" are found by enterprising death penalty appellate lawyers. Each becomes the basis for a new round of appeals, the lawyer carefully coming up with reasons why this particular ground for claiming constitutional error could not have been brought forward earlier. It is not unusual for a death penalty case to reach the U.S. Supreme Court three different times.

On one of those trips, he may get lucky. An issue may strike the court as one requiring resolution. As we have seen, the issue in capital cases in recent years has been interpretation of the eighth amendment's prohibition of cruel or unusual punishments.

After 50,000 words in Furman and after a substantial opinion in Gregg, what could there possibly be left to say about those four words which continue to cause so much controversy? A great deal.

Before the question of whether the death penalty constitutes cruel or unusual punishment can be decided, there must first be agreement on what the court's role is in making that decision. Is it merely to look at history and try to fathom what the framers of the Constitution had in mind? Is it merely to inject its own notions of morality into a 200-year-old document? Is it merely to accede to the wishes of the states' legislatures?

In McGautha, Justice John Marshall Harlan took up that fundamental issue of the court's proper role. The job of the court, he said, is "not to impose on the States, ex cathedra, what might seem to us a better system for dealing with capital cases. Rather, it is to decide whether the Federal Constitution proscribes" the state conduct which the defendant seeks to have stricken. The test, according to this view, is not whether a majority of the justices think some other system is better, or more practical, or more humane. Rather, the test is strictly whether the justices find or fail to find that the system the state adopted is constitutionally infirm.

How has the court applied that approach to eighth amendment cases? By looking at both history and contemporary social values, trying to find those elusive "evolving standards of decency" described by Chief Justice Warren.

For some, the search need go no farther than colonial experience. We need not know exactly what the framers of the Constitution believed was cruel and unusual punishment, the argument goes, for we know full well that they believed capital punishment was not. We know that because it was a punishment common at the time of ratification of the Bill of Rights. In addition, it is clear the framers intended not to preclude capital punishment, for it is mentioned in the fifth amendment ("No person shall be held to answer for a capital, or otherwise infamous crime, unless on a presentment or indictment of a Grand Jury...") and 14th amendment ("...nor shall any State deprive any person of life, liberty, or property, without due process of law..."). Surely, the American conscience was not shocked by capital punishment early on. Even "the Great Emancipator," Abraham Lincoln, authorized 267 executions as president.

But does that dispose of it?

The court appears to have said no, on three grounds. First, there is a persuasive argument that the framers of the Constitution did not imbed capital punishment into their document by providing for its just administration, they merely insisted on just administration if capital punishment was to be imposed. That means we must look elsewhere to find a definition for "cruel and unusual." Second, if all we have to do is look to colonial experience to determine what punishments were then permitted and thus determine what escapes the "cruel and unusual" prohibition, we would have to conclude that we are, today, constitu-

tionally free to employ the stock, ear-cutting and sundry other chastisements most Americans would find too objectionable to be carried out in the name of the community. Third, the framers of the Constitution were careful draftsmen who knew how to be specific when they wanted to be, as noted by Justice Brennan in a 1986 address at Harvard University. That they gave us such general guidance as "cruel and unusual punishments" telegraphs their intent that this principle should remain inviolate while its application should grow and change with the society, reflecting contemporary mores, Brennan argued.

Brennan had company. "The standard of extreme cruelty is not merely descriptive, but necessarily embodies a moral judgment. The standard itself remains the same, but its applicability must change as the mores of society change," wrote Chief Justice Burger in his Furman dissent.

So where does the court look to find those mores of society and measure change? To the decisions of state legislatures? Surely not, at least not entirely. Surely great court decisions would not be limited to the course set by legislative schooners driven hard by the winds of politics and expediency. Brennan looks to the common thread of cruelty.

That common thread, he said in his Harvard lecture, is the barbaric infliction of great pain and the significance of state infliction of that pain. The significance of the thumbscrew or the torture rack, he said, is that they treat human beings as non-humans, they deny the basic human dignity of even the vilest of human beings, making sport of them, turning them into objects instead of people, degrading them in the name of punishment. This, he believes, is the link between clear acts of barbarism and modern American capital punishment, and is why the death penalty, particularly in today's kinder and gentler nation where contemporary standards of decency have evolved, is a constitutionally prohibited cruel and unusual punishment.

Not surprisingly, there are other views.

Noting that juries continue to impose death sentences, that substantial majorities of the American public favor capital punishment as appropriate in certain heinous crimes and that legislators continue to enact death penalty statutes, Justice Powell rebuts Brennan. Given that willingness to support, enact and use death penalty statutes, it is difficult under the Warren doctrine of evolving standards of decency to find that today's standards reject capital punishment as indecent, he points out.

And there, for now, the dispute sits. Other cases, other terms, will give the court other opportunities to squarely face the eighth amendment once again and take the pulse of American opinion to determine whether as a nation we have "evolved" to any new level of support for or repudiation of punishment that takes the life of an offender.

As the country and the courts head into the 1990s, the once-raucous argument over the deterrent value of capital punishment has been muted, and the chorus is now sounding over moral issues and costs. Both those matters will be taken up and the face of death penalty litigation perhaps forever altered as the result of the work of a committee appointed by Chief Justice William Rehnquist to study the federal habeas corpus process.

In the federal system, writ requests have become far more numerous, more repetitious, more broad. There seems to be no end to litigation in some capital cases. Representation of some condemned convicts is uncertain, and often applications for stay of execution are filed at the last minute. Some of these applications are of highly dubious merit.

The result is massive litigation, massive delay, and a process called "chaotic" by Chief Justice Rehnquist.

"A fundamental reason for the delay is our unique system of dual collateral review of criminal convictions," retired Justice Powell told the American Bar Association in an address in 1988. "Of course," he said, "the criminal law is primarily a state rather than a federal responsibility. The capital cases decided since Gregg have been in state courts.

"Since the enactment by Congress of the habeas corpus statute of February 5, 1867," he said, "we have had habeas review by federal courts where federal questions are presented. And by virtue of the federalization of death penalty jurisprudence since Furman, federal claims can be raised in virtually all death cases."

Originally limited in scope and in numbers, federal collateral review has become far broader, and more popular with lawyers than billable hours. By the mid-1950s, federal habeas review had come to fully assess the merits of federal constitutional claims. By 1955, federal district courts received 660 habeas corpus petitions from state prisoners, up from 127 in 1940 — but nothing compared to the astonishing 9,542 in 1987.

"I believe," Justice Powell told the ABA, "that most judges, federal and state, would agree that the dual post-conviction remedies are abused."

The federal process to a great extent duplicates collateral review by state courts, and is both time consuming and costly. Critics say it erodes public confidence in the criminal justice system because many death penalty appeals drag on so long as to make the system appear all but impotent, and the consequential enormous expense of such an inefficient system is itself advanced by capital punishment opponents as a reason for abolition of the death penalty. But such a tortured process is quite easy to understand, particularly when one assumes that the object of the strategy of the condemned inmate—and his lawyer—is to keep the executioner at bay for as long as possible.

It works. Chief Justice Rehnquist cites an average of eight years between the commission of a capital crime and the execution. Most of that time is attributed to post-conviction appeals, many of which are felt to be redundant. At least in some areas of the country, the statistics evidence yet more delay, and the future promises more of the same.

Two cases in San Diego, Calif., provide an example. The 1978 double-murder case of Robert Alton Harris, the subject of a profile in this book, produced a conviction and sentence of death nine months from the date of the crime. Harris, after 14 appeals and three unsuccessful trips to the U.S. Supreme Court, has been in the appellate process 10 years.

David Allan Lucas, convicted of murdering three women by slashing their throats, was—after lower-court preliminary hearings—in the trial court for four years before

We need not know exactly what the framers of the Constitution believed was cruel and unusual punishment, for we know full well that they believed capital punishment was not. We know this because it was a punishment common at the time of ratification of the Bill of Rights.

being convicted and sentenced to die. On August 2, 1989, each member of the jury twice said "yes" when asked by the court clerk in Superior Court Judge Laura Hammes' court "was this and is this your verdict?" Their voices were strong, their faces reflected the awesome responsibility they had been given. Lead prosecutor Dan Williams left the court and immediately called a woman who had survived a Lucas throat-slashing to tell her the news. But the case was not, and is not, over.

How long Lucas' appeal process will take, particularly given the truckload of transcripts accumulated during his four-year trial, is anyone's guess.

Surveys of death penalty costs, at best imprecise, nonetheless give an inkling of the enormous expense that is part of the death penalty package today. Death penalty cases are said to cost from $1 million to $15 million from arrest to final appeal. Costs of keeping inmates in prison for life pale next to the cost of supporting the death penalty trial and appeal infrastructure that has become a part of modern criminal adjudication.

Some advance these costs alone—moral issues aside—as reason enough to abandon the death penalty. Others maintain that the people responsible for endless litigation which drives the costs so high and who then argue that the death penalty is too expensive are akin to children who murder their parents and then ask for mercy because they are orphans.

The strategy of winning the death penalty battle not on the merits but by wearing down the state and courts, if indeed that is what we are seeing, has drawn fire from various levels of the federal judiciary. Buried under writ applications and last minute stay requests, some courts—notably the U.S. Court of Appeals for the Fifth Circuit—are lashing back at defense attorneys. Some courts—notably the Ninth Circuit—are not.

Judge Edith Jones of the Fifth Circuit has earned a reputation of being particularly hostile to death penalty defense lawyers she believes are playing procedural games simply to stall executions of people properly convicted, whose cases have been thoroughly reviewed, and for whom no legitimate new ground of appeal is open. Other judges of that circuit

also have complained about last minute appeals having become a standard defense tactic, and have maintained that justice requires sentences to be carried out in a fair—but not unreasonably slow—fashion.

When one attorney filed what Judge Jones regarded as a spurious last minute appeal, she responded in blunt fashion:

"The veil of civility that must protect us in society has been twice torn here. It was rent wantonly when Walter Bell robbed, raped and murdered Fred and Irene Chism. It has again been torn by Bell's counsel's conduct, inexcusable according to ordinary standards of law practice," the judge wrote.

By contrast, the Ninth Circuit has developed a reputation as the Will Rogers circuit of death penalty cases: It has never seen a habeas petition it doesn't like. That circuit, with a preponderance of liberal judges, covers Alaska, Arizona, California, Hawaii, Idaho, Montana, Nevada, Oregon, Washington, and Guam.

California's death row population of almost 250, and the Ninth Circuit's fondness for keeping collateral review going as long as a defense lawyer's word processor can churn out another petition, have placed enormous burdens on the court, to the detriment of its other work. It is said that judges from outside California are not pleased about having such a high percentage of their workload revolve around California capital cases. This disaffection has reportedly fueled talk of splitting the Ninth Circuit to permit court attention to problems of the West other than whether California will ever be allowed to execute murderers.

While death cases in the Ninth Circuit stall and judicial rhetoric in the Fifth Circuit accelerates, there is a spread of concern that justice delayed as long as death penalty cases are delayed is justice not only denied but mocked. In August 1988, Chief Justice Rehnquist appointed retired Justice Powell to lead the Special Committee on Habeas Corpus Review of Capital Sentences. That is a committee of the Judicial Conference of the United States, the policy-making arm of the federal judiciary. It has the power to make court rules, and to recommend legislation to the Congress. There is no estimate of when the committee might finish its work.

Even as the study began, it sent alarm bells ringing in the community of lawyers who engage in the very practices to be reviewed by Powell's committee. They see a threat to one effective method of shutting off executions, and see no friends of the habeas procedure on the committee. The Powell committee membership includes Chief Judge Charles Clark of the Fifth Circuit, Chief U.S. District Judge William Terrell Hodges of the Middle District of Florida, Chief Judge Paul Roney of the Eleventh Circuit, and acting Chief U.S. District Judge Barefoot Sanders of the Northern District of Texas.

Defense attorneys maintain that taking full advantage of the system of dual collateral review is using, not abusing, the law, and that a high percentage of death penalty habeas cases are successful in the appellate courts. That, they say, indicates a real need for continuing the process that critics find so phlegmatic.

Virtually all participants, however, agree on one thing. The legal representation given death row inmates embarked upon collateral appeals ranges from nonexistent to slightly better than woeful. States are not obliged to provide publicly-paid attorneys to represent convicted murderers after their direct appeals are over, and most do not. A shortage of volunteer lawyers has led to condemned inmates sitting on death row mere days away from execution before an attorney rushes in to take on the case and seek appellate relief. Many of those volunteer lawyers are fresh to the practice of law, underpaid, or both.

This situation, seen from the inmate's and criminal defense bar's perspective, means that the very people most in immediate peril in the legal system are the least represented. It means last minute appeals and prolonged litigation are foreordained. Seen from the perspective of those who want executions to go forward without undue delay, it means much the same thing. To those trying to streamline the appellate system and force more timely resolution of capital cases, the shortage of attorneys preparing death penalty appeals presents difficulty in attempting to devise and enforce rules which would keep appeals moving at an efficient rate.

The Powell commission should study that aspect of the problem, as well as Chief Justice Rehnquist's suggestion that the courts require all federal claims to be consolidated in one petition, filed within a reasonable period after the direct review process has ended, rather than in piecemeal fashion as is now the case.

The lawyers who fear that the Powell commission is "loaded" with opponents to the use, or repeated use, of the habeas corpus petition take some solace in another committee studying the same collateral review system. The ABA, known for its liberal positions in virtually all criminal law matters, has formed its own task force to study habeas corpus proceedings in capital cases. That committee is made up of federal and state trial judges, academics, criminal defense attorneys and prosecutors and court administrators.

Justice Powell, in his address to the ABA's annual meeting in Toronto, told the lawyers that endless resort to collateral review is a "system no other democracy deems necessary." On whether that system of protracted litigation is reformed or not turns the question of the viability of capital punishment in America.

"It is now evident that our unique system of multiple and dual collateral review is abused, particularly in capital cases," he said. "If capital punishment cannot be enforced even where innocence is not an issue, and the fairness of the trial is not seriously questioned, perhaps Congress and the state legislatures should take a serious look at whether retention of a punishment that is not being enforced is in the public interest."

Steven J. Casey is the special assistant to the county district attorney in San Diego, California. As a journalist with the San Diego Tribune *from 1970-79, Casey won, among other honors, a national first place award in the American Trial Lawyers' Association press contest, and an Award of Merit from the California Bar Association. His articles have appeared in newspapers throughout the country, as well as in regional magazines. Casey is currently working on a news media relations textbook for attorneys.*

Casey also wrote profiles on murderer Robert Harris, and trailside killer, David Carpenter, both of which appear elsewhere in this volume.

"This Man Has Expired"

Robert Johnson

Broadly speaking, the job of a death watch officer, as one man put it, "is to sit and keep the inmate calm for the last 24 hours–and get the man ready to go."

The death penalty has made a comeback in recent years. In the late '60s and through most of the '70s, such a thing seemed impossible. There was a moratorium on executions in the United States, backed by the authority of the Supreme Court.The hiatus lasted roughly a decade, coming on the heels of a gradual but persistent decline in the use of the death penalty in the western world, it appeared to some that executions would pass from the American scene (ef:-*Commonweal*, Jan. 15, 1988). Nothing could have been further from the truth.

Beginning with the execution of Gary Gilmore in 1977, more than 100 people have been put to death, most of them in the last few years. Approximately 2,200 prisoners are presently confined on death rows across the nation. The majority of these prisoners have lived under sentence of death for years; in some cases a decade or more, and are running out of legal appeals. It is fair to say that the death penalty is alive and well in America, and that executions will be with us through the foreseeable future.

Gilmore's execution marked the resurrection of the modern death penalty and was big news. It was commemorated in a best-selling tome by Norman Mailer, "The Executioner's Song." The title was deceptive. Like others who have examined the death penalty, Mailer told us a great deal about the condemned but very little about the executioners. Indeed, if we dwell on Mailer's account, the executioner's story is not only unsung; it is distorted.

Gilmore's execution was quite atypical . His was an instance of state-assisted suicide accompanied by an element of romance and played out against a backdrop of media fanfare. Unrepentant and unafraid, Gilmore refused to appeal his conviction. He dared the state of Utah to take his life, and the media repeated the challenge until it became a taunt that may well have goaded officials to action. A failed suicide pact with his lover staged only days before the execution (using drugs she delivered to him in a visit marked by unusual intimacy) added a hint of melodrama to the proceedings. Gilmore's final words. "Let's do it," seemed to invite the lethal hail of bullets from the firing squad. The nonchalant phrase, at once fatalistic and brazenly rebellious, became Gilmore's epitaph. It clinched his outlaw-hero image, and found its way onto T-shirts that confirmed his celebrity status.

Befitting a celebrity, Gilmore was treated with unusual leniency by prison officials during his confinement on death row. He was, for example, allowed to hold a party the night before his execution, during which he was free to eat, drink, and make merry with his guests until the early morning hours. This is not entirely unprecedented. Notorious English convicts of centuries past would throw farewell balls in prison on the eve of their executions. News accounts of such affairs sometimes included a commentary on the richness of the table and the quality of the dancing. For the record, Gilmore served Tang, Kool-Aid, cookies, and coffee, later supplemented by contraband pizza and an unidentified liquor. Periodically, he gobbled drugs obligingly provided by the prison pharmacy. He played a modest arrangement of rock-music albums but refrained from dancing.

Gilmore's execution, like his parting fete, was decidedly out of step with the tenor of the modern death penalty. Most condemned prisoners fight to save their lives, not to have them taken. They do not see their fate in romantic terms; there are no farewell parties nor are they given medication to ease their anxiety or win their compliance. The subjects of typical executions remain anonymous to the public and even to their keepers. They are very much alone at the end.

In contrast to Mailer's account, the focus of the research I have conducted is on the executioners themselves as they carry out typical executions. In my experience executioners—not unlike Mailer himself—can be quite voluble, and sometimes quite moving, in expressing themselves. I shall draw upon their words to describe the death work they carry out in our name.

Executioners are not a popular subject of social research, let alone conversation at the dinner table or cocktail party. We simply don't give the subject much thought. When we think of executioners at all, the imagery runs to individual men of disreputable, or at least questionable character who work stealthily behind the scenes to carry out their grim labors. We picture hooded men hiding in the shadow of the gallows, or anonymous figures lurking out of sight be-

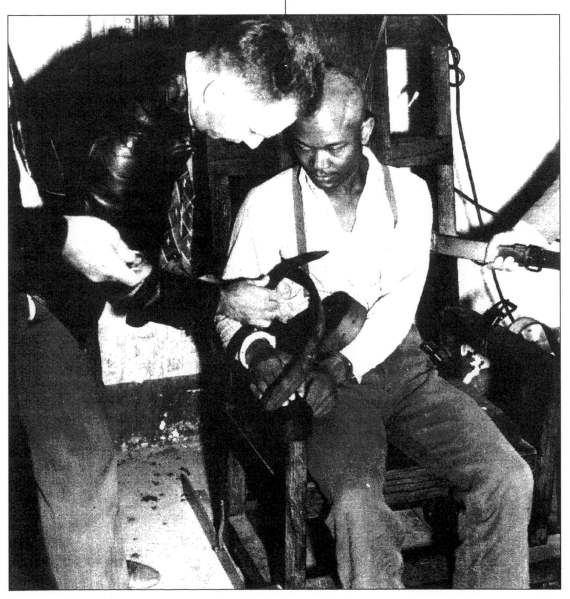

PHOTOS • AP/WIDE WORLD

Convicted wife-slayer, Willie Mae Bragg is strapped into a portable electric chair moments before he is put to death. The portable device was made necessary because Mississippi law requires that an offender be killed in the county where the crime was committed.

"It's a job. I don't take it personally. You know, I don't take it like I'm having a grudge against this person and this person has done something to me. I'm just carrying out a job, doing what I was asked to do..."

hind electric chairs, gas chambers, firing blinds, or, more recently, hospital gurneys. We wonder who would do such grisly work and how they sleep at night.

This image of the executioner as a sinister and often solitary character is misleading. To be sure, a few states hire free-lance executioners and traffic in macabre theatrics. Executioners may be picked up under cover of darkness and some may still wear black hoods. But today, executions are generally the work of a highly disciplined and efficient team of correctional officers.

Broadly speaking, the execution process as it is now practiced starts with the prisoner's confinement on death row, an oppressive prison within a prison where the condemned are housed, sometimes for years, awaiting execution. Death work gains momentum when an execution date draws near and the prisoner is moved to the death house, a short walk from the death chamber. Finally, the process culminates in the death watch, a 24-hour period that ends when the prisoner has been executed.

This final period, the death watch, is generally undertaken by correctional officers who work as a team and report directly to the prison warden. The warden or his representative, in turn, must by law preside over the execution. In many states, it is a member of the death watch or execution team, acting under the warden's authority, who in fact plays the formal role of executioner. Though this officer may technically work alone, his teammates view the execution as a shared responsibility. As one officer on the death watch told me in no uncertain terms: "We all take part in it; we all play 100 percent in it, too. That takes the load off this one individual who pulls the switch." The formal executioner concurred, "Everyone on the team can do it, and nobody will tell you I did it. I know my team." I found nothing in my research to dispute these claims.

The officers of these death watch teams are our modern executioners. As part of a larger study of the death work process, I studied one such group. This team comprised of nine seasoned officers of varying ranks had carried out five electrocutions at

the time I began my research. I interviewed each officer on the team after the fifth execution, then served as an official witness at a sixth electrocution. Later, I served as a behind-the-scenes observer during their seventh execution. The results of this phase of my research form the substance of this essay.

The death watch or execution team members refer to themselves, with evident pride, as simply "the team." This pride is shared by other correctional officials. The warden at the institution I was observing praised members of the team as solid citizens—in his words, country boys. These country boys, he assured me, could be counted on to do the job and do it well. As a fellow administrator put it, "an execution is something that needs to be done, and good people, dedicated people who believe in the American system should do it. And there's a certain amount of feeling, probably one to another, that they're part of that—that when they have to hang tough, they can do it, and they can do it right. And that it's just the right thing to do."

The official view is that an execution is a job that has to be done, and done right. The death penalty is, after all, the law of the land. In this context, the phrase "done right" means that an execution should be a proper, professional, dignified undertaking. In the words of a prison administrator, "We had to be sure that we did it properly, professionally, and that we gave as much dignity to the person as we possibly could in the process....If you've gotta do it, it might just as well be done the way it's supposed to be done—without any sensation."

In the language of the prison officials, "proper" refers to procedures that go off smoothly; "professional" means without personal feelings that intrude on the procedures in any way. The desire for executions that take place "without any sensations" no doubt refers to the absence of media sensationalism, particularly if there should be an embarrassing and undignified hitch in the procedures, for example, a prisoner who breaks down or becomes violent and must be forcibly placed in the electric chair as witnesses, some from the media, look on in horror. Still, I can't help but note that this may be a revealing slip of the tongue. For executions are indeed meant to go off without any human feeling, without any sensation. A profound absence of feeling would seem to capture the bureaucratic ideal embodied in the modern execution.

The view of executions held by the execution team members parallels that of correctional administrators, but is somewhat more restrained. The officers of the team are closer to the killing and dying, and are less apt to wax abstract or eloquent in describing the process. Listen to one man's observations: "It's a job. I don't take it personally. You know, I don't take it like I'm having a grudge against this person and this person has done something to me. I'm just carrying out a job, doing what I was asked to do....This man has been sentenced to death in the courts. This is the law and he broke this law, and he has to suffer the consequences. And one of the consequences is to put him to death."

I found that few members of the execution team support the death penalty outright or without reservation. Having seen executions close up, many of them have lingering doubts about the justice or wisdom of this sanction. As one officer put it: "I'm not sure the death penalty is the right way. I don't know if there is a right answer. So I look at it like this: if it's gotta be done, at least it can be done in a humane way if there is such a word for it....The only way it should be done, I feel, is the way we do it. It's done professionally. It's not no horseplaying. Everything is done by documentation. On time. By the book.

Arranging executions that occur "without any sensation" and that go "by the book" is no mean task, but it is a task that is undertaken in earnest by the execution team. The tone of the enterprise is set by the team leader, a man who takes a hard-boiled, nononsense approach to correctional work in general and death work in particular. "My style," he says, "is this: if it's a job to do, get it done. Do it and that's it." He seeks out kindred spirits, men who see killing condemned prisoners as a job—a dirty job one does reluctantly, perhaps, but above all a

job one carries out dispassionately and in the line of duty.

To make sure that line of duty is a straight and accurate one, the death watch team has been carefully drilled by the team leader in the mechanics of execution. The process has been broken down into simple, discrete tasks and practiced repeatedly. The team leader describes the division of labor in the following exchange: "The execution team is a nine-officer team and each one has certain things to do. When I would train you, maybe you'd buckle a belt, that might be all you'd have to do....And you'd be expected to do one thing and that's all you'd be expected to do. And if everybody does what they were taught, or what they were trained to do, at the end the man would be put in the chair and everything would be complete. It's all come together now.

"So it's broken down into very small steps...."

"Very small, yes. Each person has one thing to do."

"I see. What's the purpose of breaking it down into such small steps?"

"So people won't get confused. I've learned it's kind of a tense time. When you're executin' a person, killing a person—you call it killin', executin', whatever you want—the man dies anyway. I find the less you got on your mind, why, the better you'll carry it out. So it's just very simple things. And so far, you know, it's all come together, we haven't had any problems."

This division of labor allows each man on the execution team to become a specialist, a technician with a sense of pride in his work. Said one man: "My assignment is the leg piece. Right leg. I roll his pants leg up, place a piece [electrode] on his leg, strap his leg in....I've got all the moves down pat. We train from different posts; I can do any of them. But that's my main post."

The implication is not that the officers are incapable of performing multiple or complex tasks, but simply that it is more efficient to focus each officer's efforts on one easy task.

An essential part of the training is practice. Practice is meant to produce a confident group, capable of fast and accurate perfor-

Unrepentant and unafraid, Gary Gilmore refused to appeal his conviction. He dared the state of Utah to take his life and the media repeated the challenge until it became a taunt that may well have goaded officials to action.

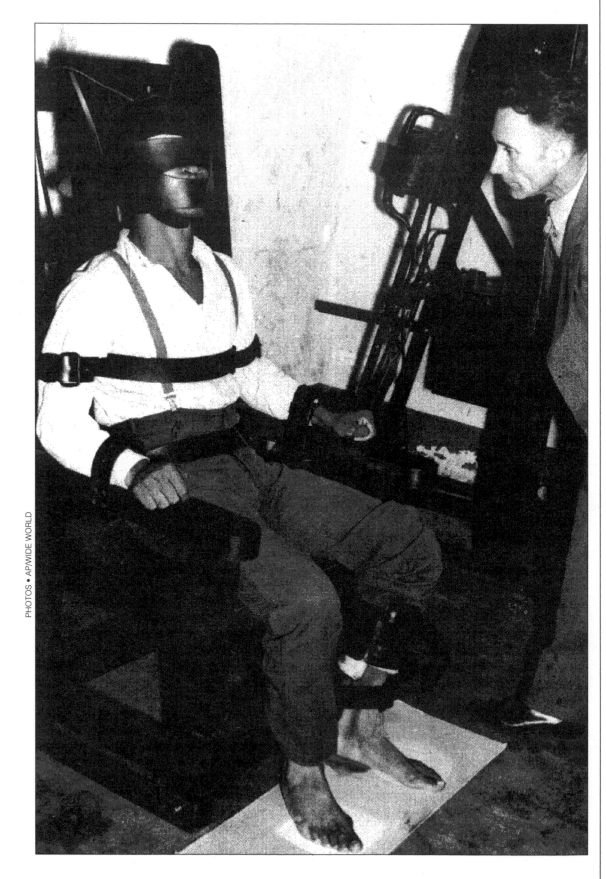

PHOTOS • AP/WIDE WORLD

After administering the deadly voltage, the executioner inspects the body. This was the first execution carried out in a portable electric chair.

mance under pressure. The rewards of practice are reaped in improved performance. Executions take place with increasing efficiency and eventually occur with precision.

"The first one was grisly," a team member confided to me. He explained that there was a certain amount of fumbling, which made the execution seem interminable. There were technical problems as well: The generator was set too high so the body was badly burned. But that is the past, the officer assured me. "The ones now, we know what we're doing. It's just like clockwork."

The death-watch team is deployed during the last 24 hours before an execution. In the state under study, the death watch starts at 11 p.m. the night before the execution and ends at 11 p.m. the next night when the execution takes place. At least two officers would be with the prisoner at any given time during that period. Their objective is to keep the prisoner alive and "on schedule." That is, to move him through a series of critical and cumulatively demoralizing junctures that begin with his last meal and end with his last walk. When the time comes, they must deliver the prisoner up for execution as quickly and unobtrusively as possible.

Broadly speaking, the job of the death watch officer, as one man put it, "is to sit and keep the inmate calm for the last 24 hours—and get the man ready to go." Keeping a condemned prisoner calm means, in part, serving his immediate needs. It seems paradoxical to think of the death watch officers as providing services to the condemned, but the logistics of the job make service a central obligation of the officers. Here's how one officer made this point: "Well you can't help but be involved with many of the things that he's involved with. Because if he wants to make a call to his family, well you'll have to dial the number and you keep records of whatever calls he makes. If he wants a cigarette, well he's not allowed to keep matches so you light it for him. You've got to pour his coffee, too. So you're aware of what he's doing. It's not like you can just ignore him. You've gotta just be with him whether he wants it or not, and cater to his needs.

Officers cater to the condemned because contented inmates are easier to keep under control. To a man, the officers say this is so. But one can never trust even a condemned prisoner

The death watch officers see condemned prisoners as men with explosive personalities. "You don't know what, what a man's gonna do," noted one officer. "He's liable to snap, he's liable to pass out. We watch him all the time to prevent him from committing suicide. You've got to be ready—he's liable to do anything." The prisoner is never out of at least one officer's sight. Thus surveillance is constant, and control, for all intents and purposes, is total.

Relations between the officers and their charges during the death watch can be quite intense. Watching and being watched are central to this enterprise and these are always engaging activities, particularly when the stakes are life and death. These relations are, nevertheless, utterly impersonal; there are no grudges but neither is there compassion or fellow-feeling. Officers are civil but cool; they keep an emotional distance from the men they're about to kill. To do otherwise, they maintain, would make it harder to execute condemned prisoners. The attitude of the officers is that the prisoners arrive as strangers and are easier to kill if they stay that way.

During the last five or six hours, two specific team officers are assigned to guard the prisoner. Unlike their more taciturn and aloof colleagues on earlier shifts, these officers make a conscious effort to talk with the prisoner. In one officer's words, "We just keep them right there and keep talking to them—about anything except the chair." The point of these conversations is not merely to pass time. It is to keep tabs on the prisoner's state of mind and to steer him away from subjects that might depress, anger or otherwise upset him. Sociability, in other words, quite explicitly serves as a source of social control. Relationships, such as they are, serve purely manipulative ends. This is impersonality at it's worst, masquerading as concern for the strangers one hopes to execute with as little trouble as possible.

The prisoner walked quickly and silently toward the chair, an escort of officers in tow. His eyes were turned downward, his expression a bit glazed.

Generally speaking, as the execution moves closer, the mood becomes more somber and subdued. There is a last meal. Prisoners can order pretty much what they want, but most eat little or nothing at all. At this point the prisoners may steadfastly maintain that their executions will be stayed. Such bravado is belied by their loss of appetite. "You can see them going down," said one officer. "Food is the last thing they got on their minds."

Next the prisoners must box their meager worldly goods. These are inventoried by the staff, recorded on a one-page checklist form, and marked for disposition to family or friends. Prisoners are visibly saddened, even moved to tears by this procedure, which at once summarizes their lives and highlights the imminence of death. At this point, said one of the officers, "I really get into him; I watch him real close." The execution schedule, the officer pointed out, is "picking up momentum, and we don't want to lose control of the situation."

This momentum is not lost on the condemned prisoner. Critical milestones have been passed. The prisoner moves in a limbo existence devoid of food or possessions; he has seen the last of such things unless he receives a stay of execution and rejoins the living. His identity is expropriated as well. The critical juncture in this regard is the shaving of the man's head (including facial hair) and right leg. Hair is shaved to facilitate the electrocution; it reduces physical resistance to electricity and minimizes singeing and burning. But the process has obvious psychological significance as well, adding greatly to the momentum of the execution.

The shaving procedure is quite public and intimidating. The condemned man is taken from his cell and seated in the middle of the tier. His hands and feet are cuffed, and he is dressed only in undershorts. The entire death watch team is assembled around him. They stay at a discrete distance, but it is obvious that they are there to maintain control should he resist in any way or make any untoward move. As a rule, the man is overwhelmed. As one officer told me in blunt terms, "Come 8 o'clock, we've got a dead man. 8 o'clock is when we shave the man. We take his identity; it goes with the hair." This taking of identity is indeed a collective process—the team makes a forceful "we," the prisoner their helpless object. The staff is confident that the prisoner's capacity to resist is now compromised. What is left of the man erodes gradually and, according to the officers, perceptibly over the remaining three hours before the execution.

After the prisoner has been shaved, he is then made to shower and don a fresh set of clothes for the execution. The clothes are unremarkable in appearance, except that velcro replaces buttons and zippers to reduce the chance of burning the body. The main significance of the clothes is symbolic: They mark the prisoner as a man who is ready for execution. Now physically "prepped," to quote one team member, the prisoner is placed in an empty tomb-like cell, the death cell. All that is left is the wait. During this fateful period, the prisoner is more like an object "without any sensation" than like a flesh-and-blood person on the threshold of death.

For condemned prisoners, like Gilmore, who come to accept and even to relish their impending deaths, a genuine calm seems to prevail. It is as if they can transcend the dehumanizing forces at work around them and go to their deaths in peace. For most condemned prisoners, however, numb resignation rather than peaceful acceptance is the norm. By the accounts of the death watch officers, these more typical prisoners are beaten men. Listen to the officers' accounts: "A lot of 'em die in their minds before they go to that chair. I've never known of one or heard of one putting up a fight. By the time they walk to the chair, they've completely faced it. Such a reality most people can't understand. Cause they don't fight it. They don't seem to have anything to say. It's just something like "Get it over with." They may be numb, sort of in a trance.

"They go through stages. And at this stage, they're real humble. Humblest bunch of people I ever seen. Most all of 'em is real, real weak. Most of the time you'd only need one or two people to carry out an execution, as weak and as humble as they are."

These men seem barely human and alive to their keepers. They wait meekly to be escorted to their deaths. The people who come for them are the warden and the remainder of the death watch team, flanked by high-ranking correctional officials. The warden reads the court order, known popularly as a death warrant. This is, as one officer said, "the real deal," and nobody misses its significance. The condemned prisoners then go to their deaths compliantly, captives of the inexorable, irresistible momentum of the situation. As one officer put it, "There's no struggle...They just walk right on in there." So too, do the staff, "just walk right on in there," following a routine they have come to know well. Both the condemned and the executioners, it would seem, find a relief of sorts in mindless mechanical conformity to the modern execution drill.

As the team and administrators prepare to commence the goods fight, as they might say, another group, the official witness, are also preparing themselves for their role in the execution. Numbering between six and twelve for any given execution, the official witnesses are disinterested citizens in good standing drawn from a cross section of the state's population. If you will, they are every good or decent person, called upon to represent the community and use their good offices to testify to the propriety of the execution. I served as an official witness at the execution of an inmate.

At 8 p.m., about the time the prisoner is shaved in preparation for the execution, the witnesses are assembled. Eleven in all, we included three newspaper reporters; a state trooper, two police officers, a magistrate, a businessman, and myself. We were picked up in the parking lot behind the main office of the corrections department. There was nothing unusual or even memorable about any of this. Gothic touches were notable by their absence. It wasn't a dark and stormy night; no one emerged from the shadows to lead us to the prison gates.

Mundane considerations prevailed. The van sent for us was missing a few rows of seats so there wasn't enough room for all of us. Obliging prison officials volunteered their cars. Our rather ordinary cavalcade reached the prison but only after getting lost. Once within the prison's walls, we were sequestered for some two hours in a bare and almost shabby administrative conference room. A public information officer was assigned to accompany us and answer our questions. We grilled this official about the prisoner and the execution procedure he would undergo shortly, but little information was to be had. The man confessed ignorance on the most basic points. Disgruntled at this and increasingly anxious, we made small talk and drank coffee.

At 10:40 p.m., roughly two and a half hours after we were assembled, and only 20 minutes before the execution was scheduled to occur, the witnesses were taken to the basement of the prison's administrative building, frisked, then led down an alleyway that ran along the exterior of the building. We entered a neighboring cell block and were admitted to a vestibule adjoining the death chamber. Each of us signed a log and was then led off to the witness area. To our left, around a corner some 30 feet away, the prisoner sat in the condemned cell. He couldn't see us, but I'm quite certain he could hear us. It occurred to me that our arrival was a fateful reminder for the prisoner. The next group would be led by the warden, and it would be coming for him.

We entered the witness area, a room within the death chamber, and took our seats. A picture window covering the front wall of the witness room offered a clear view of the electric chair, which was about 12 feet away from us and well illuminated. The chair, a large, high-back solid oak structure with imposing black straps, dominated the death chamber. Behind it, on the back wall, was an open panel full of coils and lights. Peeling paint hung from the ceiling and walls; water stains from persistent leaks were everywhere in evidence.

Two officers, one a hulking figure weighing some 400 pounds, stood alongside the electric chair. Each had his hands crossed at the lap and wore a forbidding, blank expression on his face. The witnesses gazed at them and the chair, most of us scribbling notes furiously. We did this, I suppose, as much to record the experience as to have a distraction from the growing tension. A correctional officer entered

The physician listened for a heartbeat. Hearing none, he turned to the warden and said, "This man has expired." The warden, speaking to the director, solmnly intoned: "Mr. Director, the court order has been fulfilled."

the witness room and announced that a trial run of the machinery would be undertaken. Seconds later, lights flashed on the control panel behind the chair indicating that the chair was in working order. A white curtain, opened for the test, separated the chair and the witness area. After the test, the curtain was drawn. More tests were performed behind the curtain. Afterwards, the curtain was re-opened, and would be left open until the execution was over. Then it would be closed to allow the officers to remove the body.

A handful of high-level correctional officials were present in the death chamber, standing just outside the witness area. There were two regional administrators, the director of the Department of Corrections, and the prison warden. The prisoner's chaplain and lawyer were also present. Other than the chaplain's black religious garb, subdued grey pinstripes and bland correctional uniforms prevailed. All parties were quite solemn.

At 10:58 the prisoner entered the death chamber. He was, I knew from my research, a man with a checkered, tragic past. He had been grossly abused as a child, and went on to become grossly abusive of others. I was told he could not describe his life, from childhood on, without talking about confrontations in defense of a precarious sense of self—at home, in school, on the streets, in the prison yard. Belittled by life and choking with rage, he was hungry to be noticed. Paradoxically, he had found his moment in the spotlight, but it was a dim and unflattering light cast before a small and unappreciative audience. "He'd pose for cameras in the chair—for the attention," his counselor had told me earlier in the day. But the truth was that the prisoner wasn't smiling, and there were no cameras.

The prisoner walked quickly and silently toward the chair, an escort of officers in tow. His eyes were turned downward, his expression a bit glazed. Like many before him, the prisoner had threatened to stage a last stand. But that was lifetimes ago, on death row. In the death house, he joined the humble bunch and kept to the executioner's schedule. He appeared to have given up on life before he died in the chair.

En route to the chair, the prisoner stumbled slightly, as if the momentum of the event had overtaken him. Were he not held securely by

two officers, one at each elbow, he might have fallen. Were the routine to be broken in this or indeed any other way, the officers believe, the prisoner might faint or panic or become violent, and have to be forcibly placed in the chair. Perhaps as a precaution, when the prisoner reached the chair he did not turn on his own but rather was turned, firmly but without malice, by the officers in his escort. These included the two men at his elbows, and four others who followed behind him. Once the prisoner was seated, again with help, the officers strapped him into the chair.

The execution team worked with machine precision. Like a disciplined swarm, they enveloped him. Arms, legs, stomach, chest, and head were secured in a matter of seconds. Electrodes were attached to the cap holding his head and to the strap holding his exposed right leg. A leather mask was placed over his face. The last officer mopped the prisoner's brow, then touched his hand in a gesture of farewell.

During the brief procession to the electric chair, the prisoner was attended by a chaplain. As the execution team worked feverishly to secure the condemned man's body, the chaplain, who appeared to be upset, leaned over him and placed his forehead in contact with the prisoner's, whispering urgently. The priest might have been praying, but I had the impression he was consoling the man, perhaps assuring him that a forgiving God awaited him in the next life. If he heard the chaplain, I doubt the man comprehended his message. He didn't seem comforted. Rather, he looked stricken and appeared to be in shock. Perhaps the priest's urgent ministrations betrayed his doubts that the prisoner could hold himself together. The chaplain then withdrew at the warden's request, allowing the officers to affix the death mask.

The strapped and masked figure sat before us, utterly alone, waiting to be killed. The cap and mask dominated his face. The cap was nothing more than a sponge encased in a leather shell with a metal piece at the top to accept an electrode. It looked decrepit and resembled a cheap, ill-fitting toupee. The mask, made entirely of leather, appeared soiled and worn. It had two parts. The bottom part covered the chin and mouth, the top the eyes and lower forehead. Only the nose was exposed. The effect of a rigidly restrained body, together with the bizarre cap and the protruding nose, was nothing short of grotesque. A faceless man breathed before us in a tragicomic trance, waiting for a blast of electricity that would extinguish his life. Endless seconds passed. His last act was to swallow nervously, pathetically, with his Adam's apple bobbing. I was struck by that simple movement then, and can't forget it even now. It told me, as nothing else did, that in the prisoner's restrained body, behind that mask, lurked a fellow human being who, at some level, however primitive, knew or sensed himself to be moments from death.

The condemned man sat perfectly still for what seemed an eternity but was in fact no more than 30 seconds. Finally the electricity hit him. His body stiffened spasmodically, though only briefly. A thin swirl of smoke trailed away from his head and then dissipated quickly. The body remained taut, with the right foot raised slightly at the heel, seemingly frozen there. A brief pause, then another minute of shock. When it was over, the body was flaccid and inert.

Three minutes passed while the officials let the body cool. (Immediately after the execution, I'm told, the body would be too hot to touch and would blister anyone who did). All eyes were riveted to the chair; I felt trapped in my witness seat, at once transfixed and yet eager for release. I can't recall any clear thoughts from that moment. One of the death watch officers later volunteered that he shared this experience of staring blankly at the execution scene. Had the prisoner's mind been mercifully blank before the end? I hoped so.

An officer walked up to the body, opened the shirt at chest level, then continued on to get the physician from an adjoining room. The physician listened for a heartbeat. Hearing none, he turned to the warden and said, "This man has expired." The warden, speaking to the director, solemnly intoned: "Mr. Director, the court order has been fulfilled." The curtain was then drawn and the witnesses filed out.

As the team prepared the body for the morgue, the witnesses were led to the front door of the prison. On the way, we passed a number of cell blocks. We could hear the normal sounds of prison life, including the occasional catcall and lewd comment hurled at uninvited guests like ourselves. But no trouble came in the wake of the execution. Small protests were going on outside the walls, we were told, but we could not hear them. Soon the media would be gone; the protesters would disperse and head for their homes. The prisoners, already home, had been indifferent to the proceedings, as they always are unless the condemned prisoner had been a figure of some consequence in the convict community. Then there might be tension and maybe even a modest disturbance on a prison tier or two. But few convict luminaries are executed, and the dead man had not been one of them. Our escort officer offered a sad tribute to the prisoner: "The inmates, they didn't care about this guy."

I couldn't help but think they weren't alone in this. The executioners went home and set about their lives. Having taken life, they would savor a bit of life themselves. They showered, ate, made love, slept, then took a day or two off. For some, the prisoner's image would linger for that night. The men who strapped him in remembered what it was like to touch him; they showered as soon as they got home to wash off the feel and smell of death. One official sat up picturing how the prisoner looked at the end. (I had a few drinks myself that night with that same image for company). There was some talk about delayed reactions to the stress of carrying out executions. Though such concerns seemed remote that evening, I learned later that problems would surface for some of the officers. But no one on the team, then or later, was haunted by the executed man's memory, nor would anyone grieve for him. "When I go home after one of these things," said one man, "I sleep like a rock." His may or may not be the sleep of the just, but one can only marvel at such a thing, and perhaps envy such a man.

Robert Johnson is a professor of justice, law and society at The American University, Washington D.C. He is currently working on a book entitled Death Work: a study of the modern execution process. *It will be published by Brooks/Cole in January, 1990.*
This article previously appeared in Commonweal *magazine. It is reproduced here with permission.*

IN LAW...

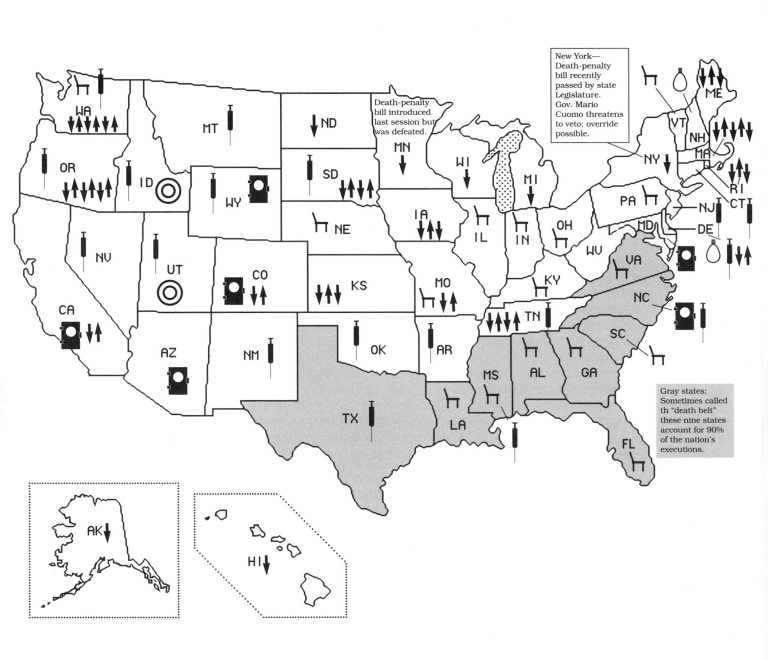

Hanging   Firing squad   Electrocution (introduced in 1890)   Gas chamber (introduced in 1924)   Lethal injection (introduced in 1977)   Death penalty abolished   Death penalty restored

New York—Death-penalty bill recently passed by state Legislature. Gov. Mario Cuomo threatens to veto; override possible.

Death-penalty bill introduced last session but was defeated.

Gray states: Sometimes called th "death belt" these nine states account for 90% of the nation's executions.

IN THEORY...

PRO

• **Deterrence:** Proponents believe that capital punishment deters crime, although studies are inconsistent in proving or disproving the idea. Proponents argue that if the deterrent effect is not readily apparent it is because the criminal justice system is too slow. Life imprisonment isn't viewed as an adequate deterrent because prisoners believe they eventually will be freed.

• **Retribution:** Only death is proportionate to some crimes, proponents hold. Further, the concept of retribution supports society's moral code, which may judge a criminal's life to have less value than other components of society, such as the general security of citizens or the life of a victim. Error in sentencing, proponents hold, is so small as to be negligible when weighed against the larger public good.

CON

• **Not a deterrent:** Death-penalty opponents cite the studies that show no deterrent effect and say that criminals rarely give prior thought to their actions.

• **Immoral:** Opponents see a contradiction when the state outlaws murder but upholds the right to kill. Further, they argue that the methods of execution violate the constitutional prohibition on "cruel and unusual punishment."

• **Not economical:** A New York study shows that each death-penalty case costs taxpayers twice as much as life imprisonment through the first level of appeals alone.

• **Unfairly applied:** Blacks and the poor are disproportionately singled out, say opponents. Poor prisoners haven't the means of engaging adequate representation.

—Reprinted with permission from the June 1, 1989 edition of the Minneapolis Star Tribune.

Sources: News services, Editorial Research Reports, "Crime and Capital Punishment" by Robert H. Loeb Jr., "The Encyclopedia of American Crime" by Carl Sifakis, "Capital Punishment, Cruel and Unusual?" by Information Aids Inc., Bureau of Justice Statistics.

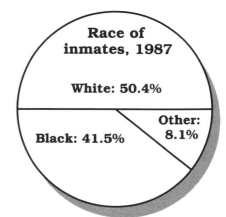

Race of inmates, 1987

White: 50.4%

Black: 41.5%

Other: 8.1%

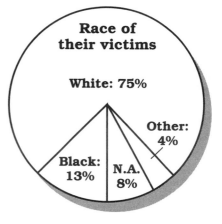

Race of their victims

White: 75%

Black: 13%

N.A. 8%

Other: 4%

...AND IN PRACTICE

EXECUTIONS

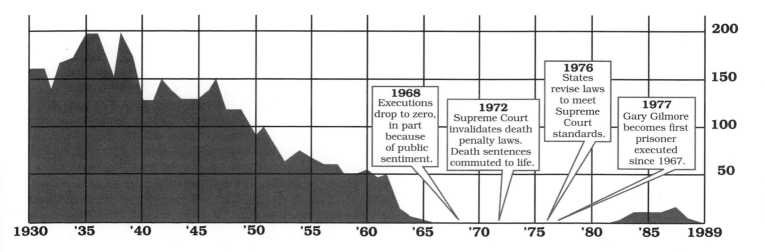

1968 Executions drop to zero, in part because of public sentiment.

1972 Supreme Court invalidates death penalty laws. Death sentences commuted to life.

1976 States revise laws to meet Supreme Court standards.

1977 Gary Gilmore becomes first prisoner executed since 1967.

1930 '35 '40 '45 '50 '55 '60 '65 '70 '75 '80 '85 1989

200 150 100 50

Martin Daniel Appel

Jeff Fleishman

The brown Monte Carlo, nicknamed U.S.S. Lexington, rattles over the thin country roads that slope and crisscross just north of Allentown, Pa. Martin Appel, wearing an Army lieutenant's shirt, sits rigidly at the wheel. Stanley Hertzog stares blankly and hunches in the passenger seat. The wine coolers an hour before have done little to level his nerves. Hertzog has a Marine corporal's hat pulled over his shaved blond skull. His big arms hang flabbily from a black sleeveless T-shirt. He wants to turn back to the night before and wander into the darkness and away from this journey.

This isn't a day for turning back. It is June 6, 1986, the 42nd anniversary of D-day, history's greatest military invasion. This is Martin Appel's day too, a day he has planned for a month. Appel, a wiry man of 5-feet 8-inches carrying a sullen face, checks the rearview mirror. Nothing except broken yellow lines

PHOTOS • THE MORNING CALL

Martin Appel is still waiting, and wanting, to die. Appel's new mission is to be the first person executed in Pennsylvania since 1962.

falling to the horizon. Appel has always prided himself on his superior intellect. He used it to mold the physically stronger Hertzog into his foot soldier. But as the car heads east, Appel wonders if he has trained Hertzog well enough. Maybe Hertzog isn't ready for a mission of such magnitude.

11:12 a.m. The U.S.S. Lexington reaches the near empty parking lot of the First National Bank of Bath. The bank of white brick and glass protrudes from a scatter of farm fields. The heavy, overcast skies mean the local Dutch farmer will work little today. Appel and Hertzog step out of the car as Appel reaches down and fingers his 9mm automatic pistol.

Discipline. Control. Confidence. All play like a chant in his mind. Hertzog trembles, his .38 caliber, bought just five miles away and two weeks earlier at an Army-Navy store, slips like a weight into his clumsy hands.

11:13 a.m. The bank doors open. Humidity hits air conditioning. Appel and Hertzog hesitate. No one notices. They walk to the tellers' counter. Teller Hazel Evans, a 55-year-old grandmother, looks up from her cash drawer and smiles at Appel. He lifts his 9mm. Two quick pops. Evans drops to the floor with what Appel would later call a "queer expression" on her face. Appel's D-day is underway.

11:50 a.m. Police, FBI and ambulance workers are rushing in and out of the bank. Evans, two bullets in her head, is dead. So is teller Janice Confer, a 47-year-old mother and avid bowler, who also has two bullets in her head. Customer service representative Jane Hartman, 33, is face-down and dead with four bullets in her body. Bank manager Marcia Hauser is unconscious, a bullet wound to the head. Customer Thomas Marchetto, a former marine, is down with wounds in his thigh and arm. Hauser and Marchetto will survive. More than $2,000, much of it in coins, is missing. A few feet above the body of Evans, $15,000 in stacked bills sits undisturbed. Blood is on the waxed floors. Friends and relatives of the victims huddle in the parking lot, and sirens break the quiet that has hung over the outlying fields for so long.

3 p.m. Appel and Hertzog are captured on their way to McDonald's.

June 9, 1986. Appel, who prior to the robbery had shot only tin cans and groundhogs, confesses to the murders. He announces he will do the "honorable thing" and face execution in Pennsylvania's electric chair. Hertzog, who shot at Hauser four times at point-blank range but killed no one, will draw three consecutive life sentences.

Martin Appel is still waiting—and wanting—to die. Appel's new mission is to be the first person executed in Pennsylvania since 1962. "It's for historical reasons," said Appel. "There's no glory in anything but first." He laughed. "You know," he said, sitting, ankles and wrists manacled, on Huntingdon State Prison's death row, "I was thinking about what I'm going to say when they strap me into the electric chair. The final statement. Well mine's going to be short and sweet. It's from the Arnold Schwarzenegger movie, "The Terminator." I'm going to say, 'I'll be back,'" he laughed.

But Appel doesn't laugh all the time. In a Feb. 25, 1987 letter to his girlfriend, he wrote: "By strict interpretation of the Bible, Jesus has already paid for my sins. Still I feel I must die to atone for what I did. And yet I know that if I didn't get caught, I would have lived a normal life and never thought about what I did. How can I be so coldblooded? I know that there's a missing part, part of a puzzle or an emptiness inside of me that needs to be filled. I'm afraid that not even you can fill it. I must become complete with God before I die. But if I do, then I won't want to die, or deserve to die. Is this making any sense at all?"

Go back to 1972.

Appel is a 14-year-old whose head seems weighted down by thick black-rimmed glasses. He is thin and odd but always gregarious. He's fascinated with model rockets and chemistry and reads Isaac Asimov. His non-stop mind

confounds his father, a simple man who spent his life working in the sprawling assembly plants of Mack Trucks Inc. "It's funny," said Appel's father, "but I never read a whole book in my life. And, well, Marty, he reads all the time."

The basement in the sturdy Cape Cod home belongs to Martin. A complete chemistry lab stands in the corner and a cardboard replica of the Starship Enterprise dangles from beneath the stairs. Martin is Captain Kirk, a sibling of the TV generation spinning visions out of syndicated dramas like Rat Patrol and Combat. With other kids he plays war games in the front yard. He always chooses to be a German soldier. "I would have been a great Nazi," he said, "because I love to give and take orders. That's why the German army was so successful. They were well disciplined and had a mission." Appel's heritage is rooted in the fatherland where his grandfather lived until coming to America in 1901.

"I wish I would have been born in the 1930s," he said. "Then I could have fought in the Korean war and got some glory and honor. I guess I was just born in the wrong decade. I almost made it in the Vietnam War. I was waiting to be old enough, but then they stopped the war. Oooh, was I mad. I think I would have held up well under fire." By his mid-teens, Appel's boyhood fantasies became more intense, more militaristic. He is not popular in school and enrolls in Air Force ROTC where he thrives on the order, structure and discipline. His keen mind and tireless determination make him commander of Dieruff High School's ROTC unit. "ROTC gave Martin recognition," said John Dillon, a retired Air Force major and Appel's instructor. "He worked hard; what I would call an overachiever."

Under Dillon's tutelage Appel dedicates his life to the military. "My dream was set," he said. "I was going to be a general, a career military man. And then I was going to retire, maybe someplace in Arizona and watch my grandchildren grow." The military strips away gawky appearances and insecurities. Men are built and their determination and will allow them to rise above the pettiness of the civilian world. Everything is neat. Orders are given and orders are followed and the mentally strong become the leaders, the ones in control.

"I almost made it in the Vietnam War. I was waiting to be old enough, but then they stopped the war. Oooh, was I mad."

There, on the front lawn and in the daylight, he raises a .357 Magnum to his head and threatens to kill himself.

That's how Appel saw it. He replaced his thick black-rimmed glasses, always a sign of weakness to him, with contact lenses. Rat Patrol and Combat were discarded for a geopolitical world he created in the likeness of the cult game Dungeons and Dragons. Into this imaginary world Appel enlisted a few misfit friends and together they devised plans to rescue hostages and start revolution in Communist countries. They turned the war games of childhood into a thinking man's battleground. Those who performed well were elevated in rank. But Appel was always commanding officer.

"It's strange," said Bill, a friend of Appel's for 20 years, who remembers the last meeting of the group. "But two weeks before the bank incident Martin promoted himself to the highest rank in our little political empire. He made himself the five-star Admiral of our fleet and said he deserved the promotion. When I look back on that now, that meant he was planning something awfully big to deserve such a promotion."

1976. Appel graduates from Dieruff High School with a shoe box full of ROTC awards and ribbons.

1980. Appel graduates as a second lieutenant in the Army from Bloomsburg State College's ROTC program. A year earlier he spent the summer training at Ft. Bragg, N.C. "I fired every weapon the Army has and even tossed a few grenades. It was the best time of my life." Some of the base's senior officers thought Appel carried his zeal a little too far.

During a routine war games exercise, Appel was in charge of a small company that was battling another "enemy" of raw recruits. The customary procedure is to accomplish the assigned mission—capture or kill the enemy and return to base with a handful of the enemy's colored arm bands.

"My problem," said Appel, "is that I executed the POWs my team captured. You see it was a waste of manpower to have the soldiers in my unit babysit the POWs we caught. And it would have taken too long to have my men escort the POWs back to base." So with a gun that fired only blanks, Appel executed the POWs, who were then forced to play dead. "My superior called me in and said, 'Son you gotta be more careful and you have to stop shooting all these people.' But I always accomplished the mission. That's the main thing, accomplishing the mission."

Appel reports to Ft. Gordon, Ga., on August 13, 1980. He has made it. In the cool predawn light he strolls past the quiet barracks and stares up at the same stars that he first discovered as a child peering through the telescope his father bought him. His uniform is pressed. Soon he will lead men just as he did in his childhood cellar where he was Captain Kirk using his imagination to send the cardboard Enterprise into a "warp factor" speed that shuttled his dreams into space.

At night he sees Gina, a single mother of two, who was introduced to him by another young officer at Ft. Gordon. They grow close and Appel, who has almost no experience with women, talks of marriage and bringing her into his military adventures. "I never met a Southern girl before," Appel said, "I like that Southern dialect. Slow and smooth."

A few weeks later Appel is sent to a NATO base in Stuttgart, West Germany, an industrial town along the Nekar River. "Marty was in for a rude awakening," said Pennsylvania State Police Trooper Charlie Marshall, who arrested Appel hours after the bank murders. "He was about to find out that first lieutenants are a dime a dozen." The superpowers at peace, and the NATO forces standing guard over Western Europe, Appel is assigned to a dining facility. "They basically made me a Pizza Hut manager," he said. Bewildered and 4,000 miles from home, he sits devoid of the glory he had worked for for so long. His dreams are being weighted down by paperwork and the Army's menial duties that are "seemingly illogical."

Appel goes AWOL. He slips out of Germany on a commercial flight as the Army scours the Stuttgart region. He heads for Georgia and Gina. "Boy, was my girl shocked to see me, especially since she had another guy. I said: 'Son of a bitch.' I went AWOL from the Army and this girl doesn't even love me anymore. Life is strange."

The military police are closing in and Appel steals a car from a dealer's lot that he is supposed to be test driving. "He just took off," said Bill. "He told me: 'Well, Bill, I didn't know where I was headed. I thought I'd just keep heading west. I was just driving in a daze with

Peter and Marcia Hauser. Marcia survived the brutal shooting at the First National Bank of Bath, but suffers from brain damage.

$1 in my pocket.'" He is pulled over by the state police and turned over to the MPs. He sits for four days in a brigg and is sent back to Stuttgart. He stands alone at attention and is given a less-than-honorable discharge. He makes an about-face and surrenders his lieutenant's bars. "I was scared," said Appel, picking at his handcuffs and staring at the cinder block wall in Huntingdon. "I thought the Army was going to be my whole career. They let me down, giving me menial work instead of letting me show them what I could do. My whole world was falling apart." Appel is a civilian.

"Martin was sad he blew it," said Bill, puffing on a cigarette and looking like the "mad scientist" Appel calls him. "You see now he could never completely succeed at anything because the Army was all he really cared about. It's strange, but he sent me a note paraphrasing Henry David Thoreau. It read: 'If a flower can't grow according to its needs, then it withers and dies.'"

Allentown in 1981 is an easy place to wither if you have lost your dream. Mack Trucks is preparing to move south and the once-busy Bethlehem Steel buildings sit like corroded shells on a scarred black earth that is webbed with rusty railroad tracks. The All-American City, as Mayor Joseph Daddona calls it is lamented in a Billy Joel pop song as a symbol of the dying smokestack industries. The displaced are crowding the homeless shelters and there is a neon sign above the center-city rescue mission proclaiming: God Is Love.

Martin Appel, the former heel-clicking officer, is peddling vacuum cleaners door-to-door, an embarrassment to his family. The job lasts three days. Next he's selling cars, "I didn't like cheating and lying to people and that's what happens when they go buy a car. You can call me a murderer and you can call me a robber, but if you call me a liar then I'd say you're sadly mistaken."

The murderer. The robber. Appel wanders in his basement, an enigma to his parents. His body growing thinner, his eyes more sunken, he drives over the broken streets, past the sturdy Allentown row houses, stopping occasionally to mix small talk and juke box music. He melts into television re-runs of The

"She crouched under her desk right in front of me," said Appel. "I don't know why she tried to hide. I just held the gun over her desk and POW, POW, she was dead."

Munsters and Star Trek. That boyish ebullience has been reluctantly traded for a stubby beard and a few Hienekens. His mother would later say: "I knew him when he was a child and he was fine. There were no problems. But then I sent him into the world, and I don't know what happened to my poor son. He got on the wrong path and he just couldn't get off."

Through a family connection, Appel is hired as a guard at Lehigh County Prison, a Civil War-era enclave that sits wedged between the Allentown Art Museum and the Eric movie theater. The job lifts his spirits. He is issued a uniform: a gray shirt with a patch of the American flag, dark pants, a whistle, a baseball cap with an LCP insignia and a silver name tag. There is structure and order in these cramped cellblocks. He gives orders and inmates obey. Appel sets a new mission: to work hard and one day exchange his gray shirt for the white shirt of a lieutenant.

"He took that prison job very seriously," said Yvonne, a 31-year-old grandmother whom Appel fell in love with. "I remember one time I had on his prison officer's shirt and when Martin came home he looked at me and got so angry. He said, 'Take that off, now! Don't ever touch that again. It can't be wrinkled.' He had all these gray officer's shirts hanging neatly pressed in his closet. He used to get dressed so methodically, staring into the mirror and then marching out the door like he was headed for some battlefield. It was cute."

Appel met Yvonne in the R&R Bar, a pungent, creaky beer joint on a ragged stretch of East Hamilton Street, just below the housing projects and the poorer wards of Allentown's Democratic stronghold. The Union vote used to live here in the days when the Union meant something. Appel is sitting at the bar and Yvonne steps in the doorway, a silhouette set in the sights between his two Heineken bottles. She is long, close to beautiful, and black with painted eyes and an ivory smile that takes more than it gives. She follows in Frankie, the prostitute, who, like Appel, is a predictable face in the usual crowd. But Yvonne is not so familiar. She is a vision, a juxtaposition of good in this dark place of half-empty glasses and wrung-out voices.

"It was a magical night," said Appel. "There was an immediate chemistry. Nothing like that

ever happened to me before." Yvonne wasn't like Gina or the 27 prostitutes Appel wrote to Bill about while in West Germany. Yvonne tells him about her "four little secrets," four children fathered by two different men. Appel surrenders his secrets too, but assures Yvonne he's a misunderstood genius who one day will capture the glory that's been eluding him. She smiles at his intensity.

At 3 a.m. they go back to Yvonne's two-bedroom apartment, quiet not to disturb the secrets that lay sleeping. The apartment is over CJ's place, a broken-brick bar in the gloomy shadows of the Bethlehem Steel plants. In the darkness, in that poor apartment that belies Yvonne's smile and colorful dress, Appel sees how welfare checks and mistakes made young can consume aspirations despite the most optimistic of smiles. Appel feels pity and love for her and commits himself to be her soldier. She is brought into Appel's imaginary geopolitical world, given a rank and becomes tied to Martin Appel forever. She is one reason he wants the electric chair.

"I know we're not married, but I know up to this point Yvonne has been faithful to me," he said one morning after playing 15 minutes of handball in the prison yard. "But if I'm around here another two or three years, who knows? I don't want to live when Yvonne is with someone else. I mean there's nothing I can do about it. The closest I can ever get to someone is through this glass. I can never touch another person again."

But for a while there aren't any other people. On his $13,000 a year prison salary, Appel takes Yvonne and her children on shopping sprees that end in a caravan of rustling bags and happy voices. There is one ritual: Appel must stop in McDonald's, his favorite restaurant. "It was the funniest thing," said Yvonne, on a recent trip to visit Appel in Huntingdon. "But when we'd get done shopping, we'd go to the second floor of the Lehigh Valley Mall where McDonald's is and buy what we called a smorgasbord of stuff. Marty loved McDonald's. He was just like a little kid. So he'd load up a tray of different burgers and stuff and we'd sit there and eat it, just laughing and laughing. I don't like McDonald's much myself. I loved him, I mean if love is something that makes you feel good for a while, then yes, I loved him."

The sustenance in Appel's paycheck can not keep pace with his spending. There are $581 worth of clothes charges at Sears. There are $51 spent in cosmetics and thousands more put on his MasterCard to refurnish some of Yvonne's apartment.

His parents bail him out and Appel is reminded that he is not an Army officer, but a $250-per-week prison guard. He and Yvonne fight more and more. Her children cry. And that first night in the R&R Bar is a phantom running through Appel's mind. Yvonne leaves him. But Appel won't allow it. He comes up with a mission to get her back. He drives to the housing project where Yvonne is staying with a friend. There, on the front lawn and in the daylight, he raises a .357 Magnum to his head and threatens to kill himself. Yvonne screams at him to pull the trigger and the neighborhood, which is used to the flash of a gun, watches intently. No police are called; an unspoken code in the projects. Finally, Appel's parents arrive and Mrs. Appel breaks down at the curb as Martin's father takes the gun from his son's head and tells Martin to get in the car. Obedient, he does. But Appel has completed his mission and the next day Yvonne comes back to him.

Trooper Marshall and Appel's father, who to this day cannot walk into a bank, blame Yvonne for the bank murders. They say she demanded more and more money from a man who had always been naive with women. Yvonne is also the wedge that forever will separate Martin and his father, a proud German who just couldn't accept his only son "going crazy" over a black girl. Trooper Marshall said: "I think Marty, who is sitting in that jail cell everyday, is smart enough to think he was used. Why else would she be with Appel. Hey, I mean the guy's no Robert Wagner. She never came right out and said she wanted money, but she sent those mental messages. You know how women have that ability."

Appel, who calls the three women he murdered "obstacles" to his mission, denies Yvonne seduced him for money. No, Yvonne did not urge me or send any vibrations or waves out saying, 'Yeah I'm going to rob a bank.'" Appel grows angry at the suggestion that he can be manipulated. Control is his credo. Order. Structure. Discipline. The inner chant never ceases.

In a shoe box, similar to the ones holding Appel's military honors, Yvonne keeps the love letters Martin sent her from prison. One reads: "I never tired of you and I never will. I desire you as much as the first night in the R&R bar! I never went with a woman as long as you. And never will. You were the beautifullest, brightest, most intriguing woman I've ever met. And I knew that I would do anything and everything to keep you mine. And I knew then and I know now that you are the woman I've searched for, struggled for, longed for, suffered for, hoped for and even prayed for. The woman whom I would idolize, cherish, exalt and LOVE to the ends of the world and time! Even unto my own end."

1984. Shame breaks out again. Just as his paychecks cannot cover his bills, Appel's prison job no longer serves as a satisfactory substitute for his bereft military dream. He is fast becoming a man desperate to exercise his authority over a world that sees him only as a misfit Poindexter, a nerd sitting at the end of a darkened bar collapsing into his overblown opinions of himself.

One night while driving the streets, another car cuts in front of Appel's. He chases the car and signals it to pull over. Appel hops out of his car, brandishing his prison identification card and screams at the other driver. Appel is arrested for impersonating a police officer. Appel's friend and passenger Lorenzo Avinger is charged with possession of marijuana and "a packet containing white powder." Appel's family suffers another humiliation as *The Morning Call* headline reads: "Lehigh Prison Guard Convicted of Impersonating a Policeman." Rage and a foolish attempt to gain respect lost him his job.

"I wanted to be a general so bad," he said, his shaved head sticking out from an oversized orange prison jumpsuit. "But then, things didn't work out. Then, of course, the impersonating a police officer thing happened and I lost the respect I had from my family and friends. It did me in. I was the great potential for my family. When I failed, that was it. So here I sit, my reputation gone. I let them down."

January, 1986. Appel is living in a trailer in a secluded mobile home park just five minutes from the First National Bank of Bath. He is driving a cab for the Quick Service Cab

"When they open that door and that electric chair is staring him in the face, I don't think he's going to walk down that hall. He's going to scream and kick and he'll have to be dragged to the chair. And that's when we'll see the real Martin Appel."

Company in Allentown. His body is a broomstick, except for his lemon-sized muscles and his beer belly. The sharp creases that had always run down his pants are rounded and imperceptible. "I really liked driving a cab," he said. "It's fascinating, the different people you meet. But the hours were very long. I'm a 40-hour a week man myself."

The cab gives him a chance to spend 10 hours a day by himself, driving over dark streets and conjuring up what he was once so close to achieving. He thinks of being a child and playing Star Trek and other games with Bill. He is 28. He thinks about looking at stars through his telescope and remembering how hard he would have to work to be noticed in this world.

He thinks about being the most decorated of ROTC cadets. He thinks about his name being scratched into the pantheon of generals from Patton to MacArthur. He knows he was destined for this, but something, some abstract force robbed him. And when he pulls the cab into the Quick Service garage, Appel comes out of his daydreams and into a world of bills, failures and other demands. This is a place where glory is not easily attained, and where a skinny, obsessive man with a few bum breaks doesn't rise to the top. Appel decides to make his own rules.

He drives the two hours to New York City to buy drugs. In Allentown, where the demand always seems to exceed the supply, drug prices can be radically inflated. "But he got ripped off," said Yvonne. "Marty wasn't much into drugs anyway and he had no idea he was getting ripped off. It's sort of cute about him. In some ways he's so innocent and then at other times he's so intense I don't understand him."

Appel is in a spin, his thoughts and words in constant flux, reeling off in different directions, an incessant energy beating through his puny 140-pound frame that is always draped in his Army field jacket. After the drug scheme he unravels another plan. Yvonne is working as a night auditor for a nearby Holiday Inn. "Marty asked me a lot of questions about the money at that place. I told him he better get that out of his mind."

He and Stanley Hertzog, who Appel befriended a year earlier over a cup of coffee in the Quick Service garage, are inseparable.

They have drinking sessions that last through the night. Hertzog is sympathetic to Appel's failures. "Yvonne didn't like Stanley," said Appel. "She thought we were spending too much time together. Can you believe that? I mean here's this beautiful girl jealous over Stanley Hertzog." Yvonne would later tell police she believed there was a homosexual relationship between Appel and Hertzog. In fact, part of Hertzog's defense for the murders would be rooted in what he claimed was Appel's ability to control him through homosexuality, but Appel denies this. "I didn't like that kind of stuff," said Appel. "There wasn't anything like that between us.

Bill, Appel's friend of 20 years, remembers Hertzog as a spacey, soft-spoken man, timid in his opinions. "One night, a rainy night," said Bill, "Stanley and I were driving through Bethlehem after dropping Martin off at Yvonne's. Stanley started pointing out all the folklore and history. He said 'Hey did you know that Ginger Rodgers once lived there?' He was very interested in that type of thing. I'll tell you this, Stanley would never have gone into that bank if not for Martin. It was the classic master-slave relationship. He looked at Martin, who was much shorter, with awe."

May. 1986. The perfect plan. It will result in a jackpot and crystalize all that is important to Appel—a merger of his military dream, his need for $15,000 to crawl out of debt and, finally, a way to keep Yvonne smiling. "I, like the Japanese kamikaze, get the satisfaction out of knowing that I've made a difference. There was simply no other way. I needed that money for myself and Yvonne. I reasoned that at least one of us would get the money and win."

Martin Appel, after years of tactical defeats, is finally planning his war. He is going to be a soldier. Like all great military plans, Appel's is inspired by history. On D-day, June 6, 1986, he and Stanley will invade the First National Bank of Bath. Appel, the commanding officer, will strafe the customers and employees and Hertzog, his corporal, will hustle through the grunt work and collect the money. Appel will be issued a 9mm automatic "because that's what officers carry." He trains Hertzog relentlessly, but in his fervor, Appel doesn't want to concede that Hertzog is not built for this. Appel even overlooks the fact that when practicing the mission, Hertzog cannot even consistently draw his gun without dropping it or banging it into a piece of furniture.

The entire plan is Appel's, including the diversionary bomb threat he will call into the Allentown-Bethlehem-Easton Airport to confuse police just minutes before the robbery. Several nights before D-day, Appel even speeds his car from the state police barracks to the bank to determine accurate police response times. "Every detail has to be worked out," he said. "That's the beauty of a military invasion."

"I had to train Hertzog and I thought I trained him well. I could instill fear in him and I hoped that would be enough to make him go through with the job and not make any mistakes. The military teaches you that when it's all stacked against you to use a frontal assault. It's the most direct and effective. Boom, right through the front door. That's what the bank was all about. We're going in the front door and blamo, we're going to shoot everyone in sight. That's simple."

June 6, 1986. 11:13 a.m. Appel's three-and-a-half-minute-D-day mission is underway in the bank. Appel fires 16 shots. Three dead. Two critically wounded. Hertzog, who would later say he never believed Appel would go through with it, is frozen, his .38 caliber dangling in his hand just above the body of Marcia Hauser. Two employees escape out the back door. Appel curses himself.

In a pulse of silence, Appel can hear teller Janice Confer, already shot twice, twitching on the floor. "I noticed she was still alive," he said. "I heard her gargling. It sounded like she was lightly wheezing or something. She was face down on the floor and trying to move a little bit. And I figured, 'Oh shit, this lady ain't dead.' It might sound weird—people say I'm not capable of mercy, but I seen the lady suffering and I figured I'm just going to put her out of it. So I aimed for her head, but the bullet hit her in the spine and killed her. My gun has a tendency to go for the spine."

The desk isn't big enough for customer service representative Jane Hartman to hide under. She tried to squeeze her body as small as it can get, hoping that somehow she will be invisible. "She crouched under her desk right in front of me," said Appel. "I don't know why she tried to hide. I just held the gun over her

desk and—Pow, pow—she was dead." Appel's inner chant played on. Hazel Evans was also dead a few feet away. Today, a plaque bearing the names of Evans, Confer, Hartman, Hauser and Marchetto is permanently bonded on the front of the bank, which sits quietly between the acres of furrowed farm fields.

June 6, 1986. 3 p.m. Appel is sitting in the kitchen of his trailer. It's 98 degrees and police and FBI are everywhere. Appel knows he must stay in control. "I remember that day sitting in my trailer with two dozen cops and FBI guys all around me," said Appel. "I sat in the kitchen drinking a soda like I was having a party, me being the host for all my guests. I wasn't even sweating. They were. It was hotter than hell in that trailer. They questioned me for six hours, constantly. One stopped and another would start. And old Marty sat there enjoying himself.

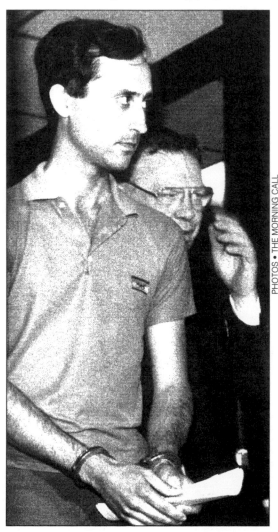

PHOTOS • THE MORNING CALL

"You can never destroy evil. Evil can't be destroyed. It can only be restrained. Evil's like trying to kill the wind. You can't kill it because you can't catch it."

You know what stands in my mind most that day? Not the killing, not the money, not even anything to do with the bank. One state trooper, after being totally frustrated in his attempts to get a confession from me says this: 'We should have sent you to Vietnam, we would have won.' I smiled for the first time in the entire ordeal when he said that. I knew I was guilty, but I was enjoying the drama of it, playing, if you will."

June 6, 1986. 9 p.m. Appel and Hertzog are arraigned for the murders at District Justice Elmo Frey Jr.'s office in Nazareth. A lynch mob forms in the dusk, screaming for the two murderers. "The people came up to the state trooper's car. It was scary," said Appel.

Trooper Marshall grew angry. "I was mad at that crowd," he said. "In a way, I guess I could understand. But I felt like going up to one of the people and handing them my gun and saying, 'Okay, you're screaming to kill this guy, well go ahead. Here.' If they would have been in that bank and seen that horrible scene they wouldn't have been calling for anybody's death that night."

The next morning someone had painted "Hang 'Em High" on the side of Appel's trailer.

June 9, 1986. Appel confesses to FBI agent Dick Fritz. "Before confessing," said Appel, "I asked to see a representative of the CIA. I figured maybe they could use me on a suicide mission to Iran or Libya of something. Maybe I saw 'The Dirty Dozen' too many times. I don't know what it is. I just felt I wanted to do something big before I die."

The next two months move quickly. Appel, representing himself, puts up no defense and asks for no trial. He tries to sell his story to the media for $5,000. There are no takers. Marchetto recovers. So does Hauser, but she has sustained permanent brain damage. In a news story about the murders, Allentown psychologist Frank Dattilio, said of Appel: "The bottom line is you're dealing with an atypical bank robber, with someone obsessed with proving to society that he was in control, in command. Somewhere in his life he fell short. He didn't cut the mustard. He was a high achiever who never made the grade." Dattilio said this threw Appel into a world of delusion in which he had to perform a grandiose act. "Appel is willing to take the death penalty be-

cause he completed his task. He has completed his mission."

Appel, a psychology major at Bloomsburg State College, writes a letter to *The Morning Call*, criticizing Dattilio's assessments: "Why must professional people like Mr. Dattilio always try to make mountains out of mole hills? They have to expand and theorize on everything. Why can't they simply take things for what they are? People rob banks for money." Speculation about Appel continues—in coffee shops, in the corridors of the courthouse and even among the prison guards who have given Appel the name, "9mm Marty." He has become the evil cause celebre of Allentown. He is found legally sane.

Sept. 3, 1986. Judge Robert A. Freedberg sentences Martin Daniel Appel to the electric chair. At an earlier hearing, Appel read a statement: "I feel only by my death can I atone for the deaths of the others. Unfortunately I am only a link in a chain and I am reminded over and over again of the German phrase, 'Auf Erfahrung gegrundet,' which means 'the necessary end to a chain of unavoidable circumstances.'" Appel will later say, "you can never destroy evil. Evil can't be destroyed. It can only be restrained. Evil's like trying to kill the wind. You can't kill it because you can't catch it."

March 7, 1988. The Pennsylvania State Supreme Court upholds Appel's death sentence. There is no appeal. Appel's death warrant goes to Gov. Robert P. Casey.

And that's where it sits. Gov. Casey has signed several death warrants but there have been no executions to lessen the ranks of the condemned on death row. Most sentences are tangled up in appeals. But some, including that of Roderick Frey, who paid two men to kill his estranged wife in 1980, may be carried out this fall. If so, Appel will lose the race for the distinction and "the glory" of being the first person executed in Pennsylvania since 1962.

July 28, 1989. Appel, 31, has started an autobiography entitled "666," the sign of the devil. "I gave it to them," he said. "I gave the prosecution the case on a silver platter. I offered no defense. I told them everything. I'm taking the chair. But you know, it's strange, but people talk about getting tough on crime, they talk about wanting to execute me for the thing I did. And I say, fine, go ahead. But look, I'm still here. I think it boils down to the fact that for all the tough talk society does, it doesn't have the balls to kill me."

Back in Allentown, the unemployment rate has dropped to four percent. A new Interstate is bringing home buyers in from New York and New Jersey. Development is closing in on the silent fields fanning out from the First National Bank of Bath. Bill plays chess with Appel through the mail, and at night sweeps floors at a department store. Yvonne tries to keep her smile strong, her children and grandchild growing. The cardboard replica of the Enterprise hangs mildewed in Appel's basement, a flimsy icon of the unreachable dream of a strange, bespectacled child.

And Trooper Marshall sits at his desk, a clutter of new cases before him, wondering about "ole Marty." He has a theory. "Marty's backed himself into a corner," said Marshall, pulling a cigarette from its pack, "Marty keeps trying to project this macho image. But nobody really knows Martin Appel. I don't know Martin Appel. You don't know him, the prosecutors don't know him, his friends don't know him and even his parents don't know him. But when they open that door and that electric chair is staring him in the face, I don't think he's going to walk down that hall. He's going to scream and kick and he'll have to be dragged to the chair. And that's when we'll all see the real Martin Appel."

Jeff Fleishman is a reporter for the Philadelphia Inquirer.

Edward Bennett

Warren Bates

Ed picked up the head of his victim and marvelled in detached wonderment that he could see the floor through the bullet hole.

"**D**on't wish me a happy birthday because it's not."

Edward Bennett was in a Las Vegas jail speaking with his father, a Sunday school teacher who, with Sunday school teacher sincerity, had tried to bring his son a cake in hopes of some small celebration of a 19th birthday. In years of birthdays past, Gordon Bennett could remember his boy raising pumpkins in the backyard of the family's red brick home in Lehi, Utah, and selling them in the front for toy money. He could remember Eddie as a ten-year-old delivering shopping coupon supplements to all the neighbors. The money earned was used to buy a Labrador puppy the youth named "Clyde". Gorden could remember the fourth-grade opera star, and the red-haired little leaguer.

He could remember Ed's early teen years, encumbered with struggles and minor disappointments; his not-so-successful endeavor to play the guitar, and the failure to revive a jalopy bought against dad's advice. Then there was the learning disability. Dyslexia. And dropping out of high school.

Still, Ed Bennett tried. He took one job as a hod carrier. Another job took him to a mink farm at the edge of the city. Gordon Bennett could remember Ed's refusal to slaughter the animals.

"He would never harm anything," he later recalled. "animal or human being."

But here he was, Gordon Bennett, the administrator of the computer science department at Brigham Young University, now in the Clark County Detention Center speaking with the son who, months earlier, had assumed the nickname "Eddie the Rotting Korpse." A shaven-headed, tattooed, devil worshiping young man with a murder charge pending. A month later, during the penalty phase of Ed's trial for the shooting death of a Las Vegas convenience store clerk, a crushed and tearful Gordon Bennett would take the witness stand and plead with jurors to spare his boy's life.

Ed,he said, was an "unopened rosebud." "If you just knew the kid's heart. I know it sounds crazy, you'd know he wants to do good."

* * * * *

It had been nearly a 400-mile trip in Joe Beeson's blue Datsun from the Utah Valley just south of Salt Lake City to the gaming mecca of Las Vegas. Ed Bennett had been chattering throughout the drive about killing someone, anyone, maybe more than one person. Joe would later tell police he thought it was a dumb idea. Real dumb.

But here he was, 17-year-old Joe Beeson, checking into a motel on Fremont Street with his friend, who was carrying a .45 caliber semi-automatic handgun under his jacket. Dumb, he thought. Real dumb.

And later, that night of Feb. 9, 1988, why did he find himself pulling the Datsun into parking lots of convenience stores, apparently scouting a place to rob, but really, literally looking for someone to kill? Just stupid, he thought. And then, for some reason, the blue Datsun, in the parking lot of a Stop 'n' Go store on one of the city's busiest non-Strip or downtown intersections. Watching. Anxiously watching his friend inside the store pretending to be a customer.

Suddenly, here he was, a young man with stature among his friends back home, by the store entrance, apparently lounging. But following. Following Ed inside.

Ed and Joe. Best Buddies. Satanic travelers extraordinaire. About to kill a 21-year-old newlywed, a store clerk named Michelle Moore.

Most friendships between teenagers in the Utah Valley are sealed by rituals of ditching class, camp-outs for concert tickets or cruising Main Street.

But the rituals that cemented the friendship of Ed Bennett and Joe Beeson were anathema to the valley, where the Mormon Church settled 140 years ago and where church members make up 90 percent of the population. At their rituals, Ed and Joe worshiped Satan. They also called themselves skinheads and dabbled in white supremacy. This, in the bountiful cradle of the Church of Jesus Christ of Latter Day Saints. Ed's hometown of Lehi, population 8,000, was quiet, somewhat poor and less sophisticated than Joe's neighboring hometown of Orem, home to 64,000, a city where lawns are long, porches are spacious and driveways are free of engine oils.

The cities are separated by a seemingly insignificant municipality called American Fork. It was here where Ed and Joe met, introduced by a mutual friend, Lewis Ivy.

The trio decided to form a rock 'n' roll band and called the group "Rigor Mortis." Joe, 16 at the time, played drums. Ed, a year older, played guitar, sang and either wrote or plagiarized lyrics.

As their friendship grew,they would spend days in the valley huddling in remote and fearful places; a condemned building in Provo that was once Brigham Young University, a craggy mountainside, a muddy creekbed. They chanted secret poetry, mutilated animals and Christian artifacts, all in hopes of pleasing the devil.

They occasionally cruised the valley in a 1950s gray hearse while listening to "black metal" rock music. A group called "Slayer," whose trademark is violent lyrics and not so subtle references to devil worship, was a favorite. An influence, one might say, of "Rigor Mortis."

Police would eventually search Ed's room and find what they believed to be some of his own lyrics. "Hate philosophy" they called it. Whatever it was, it was very disturbing prose indeed.

One excerpt from an untitled song went:

"Death is rising through the air as thunderbolts strike/blood is dripping from the walls/someone's going to die/ you hear the screams of pain and agony as children are nailed on crosses/ kill 'em, let's kill 'em dead/I cry to the depths of hell/I'm crying to you, oh lord/I need to kill somebody or tear somebody apart/I got to satisfy my need/cure this thirst for blood/so as I make this sacrifice/I'm doing it just for you/and kill this child for it is a first."

When the lyrics were published in a Las Vegas newspaper, a teenage girl called a reporter to express her concern. This was not Ed's writing, she complained. The true authors were a band called "The Righteous Pigs." Nevertheless, atop the song sheet, police found Ed's unmistakable signature, a drawing of a dagger and the initials E.R.K., Eddie the Rotting Korpse.

Ed had had the dagger and initials tattooed on his chest. Joe's tattoos were even more impressive and ornate, a dragon, a swastika with the word "skin" underneath and a serpent crawling through a skull.

A display of what police believed to be Ed and Joe's satanic handiwork was later discovered inside the once august and imposing, but now condemned Brigham Young building in Provo.

The basements and classrooms were scarred with the spray-painted slogans "Devil's Boiler Room," "Satan Lives," and inverted pentagrams. Obscene writings regarding death, homosexuality and violent sex appeared on the walls, along with black and red handprints and lyrics from black metal rock music as well as lyrics from some more mainstream heavy metal groups. Hardened feces of attack dogs that once guarded the structure covered the floors.

Devil worship, however, was only part of the youth's rebellion. They indulged in virtually all passions of juvenile delinquency; drug and alcohol abuse, petty crimes and a seemingly inexplicable infatuation with white supremacy.

High school classmates said Joe, who dropped out of high school in January 1988, was a sullen individualist who whispered

High school classmates said Joe, who dropped out of high school in January 1988, was a sullen individualist who whispered facist slogans in school hallways and proudly displayed his demonic tattoo.

PHOTOS • GEORGE FREY

The basements and classrooms were scarred with obscene writing regarding death, homosexuality and violence.

fascist slogans in school hallways and proudly displayed his demonic tattoo.

Experts later puzzled at the application of the apparently incongruous philosophies. The tenets of the nihilistic Satanism blended with the political activism of Neo-Naziism like whiskey and milk.

"It could be that all things appealed to them in various ways," said Sandi Gallant, a San Francisco police intelligence officer who has been studying the crime-cult relationship for nearly a decade. But the apparent inconsistencies, she warned, should not be mistaken for naivete.

Other authorities and friends concluded that drugs may have helped reconcile the anomalies. Ed and Joe's narcotics of choice were heroin and LSD. A preferred hallucinogen was called "fly," which they licked off pieces of perforated paper.

Others in the Mormon community didn't try to figure it out. They just recoiled at the bizarre haircuts and the weird dress of combat boots and bomber jackets. When they

were arrested, Joe was sporting shoulder length locks and Ed had his head shaved. Sometimes it was the other way around.

Despite his outward appearance, Ed was able to hide his involvement in the plutonian world from his parents. He also hid his friendship with Joe.

Joe was a leader among the Utah skinheads, a dozen-member group on the lunatic fringe of a once-genuine but now factionalized movement. The Utah skinheads were a puzzle indeed. They were apolitical. This was in marked contrast to the first skinheads who appeared on the American scene, who fashioned themselves after the anarchistic youth who appeared in London more than a decade ago. But where English skinheads used anarchy as a response to an atmosphere of political misery, the Utah skins languidly pursued a vision of formation of 13 "white only" states, which was passed off by others as a dim-witted fantasy borne of boredom and ignorance. The Utah skinheads couldn't even get high right. They took drugs, a no-no for self-respecting skinheads in Las Vegas who only drank beer. Coors, preferably.

Loyalty was generally pretty good between the Utah skins and devil worshippers. But in one case, it disintegrated, giving police the lead they needed to solve the killing of a Las Vegas convenience store clerk.

* * * * *

For $4 an hour, Michelle Moore stood behind the cash register at a Sahara Avenue Stop 'n' Go outlet, about a mile east of the Sahara Hotel and Casino. Her mother had asked her in previous weeks not to take the job. "It was too dangerous," Colleen Prentice had warned.

But Michelle needed to save money. She was secretly trying to help her husband, Frank, fulfill a dream.

Frank Moore was born with neurofibramatosis, more commonly known as Elephant Man's disease. Tumors thoroughly disfigured the left side of his face and he was a social pariah growing up in Grand Junction, Colo., where the couple eventually married in May, 1987.

Michelle lived with her own physical concern. She was over-weight. But she had a pretty face and a non-judgmental heart. She loved Frank and wanted him to accept himself more readily. She had drawn the introverted, self-conscious, aspiring art student into the world to some degree. But she also wanted to pay for his surgery.

Frank, 22, would often drop by the store about 9 p.m. and visit with his wife during the last two hours of her shift. On the night of Feb. 9, 1988, however, he stayed home and cleaned the house, hoping she would be pleasantly surprised.

Joe Beeson and Ed Bennett, meanwhile, were discussing the future.

Ed kept saying he "really wanted to do it," Joe later would tell police about his friend's desire to kill. "I said I didn't want to do it and told him it was stupid."

The two were relaxing in their Fremont Street room, drinking beer and listening to the usual musical fare. Ed, Joe said, constantly harped on about killing. Finally, Joe agreed to go out, but only after Ed had made a concession. "OK, we'll just go rob someplace."

In fact, a robbery at this point would seem practical. The lads had only a few dollars between them and they were trying to get to San Diego. Cruising in the blue Datsun, they scouted two convenience stores. One was ruled out. Bulletproof glass. Minutes later, they appeared at the Sahara Avenue target.

In his confession, Joe said he waited outside while his friend surveyed the store from the inside. When Ed walked out, they met at the foyer, Ed concealing the .45 in his leather jacket.

"There's only one person in there," Ed said, suggesting they go inside. Joe thought about returning to the car, but he never did.

Actually, Ed's attorney would later say, it was unlike Ed to be the leader. Joe, though younger, was more worldly. He had traveled the country and had, of course, the impressive police record. At age 11, Joe was arrested for shoplifting. By the time he was 17, he had run away from home several times and had been convicted of burglary, theft, forgery and escape. Joe was uncontrollable, as subtle as a sharp stick in the eye. Ed, said those who knew him, was passive.

But this night, here was Ed, taking the lead and walking inside the store, Joe in tow.

Joe loitered near a candy rack while Ed ventured into one of the aisles. Moments later, Ed approached the counter, carrying the .45. Without a word, he lifted the weapon and shot Michelle once in the forehead.

The "one person" Ed had told Joe about was a customer, Derrick Franklin, a black 17-year-old who was near the rear of the store when the shot that killed Michelle rang out. Ed passed the weapon to his buddy and told him to "get the nigger."

Joe told police he tried to make it look like he was trying to kill the teen. He briefly chased him around the store and fired twice. One bullet struck Franklin's leg; the other shattered the front window. Barely realizing he was wounded, Franklin charged out the front double doors and across the street to friends and safety.

Michelle's body lay behind the cash register. Later, it was revealed that Ed picked up the head of his victim and marvelled in detached wonderment that he could see the floor through the bullet hole.

Ed and Joe fled in the blue Datsun. They drove in no particular direction. According to later trial testimony, Ed wanted more victims. Joe was reluctant and wouldn't produce the gun, still in his possession after shooting Franklin. They eventually headed back to the motel room to watch the crime unfold to viewers of the 11 o'clock news.

Frank Moore was one of those viewers. His heart leaped when he saw the store, surrounded by yellow police tape. He tried to telephone, but heard only music through the receiver.

He recognized the song, "The Wedding Song", a hit tune from the 1970s that was played at his own wedding.

* * * * *

The whole thing was "kind of bugging" 18-year-old Jeffrey Chidester. Ed Bennett, his lifelong friend, had done some pretty bad things in the past, but this time it was something "really bad."

Actually, Chidester, an experienced police

informant, wasn't quite the friend Ed had made him to be. A year earlier, in an effort to wriggle out of a narcotics charge, Chidester gave information to an undercover American Fork detective that eventually led to drug charges against Ed and Joe.

Ed never knew who the rat was. He certainly never suspected his buddy, Jeff. After all, as fellow satanic travelers, they had spent good times together on jaunts north to Salt Lake City. There they hung out at a seedy record store called Raunch Records and frequented occult bookstores.

But now, here it was, March 5, 1988, a month after the killing and here was Jeffrey Chidester in a park in Pleasant Grove, Utah, listening to his friend, Ed Bennett, tell him about something "really bad."

Shortly after their conversation, Chidester, a devil worshipper, heroin and LSD user, police informant, Judas, and someone who was "bugged," set up another meeting at the Pleasant Grove park, this time with American Fork detective Gary Caldwell.

Three days after Chidester's rendezvous with Caldwell, Gordon Bennett awoke to police officers and detectives from Las Vegas and American Fork knocking on the door of his century-old home. His son was sleeping in his room, he told the officers, who handed him a search warrant.

Ed was given the chance to dress and met his father in the living room.

"Is it true?" Gordon asked, scanning the warrant. Ed nodded that it was.

In Ed's room, police found the lyrics, a leather jacket and Levis they believed Ed wore when Michelle was killed, two books on the occult, three adult magazines and several injection needles.

That morning, three police cars also arrived at the two-story picturesque home of Richard and Gaye Beeson. Joe's father answered the door and told police his son was sleeping in his downstairs room. As Joe put on his trousers, Las Vegas detective Dave Hatch read him his rights. When they arrived back upstairs, Joe's mother, a teen-age sister and a child were there. Richard Beeson was in shock. Joe's mother, Gaye, a professional pianist and songwriter, fiercely

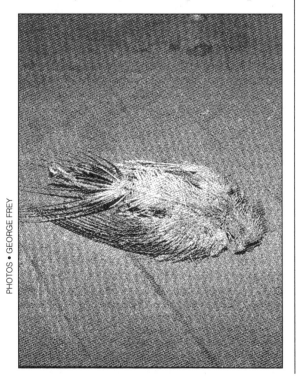

PHOTOS • GEORGE FREY

Ed and Joe chanted secret poetry, mutilated animals and christian artifacts, all in hopes of pleasing the devil.

loyal to the Mormon Church, kissed Joe as he was led away.

"Tell the truth," she said.

* * * * *

Gone were the shaved head and the hairless face, but present was a seemingly cocky courtroom demeanor. It was Sept. 5, 1988 and jury selection was beginning in Ed Bennett's murder trial.

He faced possibly the best prosecutor in Nevada in Mel Harmon, a 20-year veteran with the Clark County District Attorney's office who had pledged to get the death penalty from jurors. Joe's trial was set for the following month and prosecutors had made a similar pledge in his case.

The case against Ed was what many courtroom observers termed a "slam dunk." Harmon had Ed's confession to Jeffrey Chidester. He had Ed's palm print on the cash register's counter. He had Derrick Franklin's identification. He had a police statement by Joe regarding Ed's comments about killing people, made en route to Las Vegas. And he had ballistics reports and receipts from a Provo pawn shop that tied Ed to the weapon.

About all defense attorneys Cal Potter and David Schieck could hope for was that jurors would spare their client from death row.

Potter and Schieck, private attorneys contracted by the court to handle Ed's defense, were going to try to discredit Chidester by bringing up his fondness for drugs and devil worship. They wanted to show that he came forward only because there was a $32,000 reward posted by Secret Witness and Las Vegas convenience stores.

Indeed, Chidester had presented a problem months earlier at the preliminary hearing when he apparently lied about his double life as a police informant. He testified then that he had no prior dealings with Caldwell. But in affidavits supporting the search warrants, the American Fork detective stated he used Chidester often.

Derrick Franklin was not the best witness at that hearing either. He had trouble understanding questions posed by attorneys, gave conflicting answers and ultimately erroneously concluded that Ed chased him around the store, not Joe.

During the trial, however, Franklin was able to recall that it was indeed Joe who shot him, though he made the dubious statement that his memory had "improved with time." What was more important, anyway, was Franklin's positive identification of Ed as having been in the store.

For his part, Chidester reiterated his claim to jurors that the business of informing was new to him and denied that he went to police because of the reward. Chidester, however, readily testified about his drug use. He also testified that at the Pleasant Grove meeting, Ed told him of leaping over the store counter after shooting Michelle, supporting evidence of the palm print. He didn't give jurors the impression he was a typical teenager. But the overall impression was one of honesty.

Ed did not take the stand.

After three days of testimony, jurors deliberated three hours before returning a guilty verdict. Under Nevada law, Ed would face one of three sentences, life in prison with or without the possibility of parole, or death.

During the penalty phase, Chidester was again the focus. He testified that Ed and Joe's original plan was to go on a "killing spree," just walk into some shopping mall with guns blazing until they themselves were killed. "Ed was going to keep one shot for himself just in case," Chidester told jurors. He also testified that Ed had even asked him on former occasions to be a driver on such outings.

An American Fork police officer took the stand and brought out a fact unknown to the media, which had reported virtually every detail of the case despite attempts by police to keep a lid on things. Six days before Michelle's murder, the officer said, Ed apparently shot at two American Fork teenagers from a car driven by Joe.

When the defense's turn came, a studious looking Ed Bennett finally spoke to the jury in an unsworn statement, saving himself from cross examination.

He apologized to Michelle's mother. The last thing he remembered, he said, was arriving at the Stop 'n' Go. He couldn't recall

Ed and Joe's original plan was to go on a "killing spree," just walk into some shopping mall with guns blazing until they themselves were killed.

being inside the store at all.

"I'm not a killer. I never was and I never will be," his statement ended. "Believe it or not, I'm a caring person."

A social worker who had counseled Ed on his drug abuse problems testified that Ed was significantly depressed by the age of 16.

"He was concerned he was going to die that year," said Sharon Jensen. "He told me he had talked with Satan. He used words to the effect that he had sold his soul. He said there would be repercussions if he talked about it."

Gordon Bennett, his wife Raima present, wondered aloud if Ed was the middle child who was "scooted over."

"Edward got love, but I don't think he got enough love," he said, his Sunday school sincerity manifesting itself again for the jury. He asked jurors not to "snip off" the "unopened rosebud" that was his son.

When testimony ended, the defense played jurors 30 minutes of music by Slayer. The idea was to show how the music could have controlled and heightened Ed's emotions while impairing his judgment. Ed, according to the defense, was a product of his social environment.

Harmon, of course, disagreed.

"The defense wants you to forget Michelle Moore," the prosecutor began his closing statement. "Well, I can assure you the state of Nevada hasn't forgotten her. The chilling reality of this case is that the victim could have been anyone. The misfortune of Michelle Moore, the classic victim of circumstance, is that she was in the wrong place at the wrong time."

Harmon took Gordon Bennett's "unopened rosebud" analogy and turned it around.

Ed, he said, was "poison ivy."

Many juries take much more time deciding guilt than penalty. In Ed's case, the opposite applied. Jurors deliberated eight hours over two days before returning a verdict of death.

Michelle's family and friends cheered. Ed shrugged his shoulders, turned around and whispered "I love you" to his parents, who huddled and wept.

Jurors determined the death penalty was appropriate because the murder occurred during a burglary and robbery, created a risk to other people and was apparently random. Mitigating, but not overriding circumstances cited were Ed's youth, his lack of criminal background and his drug and alcohol abuse. During formal sentencing, Ed showed no emotion as he received an additional 55 years on his conviction of attempted murder and attempted robbery.

A month later, Joe pled guilty to a first-degree murder charge.

* * * * *

In Utah, Neo-Nazi "free Joe Beeson" graffiti had appeared on walls.

District Judge Miriam Shearing, who had presided over Ed's trial, could not oblige. She sentenced Joe to two life terms with-out the possibility of parole. Joe choked back tears. He too had apologized to Michelle's family. He also apologized to the city of Las Vegas.

There have been four executions in Nevada since the Supreme Court ruled on the penalty's constitutionality in 1977. Two of those occurred in June 1989, one involving a confessed double murderer who was convicted in late 1987 and had decided to waive his appeals.

Ed Bennett's appeals are beginning, Potter said recently. He plans to employ a double stacking argument that is currently being used to appeal many death penalty cases in the state.

In short, the argument says that because the prosecution used robbery and burglary as aggravating circumstances during a single event, too many circumstances were given to jurors for their consideration. Thus, the three mitigating circumstances jurors cited were inappropriately outweighed. Potter also said he plans to argue that the application of "random killing" as an aggravating circumstance was unwarranted because there appears to be motive if there were findings of robbery and burglary.

Potter said that what was occurring in Ed's life prior to the murder "was the only way for him to get recognition." Ed's cocky attitude in court, he said, was really a masked insecurity.

"His position was that the heavy metal music was a first amendment issue. He wanted to be a musician but he wasn't too successful at that. Ed and Joe were gaining credibility through that, but they may also have been feeding off each other. Whether the church wants to hear this or not, the Mormon religion is very non-mainstream and when kids backlash, they do it to the same extreme. Also, I think some of their own music haunted him."

Salt Lake City detective Phil Haslem tempered that view.

"It's very easy for young people who have hostile thoughts to feel like they are forced to do what they are told by church and parents," he said. "They rebel and fall back on the excuse of church coercion. "

Said Prentice after the verdict: "My daughter was a rose. My daughter was a human sacrifice. I know he would kill and kill again."

Warren Bates is reporter for the Las Vegas, Nevada Review Journal.

David Joseph Carpenter

By Steven J. Casey

For two years, terror stalked the scenic trails that meander along some of Northern California's most spectacular coast.

Hikers in shore and mountain parks were raped and brutally murdered by an unknown monster who came to be dubbed "the Trailside Killer." One ritually killed corpse after another was found off the paths in Santa Cruz and Marin counties commencing in mid-1979, driving hikers, nature lovers and families at play far from the unspoiled natural beauty of the Pacific coast. Vast areas of public land became all but deserted parks of death.

Visitors returned to the parks and the terror began to abate in May, 1981, when police arrested a man who once bragged that "to get away with murder is the ultimate challenge." He is a printer, former salesman and merchant seaman, ex-convict, child molester, arsonist, rapist and chronic stutterer. His name is David Joseph Carpenter. Convicted of seven brutal murders and an attempted eighth, and with evidence linking him to four additional trailside killings, Carpenter now lives on death row.

For virtually all of his life, David Carpenter has been driven by his own terror; a terror distilled into rage by an abusive mother and a childhood once described by state officials as "one of the worst messes" in California. That rage never left him, even as he found momentary release with his rape of perhaps 100 women and girls, and his murder of more people than we will ever know.

In 1984, following a change of venue because of massive publicity in Santa Cruz County, Carpenter went on trial for his life in a Los Angeles courtroom, charged with the murder of two women and the attempted murder of the boyfriend of one of his victims. A jury found him guilty and, in an unusual move, his fate was left to the hands of a second jury—one which merely observed all of the guilt phase of the trial and then sat in judgment on Carpenter during the second portion, the penalty phase. That jury condemned Carpenter to die, but the state wasn't through with him quite yet.

The same pervasive publicity that banished his first trial from Santa Cruz County drove his death penalty trial for five Marin County murders from that northern county to a courtroom in downtown San Diego, where a single jury judged his guilt and offered a second death verdict.

For a short while he was under two separate sentences of death. Now, the conviction in one of his cases has been set aside because of juror misconduct and he awaits retrial.

Marin County, California, is a promised land where the Golden Gate bridge touches its southern shore like the end of a rainbow.

PHOTOS • AP/WIDE WORLD

Convicted murderer, David Carpenter, has been sentenced to die in the gas chamber for the 1981 "trailside" killings.

There are more Mercedes Benz's and Cadillacs and BMW's per acre than probably anywhere else in California. When a philanthropist left millions of dollars in trust for Marin's poor, San Francisco poverty agencies, aghast, sued. Marin is a magical little kingdom, kissed by the gods and set apart from the rest of Northern California. The sun is brighter, the air is clearer, the pace less hurried, the children healthier, the men handsomer, the women more beautiful, and everyone so very much better dressed.

Physical fitness and outdoor activity are big concerns in Marin. Along Marin's miles of bay shore, joggers trot in the sunshine by fields of verdant green on one side, whitecaps slapping the rocky shore on the other. Throughout Marin, tennis is a year-round activity, and the many hills, beaches and parks afford untold opportunities for recreation and exercise.

One of the most popular recreation sites is Mount Tamalpais, affording a challenging hike to its peak and scenic views en route. At times it seems that everyone in Marin has climbed "Mount Tam" at least once.

On Aug. 19, 1979, the body of 44-year-old hiker Edda Kane was found on Mount. Tam. She was lying face down, shot once in the back of the head with a .44-caliber pistol, and was wearing only socks. The trailside terror had begun.

Carpenter, who was never charged with this murder, went the next day to his first speech therapy session in Oakland, across the bay.

On Sunday, Oct. 21, 23-year-old jogger Mary Frances Bennett was found murdered in the Lincoln Park area near Land's End in San Francisco. She was stabbed more than 25 times. That day, Carpenter was treated in the emergency room of Marin General Hospital for a cut to his left thumb. He told doctors he was bitten by a dog. Carpenter was not charged with the Bennett murder.

On the afternoon of Saturday, March 8, 1980, Barbara Schwartz, 25, was stabbed to death on Mount Tamalpais. Near her body investigators found the murder weapon and a pair of black, framed glasses with an unusual prescription.

Five hours after Barbara Schwartz' body was found, Carpenter was treated in the emer-

gency room of Peninsula Hospital in San Mateo, complaining of a stab wound to the right hand. The next day, he told his employers he had been held up near a 7-Eleven store in the town of Burlingame, and was cut in the hand during the robbery. The Burlingame Police Department has no record of any such robbery. On Monday, Carpenter walked in to the Market Street office of optometrist Dr. Donald Wright and ordered a new pair of glasses with dark frames. Carpenter was not charged in the Schwartz murder.

On Oct. 2, 1980, Carpenter's sometime girl friend, Mollie Purnell bought a .38-caliber Rossi revolver and gave it to him. It was not the first gun she gave him, she would later testify under a grant of immunity.

On Oct. 11, 18-year-old Cynthia Moreland of Cotati and her boyfriend, Richard Stowers, 19, of Petaluma, were enjoying Point Reyes National Seashore, another favorite Marin County recreation spot. They hiked along isolated Sky Trail, and it was there that they were murdered. When their bodies were discovered six weeks later, they were still lying side by side, each shot once in the head with a .38-caliber pistol.

Two days later, Oct. 13, 1980, 26-year-old Anne Alderson of San Rafael was paying a Columbus Day holiday visit to Mount Tam when she was spotted sitting in the Mountain Theater area. The following day her body was found, fully clothed, with evidence of recent intercourse. She had been shot once in the head, with the same gun used to murder Stowers and Moreland.

On Nov. 28, 1980, the day after Thanksgiving, Shauna May and Diane O'Connell, strangers to each other, were each hiking along Sky Trail at Point Reyes, very close to the site of the Moreland and Stowers murders. Their nude bodies were found the following day, laying side by side, touching. There was evidence of intercourse with May, and scratchings in the ground suggesting some bizarre rite to this day unexplained. May was raped and shot in the head three times, O'Connell once. They were murdered with the same weapon used in the Alderson, Moreland and Stowers killings.

Three days after Christmas, 1980, Anna Kelly Menjivar, a high school girl and part-

For virtually all of his life, David Carpenter has been driven by his own terror; a terror distilled into rage by an abusive mother and a childhood once described by state officials as "one of the worst messes" in California.

time clerk at the savings and loan where Carpenter maintained an account, was reported missing. A week earlier, Carpenter had taken Anna and her mother to his place of employment, Gems of the Golden West, and promised them Christmas gifts. The morning of her disappearance, the girl told her mother that she would have a surprise for her. Six months later, hikers Joseph and George Santangelo were trekking through Castle Rock State Park in Santa Cruz when they found a human jawbone. A dental comparison showed it to be the girl's. Her cause of death has never been determined, nor has Carpenter been charged in that case.

On March 29, 1981, Steven Russell Haertle, 20, and his girlfriend, Ellen Marie Hansen, also 20, were at Henry Cowell State Park in Santa Cruz County. Late that afternoon, the two University of California at Davis students hiked along the Ridge Trail where they met Carpenter, armed with a black steel revolver.

Carpenter ordered them off the trail and said he was going to rape Hansen. Hansen protested and Carpenter opened up, shooting her three times and sending her falling dead to the ground. In shock, Haertle kneeled over his girlfriend's body as he was shot in the back. Carpenter fired again, but his weapon was empty, and Haertle, wounded, heard a series of clicks. Carpenter bashed him with the empty revolver and fled to the parking lot, escaping in a reddish foreign sedan. Haertle survived, gave police an excellent description of the murderer and twice provided eyewitness testimony against Carpenter at trial.

At one of those trials, a Santa Cruz homicide detective testified that Carpenter apparently returned to the murder site a week later and urinated on the soil near where his victim's head had rested.

On May 1, 1981, Heather Scaggs and her roommate Tammy English spent Friday evening at home in San Jose, relaxing and talking. Scaggs told English that the next morning Carpenter would take her to Santa Cruz to help her buy a car, but he insisted it be a secret. Scaggs confessed some misgivings about the trip, and asked English to call the police if she failed to return by 7 p.m. the next evening.

Scaggs' boyfriend Daniel Pringle, was anxious. He urged Heather not to go, but she would not be moved. He insisted she write down Carpenter's name, address and telephone number for him and the next morning he watched her walk off toward her rendezvous.

On Sunday, May 24, Heather Scaggs' nude body, shot once through the head with a revolver, was found not far off a trail in Santa Cruz. She had been killed with the same gun used to shoot Haertle and to murder Hansen, May, O'Connell, Alderson, Moreland and Stowers.

The story of the Trailside Killer begins on May 6, 1930, only a short drive from the grisly death scenes but worlds away from the bustle and joy of the maternity ward at Stanford Hospital in San Francisco. There the first child was born to Elwood Ashley Carpenter and Frances Elizabeth Carpenter, nee Hart, a postal delivery driver and housewife. David Joseph Carpenter went home with them to 1680 Alabama Street, San Francisco, where, four years later, they would be joined by David's sister, Ann.

At the age of 6, young David started first grade at Glen Park Grammar School in San Francisco, and within a year he developed a severe stutter that would last a lifetime. By the second grade, he often appeared at school bearing obvious signs of thorough beatings.

Frances Carpenter was domineering enough to make Mussolini seem mellow. Like a drill instructor, she ordered her family about. Like a slave master, she never shied from use of the whip. Twice, Elwood Carpenter left his family, once for a year and a half, because of his wife's tyranny. Even when home, he wasn't much help to young David, making fun of the boy for his mistakes, yelling at him for his speech impediment, belittling him for his lack of athletic ability. When David's stutter grew worse, Frances Carpenter refused him treatment. Instead, she forced him to take violin lessons. And beat him.

By age 9, David had begun to turn some of those beatings toward others. He pummeled his schoolmates, twisted the ears of children at play, disrupted classes. By that tender age, he would later tell a court-appointed psychiatrist, whenever he was under severe stress he would commit a sex offense. He was tested and counseled, transferred to another school, and had his first burglary arrest, all by age 12. By 10th grade, he was accomplished at the art of arson.

Throughout his school years, children mocked David for his pronounced stutter, isolating him, ridiculing him and making him an object of derision. At home and at school, David was in constant terror and wet his bed well into his teenage years.

for forcing a 13-year-old girl into bed with him.

Carpenter finally won himself a trip to the California Youth Authority when, on July 20, 1947, he undressed and orally copulated a 3-year-old girl in the presence of her 8-year-old cousin, forcing the young boy to hold his penis. He told the little girl that he would throw her naked into a nearby creek, and threatened to stab the boy to death if either

Carpenter, stands next to public defender Larry Biggan during an arraignment in a Santa Cruz courtroom on charges that he murdered Ellen Hansen.

His only relief lay in escape. At 15, he ran away from home, heading to his family's summer house at Boulder Creek, a lovely vacation spot deep in Santa Cruz County. After 10 residential burglaries in the Redwood Grove area of Boulder Creek, he was arrested and sent to the Napa State Hospital for psychiatric evaluation. There, David spent more time on the hoof than he did on the couch, escaping three times until he was finally housed in the "disturbed" ward.

During one escape, he wrecked a stolen car. During another, he undressed a small girl. During the third, he practiced his burglary skills, again in the Santa Cruz mountains. At length, Carpenter was released from the hospital and, despite a recommendation he be taken from his home, was dropped back into that family cesspool. At age 16, he ran away again, and was later arrested in San Francisco

reported him. Investigators looking into that incident were told of similar child molestations Carpenter had visited upon his neighbors.

Classified as incorrigible, Carpenter was five times arrested on sex charges, escaped once from Juvenile Hall and twice walked away from the same facility. His teenage years, he was later to brag to a psychiatrist, were filled with rape. He said that before his 18th birthday he had sex with 50 young girls and women, sometimes by force, sometimes by consent.

Released from the youth authority at 18, he was paroled to his parents' custody and they all took up folk dancing. "Acquaintances who knew Carpenter during this period of his life have described him as being bright and having a pleasant personality," one biographical report says of him. "He was described as having a great sense of humor, which he used to

On Aug. 19, 1979, the body of 44-year-old hiker Edda Kane was found on Mount. Tam. She was lying face down, shot once in the back of the head with a .44-caliber pistol, and was wearing only socks.

the amusement of those around him." Indeed, his IQ tested at 125 and 126 and he was determined to control every social situation.

"Carpenter also had a reputation among his peer group of being very aggressive sexually in his relations with women," the biographical study says. It adds, in language which now seems quaint, "on numerous occasions, different women were in the position of having to fight off his advances in order to protect their virtue."

From 1950 to 1952, Carpenter was arrested for attempted rape and acquitted, and bounced from one entry—level job to another. Turned down by Selective Service because of his extensive criminal history, he signed on as a purser trainee with Pacific Far East Lines, a San Francisco steamship company.

Carpenter did clerical work on the S.S. Hawaii Bear, the S.S. Fleetwood, the S.S. Canada Bear and the M.S. Surprise, sailing throughout the Pacific to the Orient. During a voyage in early 1955, passenger Roberta Patterson complained to ship's Captain M. P. McManus that Carpenter acted improperly toward her 14-year-old daughter. Approximately 26 years later Mrs. Patterson was to remember that incident when she saw a composite picture of the then-sought Trailside Killer. Her recollection of David Carpenter prompted one of three tips to police which led to his arrest in northern California's most vicious serial murder case.

In the early 1950s, Carpenter expressed a romantic interest in Wilhemina Heatlie but was spurned. Jilted, he proceeded to impugn her character to others in their circle of acquaintances, and turned his attentions to her younger sister, Ellen. On November 5, 1955, David Carpenter and Ellen May Heatlie were married in San Francisco by Municipal Court Judge Claygon Horn. Son Michael David Carpenter was born 10 months later, daughter Gabrielle Louise followed in July 1958, and the family soon moved into a home they purchased in Redwood City, giving sellers Robert and Lillian Clancey a trust deed for $4,705.37.

Working full time for the steamship line, Carpenter also started a messenger and delivery service in San Francisco. Not all hard work paid off, however, for in 1957 he lost $10,000 in bad stock investments.

In 1960 the Carpenter family grew by one, right before it disintegrated in a spasm of terrible violence.

Lois DeAndrade, a 32-year-old casual acquaintance of Carpenter, was walking from home to the bus stop near the intersection of Green and Octavia Streets in the Pacific Heights section of San Francisco a little after 8:30 a.m., July 12, 1960, fretting about being late for work. Carpenter drove up next to her, and said he had just dropped off his wife and children at the Presidio, a sprawling Army base on some of San Francisco's most choice real estate. He asked if she would like to ride over and see his new baby, Circe Ann, after which he would drive her to work.

They drove into the Presidio, then Carpenter wandered about almost aimlessly, apparently not knowing where he was going. DeAndrade nervously complained about the time, and Carpenter stopped in a deserted area. DeAndrade, by then thoroughly frightened, bolted from the car. Carpenter chased after her, grabbed the terrorized woman's arm and dragged her back inside the car. He threw her down on the seat and straddled her as he reached into the glove box for a clothesline. She thrashed and cried, begging him to let her go and asking "Why are you doing this to me?" "I have a funny quirk that needs to be satisfied," he told her, as he retrieved a hammer from underneath the seat.

DeAndrade saw a car nearby and she screamed as she reached out for the horn. Carpenter lunged at her with a knife, which she caught with her hand as she stumbled from the car. Carpenter leaped after her, flailing at the air with the hammer and striking her in the head six times.

Jewell Hicks, a military policeman on patrol, had watched Carpenter's car wander around the Presidio and then vanish from sight. He decided to check it out and became increasingly suspicious when he saw the car parked under a tree by the underbrush. Approaching, he heard a scream and saw Lois DeAndrade on the ground, Carpenter smashing her head with the hammer.

Hicks ran to the car and Carpenter swung his hammer at the MP. Hicks pulled his gun and Carpenter seemed to give up but, when Hicks was on the radio, the rapist pulled a fountain pen gun that fired a .38 projectile and got a shot off at Hicks. Carpenter started to run and Hicks shot at him twice, hitting him once in the thigh.

At Letterman Hospital where both were taken for treatment, Carpenter told DeAndrade "I won't hurt you now; I can't hurt you."

Small comfort. She had a bilaterally fractured skull, visual disturbance, and sliced fingers. Doctors performed brain surgery and fashioned plates for each side of her head.

Carpenter was sentenced to 14 years in federal prison. Ellen divorced him, taking custody of the three children and all community property, and an order for $1 monthly alimony and a like sum for child support.

After eight years, Carpenter was released on federal parole and started a welding class in San Francisco, collecting grants under the Manpower Development and Training Act. He met Helen Hunt Abbott, a 34-year-old divorcee working as a college clerk-typist whom he met while both were involved in a therapy group. Married Aug. 1, 1969, the couple divorced in 1970.

The nights are black in Boulder Creek in the dead of winter, and just after 10 p.m. on Jan. 27, 1970, 19-year-old Cheryl Lynn Smith was making her way down a dark Santa Cruz County highway to her parents' home. Alone in the car, she was driving south on Highway 9 when, about 10 miles north of Boulder Creek, a speeding car smashed the rear of her vehicle. Both cars pulled to the shoulder of the road and the other driver ran up, apologizing to the frightened teenager for causing the accident.

Smith got out to survey the damage to her car, turning her back for just a moment on David Joseph Carpenter. He snatched her, took a club from under his coat and yelled at the squirming woman: "I want to rape you. I'll have to kill you if you don't come with me."

He then dragged her up a small incline where, threatening her with a knife, he forced her to partially undress. Dragging her further up the hill, Carpenter made her finish undressing and she started sliding down the hill in a frantic effort to flee. Enraged, Carpenter lashed at her with the knife and she felt blood dripping from her body as she crouched on the ground. Suddenly, he stopped hitting her and her first thought was that he was scared.

He walked her back to the parked cars, gave her his jacket to wear and told her "You are hurt and bleeding. I'll follow you home and bandage you up, if you promise not to call the police."

She promised. Right then, she would have promised him sex at high noon in Union Square if it had meant a chance to get away.

She drove off in her car, Carpenter following in his. Soon, she ditched him and raced for the police.

Carpenter fled to Daly City, slept the night in an abandoned house and early in the morning on Jan. 28 he hitch-hiked to Santa Cruz where he broke into a home at 6821 Empire Grade Road. About 2:30 p.m., a schoolteacher and her two young sons came home to find Carpenter staring down a 16-gauge shotgun at them. He sent the boys to their room and took their mother to his cabin hideout. There, he raped the captive woman, then drove her back to her home and let her go.

The following morning just moments after 8:00 a.m., Sharon O'Donnell, 25, was in the parking garage of her Daly City apartment complex when she met a rifle-toting Carpenter who forced her into the Mercedes Benz he had stolen in Santa Cruz, and tied her hands. As he checked over the car, O'Donnell sprang from the seat and ran from the garage.

Carpenter then took O'Donnell's Volkswagen and headed for California's Mother Lode country in the Sierra foothills.

On Feb. 3, 1970, the one-man crime wave continued. Lucille Davis was at work, cleaning a house in the gold rush town of Murphys when she heard a knock on the back door. Carpenter stood at the door, a long-barreled pistol in his hand. He tied the charwoman to the bed, robbed her of $3 and her car, and left.

Forty minutes later, a 25-year-old housewife in the town of Angels Camp heard a knock on her back door. Expecting her husband home for lunch, she opened the door only to find Carpenter, brandishing a long-barreled pistol. He forced her and her infant son into her car, robbed her of $3—thereby doubling his take for the morning—and took the pair with him to a deserted area where he raped the woman. Soon, he left his victims and hitch-hiked to Modesto, Calif., where an alert sheriff's deputy spotted him in a Greyhound bus depot.

Held in the Stanislaus County Jail, Carpenter escaped with four other inmates. A day later, the little criminal band was recaptured while trying to get food.

This crime spree took David Joseph Carpenter for the first time inside the California state prison system, where he became convict B-27305. He also became something of a star inmate.

When he got to prison, "Stuttering Dave," as the inmates called him, always adjusted well. Despite his speech impediment, he won debates with other convicts, he excelled in class and at his work assignments, he completed the Dale Carnegie Course, enrolled in the Gavel Club, the Investment Analysis Group and Alcoholics Anonymous, and took college—level courses in philosophy and personal finance.

But it was at group therapy that his star shone brightest.

Diagnosed as having a personality disorder "manifesting itself by hostility toward women" and as a sexual sadist, David Carpenter threw himself into group therapy in prison. A female therapist came into the sessions, teaching him how to cope with the demons of his past that had erupted in violent rage. It was, he insisted, in a 1975 letter, working.

"I was able to get down to gut level dealing with my sexual hang-ups and learned how to deal with women on the same level as everyone else," he wrote. "I do not have any hostilities towards women any more, nor will I ever have to rape another woman, or use force against them. because I feel adequate now and do not suffer from the stresses and strains that I have for these past many years. I am presently working on my speech problems, and I feel more confident in myself than at any point in my life."

By 1974, prison records show Carpenter working in three different therapy groups, and assisting other patients. Dr. Carl Swedenburg, his reviewing clinical psychologist, reported Carpenter "developing insight" into his problems and showing great improvement. The following year, Carpenter began work as Swedenburg's co-therapist in the LaMarch Unit of the California Medical Facility, a prison at

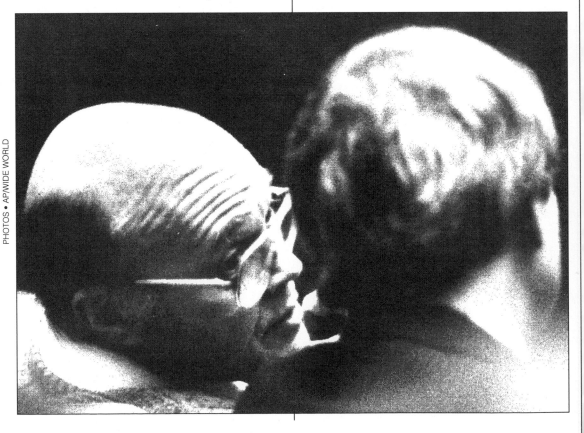

PHOTOS • AP/WIDE WORLD

Carpenter glances at his attorney in a Los Angeles County Courtroom. A jury recommended Carpenter die in the gas chamber for the shooting death of two women in Northern California.

Vacaville. Swedenburg told the parole board that Carpenter was approaching maximum benefit from therapy, and was likely to continue his improvement if released from prison. Correctional officers joined in that assessment, and several staff members wrote letters to the parole board on Carpenter's behalf. Skeptics would later say the shrink and the guards were thoroughly conned by a master at manipulation. They would argue that he led them to the behaviors he wanted, that it didn't happen the other way around.

On Feb. 28, 1977, Carpenter was released from state prison, into the custody of the U.S. Marshal as a federal parole violator. He served 27 months at the federal prison at Lompoc, Calif., a period remarkable for his learning to control his stutter, and was released on parole to San Francisco on May 21, 1979.

Swift Air Flight 441 from Santa Barbara touched down at San Francisco International Airport on time at 11:30 that May morning, and David Joseph Carpenter came home. For 49 years, the Trailside Killer had been growing in his cocoon. In weeks, that vampire moth would fly.

The trials of the Trailside Killer were, in a sense, backwards.

In 1984, Santa Cruz District Attorney Art Danner took the Hansen and Scaggs murders to trial in Los Angeles, after a torrent of publicity drove the case from Santa Cruz County. The trial stretched into 1985, and the jury returned a verdict of death.

Starting in 1988, Marin County Deputy District Attorney John Posey tried Carpenter in San Diego, following another change of venue, for the Moreland, Stowers, Alderson, May and O'Connell murders. He, too, obtained a death verdict although that was subsequently stricken by the trial judge.

Raymond Cameron, a career police officer and investigator for the District Attorney in San Diego County, holds a Ph.D. in psychology and is frequently loaned to other California prosecutors as a forensic consultant, often assisting in jury selection. Cameron helped Danner pick the Los Angeles jury for the trial of the Santa Cruz murders.

"The defense at the penalty phase was going to be the terrible home life Carpenter had when he was a child," Cameron recalled.

"And it *was* horrible, no question. But the defense wanted to sell that to the jury as a reason not to execute him, and they were shopping for sympathetic jurors—social-worker types.

"There was a woman on the panel, a black woman who was a supervising social worker and the defense asked her if she had ever seen children so badly damaged by awful homes that they seemed destined for a life of crime. She said oh, my, she had, indeed. That's good for the defense. But then she went on, saying she had seen others from similar homes who grew up to be lawyers and doctors and judges. That's good for us.

"In any jury selection, there's a certain amount of bluffing that goes on, because both sides are limited on the number of peremptory challenges they have and each is trying to get the other to use one of its challenges—fire one of its bullets, as they say—to kick a juror neither really wants.

"Well, the defense after questioning this woman passed. That left it to us, and Art Danner stood up and said he accepted the jury. Carpenter leaned over to his attorney and motioned to the just-seated woman. 'She's gonna kill me,' he said. And you know what? She became the foreman of the jury, and they convicted him and gave him a death sentence."

In addition to jury selection work, Cameron also reviewed Carpenter's criminal and psychiatric history, and tried to anticipate what course the defense would take. He provided Danner with insight into Carpenter's warped personality and estimates of how he would present himself to the jury.

"Review of Carpenter's history and his behavior from childhood through adulthood clearly demonstrates that Carpenter is an individual who rapidly learns from his mistakes," Cameron wrote. The way Cameron saw it, Carpenter's violence escalated as he learned, first, that hollow threats would not protect him, that guns worked better than knives, and that surviving victims would identify him. "Therefore, to continue his attack upon women would necessitate their elimination once he had completed his attack. He knew it was much simpler to eliminate the victim than to attempt to overcome investigation, identification and prosecution in court."

Classified as incorrigible, Carpenter was five times arrested on sex charges, escaped once from Juvenile Hall and twice walked away from the same facility.

Cameron also counseled that Carpenter would attempt to turn his stutter to his advantage, "making repeated apologies to the court and jury for his inability to adequately articulate his responses." The way to overcome that, the psychologist opined, would be to ask short, penetrating questions, depriving Carpenter of the control over the courtroom he so desperately sought and making him angry and frustrated. When very relaxed, or exceptionally angry, Cameron said, Carpenter loses his stutter.

That happened as trial began and a lovely female sheriff's deputy joined the courtroom as a new bailiff. Carpenter quickly set out to dominate her. "He was always after her to get him this or bring him that," Cameron said. "Soon, she'd had enough. She really got in his face, and here's a guy who just can't stand to be bossed around by a woman. 'Listen, asshole,' she told him, 'sit there and shut up.'

"Later on, she remarked to me that he always stuttered badly, but never when he talked to her. I told her it was because he hates her, that he's fixing all his energy and all his hate on her, and when he does that he speaks perfectly."

Danner produced a parade of witnesses to link Carpenter with the hideous crimes, but the surprise of the trial waited for Defense Attorney Larry Biggam, who admitted to the jury that his client committed the murders. The guilt issue clearly won by the prosecution, Biggam's aim was to spare Carpenter's life.

His witnesses told the jury that David's mother was "an aggressive and vicious, domineering woman" who often beat him severely and constantly made him feel a failure, that he couldn't get his bearings when he was released from prison into the turbulence of the 1960s civil rights and feminist movements, that in prison Carpenter was always a model inmate.

Danner called two prison guards—both women—to testify that Carpenter threw temper tantrums and led other inmates in small revolts, and glared pure hatred at them when they took action.

"I don't want it to be unclear in any regard, that the people demand death for David Carpenter," Danner told the jury in his penalty phase argument. "This defendant, as he sits over there, right now, still thinks he had the right" to murder those victims, the prosecutor said.

The jury and the judge agreed. Los Angeles Superior Court Judge Dion Morrow heard from Heather Scaggs' mother, Mary Scaggs, before he pronounced sentence. In a tiny, quivering voice, the petite woman told the court "I'm a Christian. I'm asking for his life, as did the jury, not [for] his soul." Judge Morrow was of the same mind, saying "The defendant's entire life has been a continuous expression of violence and force almost beyond exception." Carpenter sat silently, resting his head on his arm. "I must conclude with the prosecution," said Judge Morrow, "that if ever there was a case appropriate for the death penalty, this is it."

Between trials, Carpenter was the subject of rare death row interviews with an Oakland television station and the Point Reyes newspaper.

Ignoring his attorney's advice, he talked to KTVU reporter Elaine Corral, telling her he was innocent of the Scaggs murder. "They knew before they arrested me I didn't kill Heather Scaggs," he said. "As they pulled the bullet out of her head, they knew I hadn't killed her." He told Point Reyes *Light* publisher David Mitchell that he had missed his early morning appointment with Scaggs because he overslept after a night of heavy partying.

He insisted he was charged with the murders just because he was an ex-con who did 20 years for sex crimes. "My record sucks," he told the television reporter, insisting he was innocent of the murders. "I've never denied what I've done. On everything that I've ever done, I've always pled guilty. There was never any question I was guilty and that was it. But I have fought this case from the very, very start."

That fight continued in San Diego, where the Marin County murder trial opened Jan. 5, 1988 in the courtroom of Superior Court Judge Herbert Hoffman, a federal prosecutor recently appointed to the state bench.

Marin County Deputy District Attorney John Posey and his team faced what even other judges regarded as bullying from Hoffman as they set out to prove that Carpenter shot to death Moreland, Stowers, Alderson, O'Connell and May, making a ritual of the killings and inflicting psychological torture on them. The prosecutor played for the jury a tape recording of Carpenter's television interview, in which Carpenter said, "If I pulled the trigger once, then I had to pull the trigger each time and kill everybody."

"You have seen real evil," Posey told the jury, "and it's sitting right there."

The jury agreed, and on May 9, 1988 convicted Carpenter of five counts of first-degree murder, two counts of rape and one count of attempted rape. They had deliberated but seven hours.

On June 26, 1988, the jury returned a verdict of death, and on July 19, Judge Hoffman affirmed that verdict, pronouncing a death sentence on Carpenter, finding him to be a vicious serial killer who offered perjured testimony and altered evidence as he concocted a series of alibis.

"I have never seen anyone like him," prosecutor John Posey said in a private conversation in 1989. Posey has lived with the specter of Carpenter for years, has studied his every move and has visited all the murder sites. Posey may know Carpenter better then Carpenter does.

"If there is such a thing as true evil, in my opinion it is David Carpenter," Posey said. "What's so disarming about a personality like Carpenter is that he can be whatever he wants to be, given the circumstances."

On June 13, 1989, the conviction and death sentence of David Joseph Carpenter for the Marin County murder series was set aside.

Judge Hoffman ruled that jury foreman Barbara Durham knew about Carpenter's conviction and death sentence in the Santa Cruz case, information carefully kept from the jury in San Diego so as not to compromise its independent decision making. Durham had allegedly told a friend about the Santa Cruz case once over dinner during the trial.

"Despite the strength of the prosecution's case," Hoffman said from the bench, "every defendant is entitled to a verdict by 12 fair and impartial jurors. That's what this whole system is about; not 11 impartial jurors, not 9, but 12."

Saying that Carpenter is "without question" guilty, Hoffman said "this is an absolute travesty that such a result could happen in such a case," and he referred Durham to state and local prosecutors for possible criminal prosecution of what he called "serious juror misconduct." After 10 years of trailside killings, a seven-month trial in San Diego and an expense of well over $2 million, according to Marin County officials, the five-victim homicide case was ordered to begin again.

Posey said he would appeal. The Trailside Killer case goes on.

Casey also wrote Standards of Decency and a profile on murderer, Robert Harris, both of which appear elsewhere in this volume.

J.C. Hadley

Cathy Donelson

"J C. Hadley shot and killed Deputy Howard Dutton on Oct. 1, 1987."

That's the last hand-written notation at the bottom of a two-sheet record in the Robertsdale, Ala. Police Department files. What the note doesn't reveal is Hadley's acquaintance with Dutton, who had befriended him following Hadley's release from prison on charges related to an attempted arson. Hadley had done odd jobs at Dutton's Robertsdale residence, and often referred to Dutton as his buddy. With three dozen arrests in 10 years, Hadley uncontestably had the most extensive police record of anyone in the rural, south Alabama town of 2,300.

PHOTOS • CATHY DONELSON

Although the jury had reached a unanimous decision of life without parole, the judge sentenced J.C. Hadley to die in Alabama's electric chair.

After his conviction on capital murder charges last winter, the 53-year-old Hadley told his trial jury he'd rather die than spend the rest of his life in prison. "I want the chair," he said. "And I don't want to sit up there no six, seven years to get it."

A week later he had a change of heart. Facing the judge at the sentencing hearing, he asked for mercy, saying his children had talked him into wanting to live to know his grandchildren. Although the jury had made a unanimous recommendation of life without parole, the judge sentenced J.C. Hadley to die in Alabama's electric chair.

In what amounted to a test case, Hadley's was the first conviction and death sentence under a newly enacted Alabama law called the Undercover Policeman's Protection Act. Prosecutors think it may end up before the U.S. Supreme Court.

Born the sixth child of a turpentine worker who died at the reputed age of 105, Hadley is related to an old-fashioned family clan with numerous members and complexities of interfamily kinship living in a backwoods riverbottom of north Baldwin County. Many Hadleys live together in what is termed a compound by a state criminal justice system officer. "And it isn't like the Kennedy family compound at Hyannis Port," he noted.

Once known as the Old Southwest in pioneer days before Texas was settled, the area has provided county authorities with several crimes and murder cases that read like something out of southern Gothic mystery novels. It's a land where people fight game cocks and pit bulls and cling to the old Indian custom of burning off the woods—not necessarily their own—in the spring to improve the turkey hunting. State health and welfare department workers, who say the pregnant women up there still eat clay, are as reluctant to go there on government business as are the revenuers, given the settlement's history of bootlegging.

This is the mileau that spawned Hadley, who was drunk and holed-up in a back alley, threatening to kill himself, when Dutton and other officers arrived to try to dissuade him. J.C. had blown a bumbling attempt to commit suicide at least once before. Not long before killing Dutton, he had been released from prison, where he served part of a five-year term following a suicide threat authorities claim also endangered the lives of policemen. That incident was either ironic, pathetic, bizarre, ridiculous or dangerous, depending on the prosecution or defense view.

One October day in 1981 Hadley doused himself and the shack where he lived behind his mother's house with a gallon of gasoline and unsuccessfully tried to set a fire. He flicked his lighter in front of police officers who had been summoned, but it failed him.

He was arrested and charged with attempted arson. The wooden shed is still standing, barely. Stuffed with junk and open to the elements, it looks like it should have been easy enough to burn, but doesn't appear to be a fit habitation for a man. It sits in decay off the alley a few yards from where Hadley shot Dutton seven years later.

Robertsdale Police Chief Robert E. Williams, who witnessed the shooting, says he seriously considered leaving police work afterwards because he felt so guilty. It had happened in his town.

And he feels guilty because he is convinced the shotgun blast was meant for him. Hadley, with his record 36 arrests, was none too fond of the chief. "He threatened to kill a police officer on three different occasions," Chief Williams said. He declined to name the officer, but sources in the department say it was the chief.

Nonetheless, he and Hadley had exchanged greetings the morning of the shooting. Chief Williams waved at Hadley as he drove by the house. "He was sitting on the porch. He raised his hand and kind of half-waved back," the chief recalled. "You could tell there was something wrong by the way he hung his head."

The day ending in the death of the first Baldwin County law enforcement officer killed in the line of duty had been bad from the start for Hadley. The morning mail brought a letter denying him the government benefits he had applied for, and his girlfriend had left on an errand and had been gone for three days. Nothing was going right. He began drinking early in the day.

The main thing wrong with Hadley was his drinking, according to those close to him. He had become frustrated while trying to fix a toilet at his mother's house, and developed one of the violent headaches that plagued him. "He grabbed his head, started hitting himself with a pipe wrench and asking for help," a relative said. Hadley had gotten religion when he was in prison, so a family member went for a minister who worked at a nearby tire store to try to calm him down and pray with him.

Later in the day a county deputy saw Hadley—a former felon who previously had threatened his own life and others—buy three double-aught buckshot shells over the counter at the local hardware store. He did not interfere, he told defense attorneys who questioned him, because it isn't against the law to buy ammunition.

At 10:18 that night, Hadley shot Deputy Dutton in the stomach at close range with one of those shells as Dutton was trying to talk him into giving up his shotgun and surrendering to the police.

Officers on the scene returned fire, wounding Hadley, who was taken to a hospital where he was placed under 24-hour guard. According to his son, Hadley refused to believe he could have killed his friend, when Hadley was served with a capital murder warrant the next day.

His sister believes Hadley would have gone back to his shed to sleep it off as usual and never shot anyone if police hadn't "swarmed in" on him. "He was fine until he got to drinking, then it run him crazy," his sister Nona Parnell said. "I think it got to where he would drink too much and his wife left him." Hadley started drinking heavily, she said, after his wife left him with three children under school age. Hadley's wife's body was found hanging in a New Orleans motel room a

Hadley was the first person tried in Alabama under a law passed two months before he gunned Dutton down in the alley. The act carries the death penalty for the slaying of a policeman on duty— even if the killer was unaware the person was a police officer.

The shack behind Hadley's mother's house. This was where Hadley lived and was the object of his 1981 arson attempt.

PHOTOS • CATHY DONELSON

couple weeks later.

"I don't think he even got to see her. It just tore him up," she said. "He was not a mean boy. The boy has had enough to make him go crazy." At 66, Mrs. Parnell is the oldest of the 10 children of Mathilda and the late John Hadley, Sr.

Suicide, booze and trouble has followed the family. After Hadley's first wife's death he married a woman from Florida. "Then she passed away and that messed him up," his sister said.

Still, said E.B. Ball, an attorney who defended Hadley, "He's not the classic cop killer. There was no motive; everything worked together for the bad this time."

"There was a good side to Hadley and a bad side," said a pool room acquaintance who noted the man had no close friends. "He was a good man, but it seemed like he liked trouble and it seemed to follow," she said. He never held a steady job that anyone can recall and pool games were his recreation.

Hadley was fairly good at pool, according to an observer at Duck's Pool Hall in Robertsdale where he liked to spend his free time. However there were times he was asked to leave because he had a reputation for getting into knife fights and being unpredictable when he was drinking.

Hadley's penchant for trouble was no secret in town. His first recorded arrest in Robertsdale was for public drunkeness in 1976. That was the year Bob Williams became chief and started keeping arrest records. The record shows Hadley had numerous arrests related to alcohol, disturbing the peace, menacing, criminal trespass, many driving violations and assaults, including assault with a knife.

He has a long history of alcoholism and an IQ of about 70, according to one of his attorneys. "He's a lifelong alcoholic. We had strong testimony his alcoholism coupled with borderline mental retardation made it impossible for him to form an intent to kill," said Ball, one of the county's foremost criminal defense counsels. Hadley was admittedly drunk at the time of the shooting, with a .028 blood alcohol content. That's more than two and a half times legally intoxicated.

Ball says he believes Hadley doesn't know what happened. "Even after the trial was over he couldn't comprehend he had killed his friend, Howard Dutton," the lawyer said. "He would say, 'I can't believe they say I killed Howard'."

Hadley was the first person tried in Alabama under a law passed two months before he gunned Dutton down in the alley.

The act carries the death penalty for the slaying of a policeman on duty—even if the killer was unaware that the person was a law enforcement officer.

Hadley, on trial for his life, testified he had been drinking heavily the night of the murder and did not recollect anything after he left Duck's and crossed the highway. "I remember getting to the red light and feeling funny," he said. "The next thing I knew I was in the hospital." He said he first thought he'd been in an automobile accident and didn't realize he had been shot.

He said he liked and respected the deputy, whom he considered a friend, and couldn't believe he had shot him.

which could cause him to become psychotic under the influence of alcohol or stress and that he did not meet the state's test for sanity. Alabama law holds a sane person is able to understand the criminal nature of his acts when committing a crime.

At the end of the week-long trial at which spectators were required to pass through a metal detector and heavy security, the Baldwin County district attorney said the guilty verdict sent a strong message that the voluntary intake of alcohol wasn't a defense for a criminal act.

It had taken two days to select a jury for the capital trial because possible jurors were asked detailed questions about their views on

PHOTOS • CATHY DONELSON

Hadley's mother's house. It was on this porch the morning of the shooting that Robertsdale Police Chief, Robert Williams saw Hadley and exchanged greetings with him.

During the trial, two mental health experts gave conflicting reports. One said Hadley was insane when he shot the deputy and another said he wasn't. The director of psychiatry at the state's evaluation center, the Taylor Hardin Secure Mental Health Facility at Tuscaloosa, said the defendant was examined for a month after the killing and he, along with two other psychiatrists and a psychologist, agreed Hadley had mental problems but was sane.

A psychologist testifying for the defense said Hadley had a variety of mental disorders

the death penalty. It was about the time of the Ted Bundy execution in neighboring Florida, but Hadley's prosecutors expressed surprise about the "eye-for-an-eye" beliefs stated by prospective jurors who professed to also be very religious. Only one woman among the 60 people questioned said outright she was opposed to capital punishment.

During the trial Hadley, who wore blue jeans and a plaid cotton shirt, sat with his hands folded, staring grimly at the jury box and listening to witnesses. His grown son and daughter, who sat nearby, puzzled onlookers

If Hadley didn't remember what happened after he left the pool hall the night of Oct. 1, several witnesses did. A store clerk said Hadley came into the store and asked her to call the police because he was going out back to kill himself.

by giggling a few times when things were said in testimony which, under different circumstances might have seemed humorous. They also shot each other hopeful, timid smiles from time to time.

If Hadley didn't remember what happened after he left the pool hall the night of Oct. 1, several witnesses did. A convenience store clerk said he came into the store and asked her to call the police because he was going out back to kill himself. Sgt. Leroy Bishop of the Robertsdale Police Department said he called for back-up after he spotted the subject in an alley holding a shotgun.

Shortly afterward, four members of the five-man department, including the chief, arrived along with Deputy Dutton, who was patrolling the area. When the deputy approached, Hadley told him to stay back, saying, "Don't make me kill you."

As Deputy Dutton walked toward Hadley holding a flashlight in one hand and keeping the other hand raised to show he was unarmed, a shot blasted. "He had his pistol holstered and secured, hand up, then we heard Hadley's gun go off," the police officer said.

Then Sgt. Bishop fired three shots in the dark and one brought down Hadley. By the unconscious man, police found empty beer cans and a half-gallon jug of Mogen David, a high-alcohol content wine often called Mad Dog 20.20.

Today the crime scene doesn't look the same. The warehouse behind Hub City Tires where Hadley sat with a loaded shotgun is being demolished. His 84-year-old mother whose memory comes and goes has moved away from her home next door to stay with her oldest daughter. She's not alert enough to offer any insight into Hadley's life, though she helped him rear his motherless children.

Hadley's sister says he's under a doctor's care at the prison. "He won't let me know much about him now," Mrs. Parnell said. "But I can tell from the way he talks he's down."

After his eight-woman, four-man jury returned a guilty verdict which carried a life or death sentence, Hadley told Baldwin County Circuit Court Judge Charles Partin he'd rather die in the electric chair as soon as possible. At his March 9 sentencing hearing

he said he had changed his mind "on account of my young 'uns and my grandchildren." He said his children came to his county jail cell and said, "Daddy, we don't want to see you die in the electric chair. We'd like you to see your grandbabies and don't want to tell them their grandpa died in an electric chair."

David Simon, another of Hadley's defense lawyers, said his client clearly had low intelligence, was highly intoxicated and did not realize who was in front of him when he fired. Arguing it wasn't correct police procedure to walk into the line of fire of a suicidal person, he asked the judge to send the man to prison "for the rest of his natural life."

The prosecutor countered that the buckshot spray could have killed other policemen or passersby and said it had been an act of cold-blooded murder. Saying he had drafted the capital murder indictment with a heavy hand, DA Whetstone asked the court not to follow the jury recommendation, but to sentence the convicted man to death.

"Sure, a lot of people say he killed a police officer, so pour the coal to him, let him die," Simon said. Asking the judge to spare Hadley, he said "We're killing the retarded in an act of warfare against poor and incompetent people."

Despite Simon's plea that Hadley was in poor health and would have to beat the odds to live long enough to sit in the electric chair, Judge Partin handed down a death sentence, saying, "In the court's opinion, the law must be followed and an example must be set."

The issue of mental capacity and retardation of criminals was recently considered by the U.S. Supreme Court which did not outlaw capital punishment for retarded killers. In a case decision released June 27, 1989, Justice Sandra Day O'Connor wrote: "While a national consensus against execution of the mentally retarded may someday emerge reflecting the evolving standards of decency that mark the progress of a maturing society, there is insufficient evidence of such a consensus today."

Alabama officials have not shown a reluctance to move ahead with scheduled executions when court appeals have run their course in capital cases. When the last court has spoken, the state Attorney General's Office submits a request to the Alabama

Supreme Court to set a date.

Electrocutions, which are set by law to take place at 12:01 a.m. on a Friday, have been carried out at a rate of about one a year for the past few years. The last state execution took place this spring in the chair called "Yellow Mama" by some, but a death row prisoner commented recently, "We just call it the electric chair."

Gov. Guy Hunt, a Primitive Baptist minister and former probate judge who is the state's first Republican governor since the Reconstruction days following the Civil War, has not granted any reprieves or pardons after holding clemency hearings in his office with the family members of three condemned killers. He has said the courts and juries have spoken.

The law under which the deputy's killer was sentenced may eventually be called into question. In late June an appeal of his case, consisting of seven volumes of documents, was relayed in boxes by Alabama State Troopers from coastal Baldwin County up the interstate highway about 150 miles to the Court of Criminal Appeals in the capital, Montgomery. In Alabama the death penalty carries an automatic appeal and Hadley's lawyers say they think there is reversible error on the record in his case.

If so, Hadley may well sit behind bars for the next six or seven years before he gets the chair he changed his mind about—if indeed that will be his punishment for killing his friend, a law enforcement officer who died trying to help him for the last time.

Cathy Donelson has worked in Mobile, Ala. as gulf bureau chief of the Montgomery Advertiser *since 1984. She is the author of two books, including "Mobile, Sea Port City," and the former publisher of* Gulf Coast Magazine.

Robert Alton Harris

Steven J. Casey

By mid morning on Thursday, July 5, 1978 John Mayeski and Michael Baker, both 16, were less than half an hour away from summary execution at the hands of Robert Harris.

Before adding murder to his criminal resume, Harris' list of offenses included wife beating, auto theft, burglary, drunk driving and manslaughter.

Beneath the flight path into Miramar Naval Air Station, where Top Guns and weekend hot dogs bank their screaming Skyhawks west onto final approach, the bulging San Diego tabletop called Kearney Mesa holds much that is most depressing about Southern California.

As Gertrude Stein has said about Oakland, California "there's no _there_ there." No sense of place, or community, or soul. It is flat and dry and desolate. On its arid expanse have been laid wide boulevards, now always congested, lined with car dealerships and chain restaurants and the kind of shopping centers that look like they must have been built from plans ordered by mail.

PHOTOS ©UNION-TRIBUNE PUBLISHING CO.

North of Miramar by four miles is a housing tract called Mira Mesa. A tightly packed cluster of "affordable homes" utterly without style, Mira Mesa was built on Kearney Mesa jackrabbit land as one of San Diego's scrubby suburbs.

The July 4th holiday had been warm in Mira Mesa and in all of San Diego in 1978, and on July 5, a Thursday, at mid-morning the temperature was promising to reach 85 degrees. It was a day filled with excitement for two Mira Mesa teenagers, Michael Brian Baker and John Fitzgerald Mayeski. The 16-year-old pals had planned an afternoon of fishing at nearby Miramar Reservoir. His driver's license freshly issued, it was John's third time out with his dad's Ford Galaxie.

John Mayeski and Michael Baker lived on Westonhill Drive, John with his parents at 11047 and Michael with his mother just a few blocks up at 11453. The two boys shared much in life. Both endured teenage orthodontia—Michael's braces had come off not long before, John still had his. They were classmates, soulmates, and shared a love of fishing. Both were typical teenage products of the Southern California late 1970s, perhaps exceptional only in their preference for outdoor activity over drugs. Michael wore his light brown hair at shoulder length, John's blond hair was closer cut.

At about 10:30 that Thursday morning, John proudly wheeled up at Michael's house in the four-year-old green Ford with the personalized license plate "MAYSKI." The lads drove along Mira Mesa Boulevard, the main arterial through the neighborhood, to Black Mountain Road where there is a Jack-in-the-Box outlet. It was not much before 11 a.m. that morning when John and Michael pulled in the parking lot and walked inside to place their orders, chattering about the day's activity ahead.

They walked with the languid movements of youth, dressed comfortably for a day's outing, John wearing a light brown, short-sleeved pullover shirt with a red border along the base of the sleeve, blue denim pants with a large yellow comb sticking out of the back pocket and brown athletic shoes with lighter brown stripes along the side. Michael dressed still more casually, in a blue T-shirt with a seagull on the back, a pair of corduroy Levis and blue tennies with white stripes. They carried little money and only Michael had any identification, a photo ID from the Mira Mesa Junior-Senior High School. John's new driver's license was apparently forgotten in the flush of excitement.

They came out of the Jack-in-the-Box, their wrapped, thick, wet hamburgers in their hands, and climbed into the Ford. They were ready to head for the reservoir when they noticed a handsome young man with cold grey eyes approach the car as if to ask for help.

The two lads with all the hostility of puppies looked expectantly at Robert Alton Harris as he bent over the car door to speak. "Don't move," he said. He pulled a 9mm semi-automatic pistol from his waistband, pointed it at John's head and without another word climbed into the back seat of the Ford.

John and Michael had less than a half-hour to live.

About the time John entered Michael's driveway, 25-year-old Robbie Harris and his 18-year-old brother Danny were only two minutes away, leaving the modest rented home of Robbie's girlfriend, Rebecca Eddleman, a counselor to ex-convicts.

Idlers and petty criminals since childhood, the Harris brothers this day had serious business ahead: They were about to rob a bank. Still tired from a long drive south from the farming town of Visalia in California's central valley, the Harrises had slept in until about 9:30 a.m. They lounged around the house watching daytime television until boredom drove them out to a nearby Thrifty Drug Store where they each bought an ice cream and where, Danny would later say, the idea for the bank robbery was born.

Not quite. The life of Daniel Marcus Harris

PHOTOS ∙ UNION-TRIBUNE PUBLISHING CO.

Robert Harris is escorted from the courtroom. Robert and his brother, Danny had been petty criminals since childhood.

PHOTOS •UNION-TRIBUNE PUBLISHING CO.

At one time, Robert Harris had served time for beating a friend to death.

lose control of himself, right there in the car.

July 2, they went into the area around Brown Field which is a .22-short shot from the Mexican border on another mesa, occupied almost exclusively by lizards, illegal aliens and border patrol agents, and there they tested their weapons. July 4, they found a place near their Mira Mesa home and shot some more.

The morning of July 5, the brothers burned eye holes in the ski masks they planned to use in the bank robbery and only then did they go out to get ice cream—and to case the bank.

"It was a weird thing," Danny later told Chief Deputy District Attorney Richard Huffman about all that practicing with the guns. "We used them like combat maneuvers, I guess, or something to be able to use them... without aiming them and stuff like that."

Huffman is a man of great patience, particularly with a killer's brother who is going to be the prosecution's star witness. But even for a patient man, listening to Danny Harris can be a test. The exasperation in Huffman's voice was clear.

"Were you preparing yourself in any fashion for the bank robbery?" he asked.

"I'd say we was."

"How," Huffman persisted.

"Robbie said he wanted something like a... battle plan, that if it came down to a shootout or something, that we'd be more or less prepared for it."

It was, after all, going to be a big day and they needed to be ready. They had a bank to rob and boys to kill.

Robbie and Danny Harris left Rebecca Eddleman's in Robbie's newly-purchased 1963 Ford, drove down Westonhill past the Mayeski and Baker homes, on to Mira Mesa Boulevard where they headed east toward Black Mountain, scouting the area like two bozo desperados on their way to the bank. At 9045 Mira Mesa Boulevard stands the San Diego Trust and Savings Bank branch that so tempted the Harrises that they decided it was where they would make their debut into big league robbery.

More accurately, Robbie decided. Danny Harris, a slightly-built, nervous kid, was probably incapable of deciding anything more

has not been characterized by candor, and in truth the plan to rob the bank was far advanced by the time they purchased ice cream. They had first agreed on bank robbery back in June, Robbie promising Danny that the bank was picked, the guns secured, a gang of confederates at the ready, and riches just ahead. As always with Robbie's promises, it was smoke. There was no gang. No guns, No getaway car. No bank picked out. Nobody but Danny, Robbie, and the dream of losers.

On July 1, they had used the occasion of a family picnic in Visalia to sneak into a friend's apartment and steal his guns for use in the robbery. On the long night of July 1, during the drive to San Diego after the picnic, Robbie got in his first practice. With Danny asleep in the front seat and Robbie at the wheel, he broke out the stolen rifle and shot out his own back window. Danny thought he would

complicated than what to have for lunch. All through his young life he had been ordered about by family members or led about by friends and acquaintances, always ready to do whatever someone else asked, always ready to snivel and whine and snitch when those things went sour. Danny was in awe of his older brother who, once as slender and eager to please as Danny, had filled out by pumping iron while serving a prison sentence for beating a friend to death.

Robbie also decided that they needed a getaway car other than his own, so the two loitered in a nearby shopping center parking lot waiting for an opportunity.

Soon, the perfect victim arrived, an old woman who trundled into the Longs Drug Store. Robbie turned his attention to her green Chevy Nova, while Danny contributed to this criminal enterprise by buying a donut. Robbie popped the car hood but could not get the car started. He cursed as he sweated, scraping his knuckles on the engine and getting increasingly frustrated.

A police van cruised by, scaring Robbie into closing the Chevy's hood and climbing in his own car where he sat, stewing. The old woman came out of Longs and headed for her car, then suddenly veered off and went into the Safeway supermarket, a decision Robbie thought would surely cost her a car. He needed one, and he needed it now.

And then he saw it. It was a Ford Galaxie, and it had two boys in it.

"There was two boys in it, about my age I guess they were, maybe a little bit older, maybe a little bit younger," Danny said the next day. "And my brother looked back at me 'cause I was in the back seat, and he said 'we're going to get a car now.' I thought he was going to steal a car."

Whatever he may have thought, Danny also handed Robbie the automatic, as the elder brother headed for the boys' car.

Robbie ordered Baker to drive less than a mile, to the then seldom traveled intersection of Erma Road and Scripps Ranch Boulevard. There, a fire trail takes off up a rugged hillside, then goes over the crest and into a wash where there was litter from occasional transients and teenaged visitors on missions of delinquency. Danny, who followed in Robbie's car, told Huffman that this area was "one we was at the day before," firing their guns.

As Danny parked, Robbie and his two captives trudged up the rough rock trail. Their mood was surprisingly cheery, for Robbie had reassured them he meant them no harm. He asked if the boys had any marijuana, and was disappointed that they did not. They continued walking, talking lightly, and short of the crest of the hill stopped to rest. Danny had by then caught up, and he and Robbie talked with John and Michael about their planned robbery, and the use of the getaway car.

"I got out of the car with the rifle, we got the pistol and the rifle because we were going to rob the bank...and, ah, so we walked them up there and everything, and just talked to them real friendly like and I didn't even know, we thought we was going to let them go, at least I did, and they did too," Danny said.

Whether John and Michael were buying any of that is something we'll never know. We do know that for whatever reason, possibly terror, they agreed to wait at the top of the hill until well after the Harrises had driven off, then walk slowly down and into town before making their stolen car report. They also volunteered to tell the police that their abductors were black, so as to help cover the trail of these white robbers.

As agreed, John and Michael arose and started walking into the bushes, climbing toward the top of the hill where they would wait. Preoccupied with his future as a bank robber, Danny gazed off toward town, wondering how he was going to pull off the biggest caper in his sorry little life.

Michael Baker started off first, John Mayeski behind and for some reason still clutching the hamburger he'd bitten into before he was kidnapped. Michael stepped out into the bush as a shot rang out, crashing into John's back and tearing through his lungs.

"I heard the shot and as soon as I heard it I turned and saw the guy, the blond haired guy, look at me. Blood came out of his mouth and everything, and I thought he was shot in the shoulder," Danny said. "And he fell down on the ground, kind of spun and hit the ground, and it just shocked me when I looked at it. And the look on his face—you know, his eyes bulged out real big and everything."

As always with Robbie's promises, it was smoke. There was no gang. No guns, No getaway car. No bank picked out. Nobody but Danny, Robbie, and the dream of losers.

A patrol officer leveled a 12-gauge shotgun at Robbie and yelled "Freeze where you are. Put your hands on top of your head." That officer was Steven Baker, Michael's father. As he led Robbie away, Steve Baker had no idea that his son lay murdered nearby.

And the world went mad with action and anger and fear.

Robbie fired again at John, again hitting him in the back. John fell to the ground, unbelieving and still clutching the wrapper from his hamburger. The partially eaten hamburger fell into the dirt under his right knee. Michael ran screaming up the trail, Robbie chasing after him with the automatic. Michael plunged onto a dirt embankment and, breathing heavily, cried and screamed for mercy as he desperately clawed at the earth, flinging dirt and writhing at the earth as he tried to scramble up over the top to safety.

It was so futile, Michael made it only 33 feet when Robbie reached him and told him contemptuously to "Quit crying and die like a man." Then he pulled the trigger four times and Michael Baker was no more.

Robbie raced back to the mortally wounded John, where Danny stood, stunned. Robbie took the 9mm pistol in his left hand, extended both of his arms straight out until the barrel of the gun just kissed John's head, and fired. But not before he protected himself with his right hand.

"He kind of used it as a shield," said Danny. "He put it up behind the back part of the pistol so, I guess, that if any parts of the Mayeski boy's blood or hair or skin or something came off it wouldn't go back on him."

Danny Harris dropped his rifle and fled to the car. Robbie gathered up the weapons and drove the dead boys' car back to the Eddleman residence, and Danny brought home his brother's Ford. Danny ran to the bathroom and got sick after he walked into the living room and found Robbie eating Michael Baker's hamburger. Robbie laughed, and called him a sissy.

Fifteen minutes later, the Harris brothers made the first of two trips to the bank. Parking in the lot, they ran up to an automated teller machine by the bank's door, but Danny couldn't bring himself to go inside. They went back to the car, rested, and tried again to approach the bank. This time, Robbie asked Danny if he had brought a pillow case for the money they expected to get, and Danny had not. So the would-be robbers went back to Eddleman's and picked up a pillow case, and returned to the vicinity of the bank. There, they

decided that before the robbery they should find the police ambulance stationed in that area, and ambush and kill the two officers in it as a diversion.

For 10 minutes they hunted for the officers, without success. Again, they went back to the bank and, again, Danny chickened out. As Danny got up his nerve for the coming robbery, Robbie joked about how much fun it would be to dress up as policemen and tell the Mayeski and Baker families that their sons were dead. He pulled the automatic from his waistband, and found fragments of John's scalp and hair on the barrel. He giggled as he flicked it out the window of the car, and observed that he really blew the kid's brains out.

Convinced by Robbie that with two boys dead on the hillside they had nothing to lose, and spurred along by his command "If you don't do it, I'll whip your ass," Danny went inside the bank with Robbie. Together the two controlled the crowd of customers, intimidated a teller with weapons and made off with $2,983. As they ran out the door, two bank customers standing outside heard shouts of a holdup and gave chase. The Harris brothers roared off in the Ford with the MAYSKI plates, and in separate cars heroes Harry Rogers and Robert Pineault followed, tracking the two through Mira Mesa to Eddleman's house. Within minutes of the bank robbery, police surrounded the residence and, quietly staking out the house, snatched up first Danny and then Robbie as they wandered, unsuspecting, outside.

A patrol officer leveled a 12-gauge shotgun at Robbie and yelled "Freeze where you are. Put your hands on top of your head." That officer was Steven Baker, Michael's father. As he led Robbie away, Steve Baker had no idea that his son lay murdered nearby.

Interrogation of Danny Harris by police and FBI agents simply completing work on a botched bank robbery led to the stunning revelation of the two murders. That, in turn, led to a quiet but bitter fight between the District Attorney in San Diego and a United States Attorney who threatened to try the bank robbery case in federal court even if that meant trampling over the District Attorney's murder evidence in the process.

Ed Miller, San Diego's District Attorney,

was livid. So was Chief Deputy D.A. Richard Huffman, Miller's designated death penalty prosecutor, who succeeded in getting the state murder trial date set a week before the federal trial was scheduled. Soon, the Harrises went to federal court to plead guilty to bank robbery, in plea bargains that gave Robbie 25 years and Danny six. With that, the sole legal stage was state court.

There, the evidence was overwhelming. Before trial, Robbie Harris had confessed twice to investigators, once to a psychiatrist, once to a jail inmate and again to his younger sister. Murder weapons, cash from the bank robbery and other physical evidence was found at Eddleman's house. Gunshot residue was all over his hands. And then there was Danny's chilling testimony against his brother.

Huffman tried his case against skilled defense attorney Tom Ryan whose biggest challenge was controlling his client, the drama playing out over six weeks before Superior Court Judge Eli Levinson. Slowly, methodically, Huffman built his case against Harris, getting an unexpected break when the defendant decided to testify. Robbie insisted he was innocent, insisted he killed no one on July 5. He said his confessions were all lies, police testimony was all lies, that it was Danny's fault.

After a day of deliberation, the jury told Harris what they thought of his story, bringing in verdicts of guilty of two counts of first degree murder, kidnapping and robbery.

The trial then shifted to the penalty phase. The jury heard evidence about Robbie's childhood, previous crimes, crimes committed in jail while on trial, and testimony from Robbie himself, in which he said his denials of guilt were a pack of lies, and that he did the murders but he was sorry.

The fifth of nine children, Robbie was born to violence.

On the night of January 15, 1953, Evelyn Harris was six and a half months pregnant when her husband, Kenneth, came home drunk and insanely jealous. Accusing her of infidelity, he ranted that the baby in her womb was not his. He threw her to the ground and kicked her. Hours later, Robbie was born and spent the first months of his life in an incubator.

His parents were a cold-hearted mother who herself was convicted of bank robbery and an alcoholic father who twice was incarcerated for molesting his daughters. In his early years, Robbie moved with the family from labor camp to labor camp, as his ex-Army warrant officer father sought work as a fruit picker. Usually, the family stayed in the fields working, the elder Harris stayed in the camp, drunk.

All the children were subject to abuse and neglect, but Robbie, who by some sibling accounts was the most sensitive of them all, was singled out for particularly harsh treatment. From his mother when he cried out for love or reached out to wrap his tiny arms around her leg, he got the back of a hand or a bloodied nose. From his father he got disgust and cruelty, and never recognition that he was his father's son.

In trouble with juvenile authorities since age 10, and a chronic sniffer of glue, paint or virtually any other substance, Robbie left home at 14. He lived a while with a brother, then hitch-hiked to Oklahoma where he lived with a sister before he and a friend stole a car and went to Florida where they were arrested.

PHOTOS •UNION-TRIBUNE PUBLISHING CO.

Harris in handcuffs in a courthouse corridor during his trial.

Robbie took the 9mm pistol in his left hand, extended both of his arms straight out until the barrel of the gun just kissed John's head, and fired.

He was sent to a federal youth detention facility in Kentucky, where officials tried to help him by putting him into a course of study on rocketry. He repaid them by stealing rocket fuel and taxing all his 109 IQ points trying to make bombs.

He escaped, tried to escape again, was a constant discipline problem, was transferred from one institution to another and tried, or feigned trying, suicide. Recording Robbie's history for Huffman, District Attorney Investigator Ray Cameron wrote that "he broke his fist, removed the cast, rebroke the fist, then shoved a pointed piece of plastic into his penis requiring surgical removal, stuck his hand into a movie reel, has attempted numerous escapes, has become intoxicated on solvents and fought with correctional officers."

Released from federal custody, Robbie went to join the family in Visalia and even they were stunned at what he had become. He was bigger and stronger, he had lost his innocent quest for love, he tortured animals, he was cold and hard. Up and down California, Robbie left a record of drunk driving, minor burglaries and at least one armed robbery in which he and a crime partner rolled a hobo in a train yard, beating and cutting their victim before taking his blanket roll, money and gun.

Three years later he was living in the desert town of El Centro, when he beat his next door neighbor to death, hitting and stomping the weaker man. Originally charged with murder, Robbie pleaded guilty to voluntary manslaughter and had spent less than three years in prison when he was released in January 1978—five months and 26 days before he murdered John Mayeski and Michael Baker.

Along the way, he had married and fathered a son. The marriage ended, and he told a psychiatrist "Well, I guess the reason why she, they, left was because I beat her up pretty bad one day."

All this the jury heard in the penalty phase of his trial. The jury also heard that a shank and a garrotte were confiscated from Robbie's cell before his trial, and that during trial he and several other inmates held a kangaroo court. There, "Judge" Harris tried an inmate in their jail tank for the "crime" of cowardice, found him guilty, and sentenced him—under pain of death—to multiple sodomies and to orally copulate three of his accusers, as well as "Judge" Harris.

The jury also heard from psychiatrist Wait R. Griswold, who diagnosed Robbie as a sociopath and described him as "immature, emotionally unstable, callous, egotistical and manipulative." Griswold testified Robbie had started laughing when asked if he derived pleasure from murdering the boys. "Well, it seemed funny at the time," he quoted Robbie as saying.

His family came to visit him in the jail while the trial was on, and Robbie told them he would get the death penalty, and he had accepted death.

"Hey, mama, I wanta tell you something," he said to his mother, "okay? Okay, remember when I was about seven, eight years old, I told you this voice kept telling me that I was gonna die, gonna die, gonna die? And I told you there was this voice I was hearin,' right? Okay, and I said it was just in my head? Okay, now, I been havin' these dreams and, man, they're beautiful dreams, mama. I mean just growin', this forest, this beautiful forest and this pond, and about going to different worlds and stuff and I think, I think this is my time to go, mama."

He added an element of his dream when he talked with his sister, Glenda.

"Now, I been havin' these beautiful dreams, I mean beautiful dreams about going to different worlds, different dimensions and, and they're really, really beautiful, and there's a beautiful, well, she's naked, but, you know, she's sitting on a horse…the beautifullest horse I ever seen in my life. And she's waiting for me and there's a big pond and trees and lily pads and it's, it's sanctuary. It's peace of mind, you know…

"Now, I guess because I killed those two kids, they were only 16 years old, and robbed the bank, and kidnapped them, was because I really wanted to die. I know by doing this and getting caught that I would die. And this is what I want. See? When you die you to to a beautiful place and that's where I'm gonna go…I can go where that horse is at and this girl and live there and be, be happy, you know, really be happy. There'll be no guns, no weapons, it'll just be beautiful and that's where I want to go, okay?"

Talking to another sister, Debbie, he insisted that death was his way of coping.

"Everything fits, fits in place. I'm not meant

for this world. I'm not. Matter of fact, since I was a little bitty sucker, I just didn't, couldn't handle the world around me and all the other shit, so now when I go, I'll be happy. I'm not upset. I'm not nervous. Matter of fact, I'm happy. I really am."

Two and a half hours after retiring to deliberate, the jury returned to the courtroom with a verdict of death.

In a rare Death Row interview, Robert Alton Harris in 1989 reaffirmed that attitude of a decade earlier and, perhaps unknowingly, gave himself the same command he gave Michael Baker. Robbie said when the execution came he would "die like a man."

That execution, however, is still uncertain. Widely expected to be the first murderer put to death in California's gas chamber since the 1967 execution of cop-killer Aaron Mitchell, Robbie Harris has filed 14 appeals since his death sentence was pronounced, making three unsuccessful trips to the United States Supreme Court.

For awhile, the most promising argument for him seemed to be a claim that the death penalty is applied in a racially discriminatory manner. That argument is advanced in the case of black killers, who claim too many black murderers are sentenced to die in comparison with the number of white murderers under sentence of death. Most people would not think that affords a white lad like Robbie Harris much comfort; most people have not contemplated the creativity of the legal mind. Robbie's appeals were based, in part, on the claim that killers are sentenced to die in disproportionate numbers if their victims are white. In both his case and another, the U.S. Supreme Court removed that as an issue.

At present, the Harris case is bouncing between the U.S. District Court in San Diego and the 9th U.S. Circuit Court of Appeals, on the issue of whether Dr. Griswold's trial testimony was proper. Some say the U.S. Ninth Circuit is a liberal court determined to permit no executions in the Western states it controls. Nonetheless, even passionate foes of the death penalty agree that Robbie's legal recourse has been about exhausted, and most observers predict he will be executed by mid-1990.

That will, or so it is claimed, set off a series of executions in California, executions now being held up because Robbie's case is being used to raise and decide legal issues—real or imagined—common to all.

As the appellate process drones on, memories dim, faces change. Prosecutor Huffman, later named the California District Attorney's Assn. "prosecutor of the year," was appointed by California's governor first to the Superior Court bench and later as a justice of the state's Court of Appeal. Deputy Attorney General Mike Wellington, who handled 10 years of appellate litigation on Robbie's death sentence, in 1989 was appointed a Superior Court judge.

Since the murders, San Diego has grown out to Mira Mesa, surrounding it and gobbling up its canyons and hillsides. The view from the crest of the hill off Erma Road is still magnificent, as all of Kearney Mesa spreads out below and you can see from well past Miramar Naval Air Station to the south, almost all the way to the bustling city of Escondido to the north. Nothing is left of the arroyo where John Mayeski and Michael Baker were murdered. The knoll has been eaten away by bulldozers, which have scraped a road snaking up the reshaped hill. The storm drains have long since been moved, the rough rock is now paved. Winding up that road is a handsome brick wall and at its summit an electronically controlled wrought iron gate, marking the entrance of what has been elegantly named Nob Hill, an upscale condominium development that likely does not know it has been born on the very spot two young boys were taken to die.

Casey also wrote Standards of Decency and a profile on trailside killer, David Carpenter, both of which appear elsewhere in this volume.

Jesus Rodriguez Jimenez

Laura Laughlin

Court records show Jimenez took Marisol into a bedroom to give her some candy, then strangled her until she went limp.

The Arizona Attorney General's Office publishes a booklet profiling the men awaiting execution on death row at the state's maximum security prison in Florence.

Among the 76 faces included in the latest edition of the publication are many that could make a person's skin crawl. These are men who appear quite capable of the kinds of atrocities that prompt judges to order them to die in the gas chamber.

The photograph of Jesus Rodriguez Jimenez is an exception. It depicts a nice-looking youth with dark, sad eyes and a thin moustache, the kind skinny, baby-faced young men sometimes grow to make them appear older.

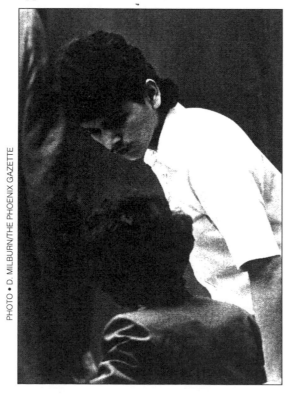

PHOTO • D. MILBURN/THE PHOENIX GAZETTE

Jimenez, 18 is escorted into the courtroom at his 1987 trial for the murder of Marisol Diaz. Now 19, he is the youngest person on death row in Arizona.

But 19-year-old Jimenez, the youngest resident of Arizona's death row, doesn't have to rely on facial hair to prove he is an adult. The Mexican national earned his entry into the grown-up world when two months after his 17th birthday, he invited 5-year-old Marisol Diaz to his house, strangled her, stabbed her more than 16 times in the chest, vagina and rectum and finally plunged a knife into her mouth, leaving it lodged in the vertebrae behind her throat.

The vicious slaying of the little girl who lived next door to Jimenez was an aberration. Jimenez never had been in trouble with the law. Those who knew him said he was kind of a loner, but seemed to be a nice, gentle soul. Even the mother of Marisol Diaz testified at Jimenez's trial that she had no reason to fear the boy who lived with his aunt and uncle next to her home in Phoenix. Jesus enjoyed playing with kids on the block and her children often went to his house to visit him.

The oldest of three children who were shuffled from home to home all their lives, Jimenez was born Sept. 7, 1969 in Sonora, Mexico.

He never knew his father. His mother was an alcoholic nightclub singer who reportedly tried to sell him to Americans when he was a baby. An aunt told Jesus she hid him in the mountains to foil the deal. But no one was able to save him from a miserable childhood.

Raised for a time by grandparents, he returned at one point to live with his mother, who placed him in a boarding house. Jimenez said he was let out of the facility one day a week to see his mother, who would frequently be either not at home or drunk.

When his mother married a Mexican customs officer, Jesus moved back to a stormy household marked by heavy drinking, violent fights, breakups, reconciliations, and life with a stepfather, who told him he was bad, stupid and worthless.

In 1984, Jesus was sent to Arizona to live with an aunt and uncle in Phoenix. When he enrolled in North High School, he immediately encountered difficulties. He struggled not only with the English language, but also with the content of the classes.

would again have to obey the voices' commands.

Jimenez, who was classified by the school as a slow learner and was on a waiting list for special education classes, made an appointment with a counselor and told the man about the voices and what they were telling him to do.

"I wanted to ask for help," he said. "Later, I

PHOTO • R. GATES/THE PHOENIX GAZETTE

Marisol's mother tearfully relays the events of the last day she saw her daughter alive.

"The words do not stay in my head," he explained to the detective who questioned him the day he killed Marisol. Jimenez, a high school sophomore when he was arrested, said he had received all F's on his last report card.

Some words, however, did remain in his head, echoing the messages he had heard in Mexico. Voices told him he was stupid, bad and good for nothing. And sometimes, he said, they ordered him to hurt someone.

Five days before he killed Marisol Diaz, Jimenez decided to tell his school counselor about the voices. Responding to them, he had tried to stab a male friend and he feared he

felt better that I had told him, but always a little ashamed."

Judge Edward C. Rapp, the Maricopa County Superior Court judge who ordered Jimenez transferred from juvenile to adult court, lamented in his order that the counselor did not report Jimenez's revelations to anyone—"especially the aunt or uncle, a report which might have headed off this tragic event."

Three days after seeing the counselor, Jimenez decided he had no choice but to obey the voices. And he selected Marisol as the one he would hurt.

Prosecution experts agreed that Jimenez was mentally ill, but said his problems did not rise to the level of insanity. Even the witnesses hired by Ray could not convince the jury that Jimenez was insane when he murdered the little girl.

"I do not know why I did it, but I planned it and this is the way I did it," Jimenez told a detective in Spanish after the murder.

This is how he carried out his plan: On Nov. 30, 1986, when his aunt and uncle were out of town, Jimenez telephoned Marisol at about 2 p.m. Earlier in the day, Marisol and other children had been playing marbles outside with Jimenez. Marisol's mother said her little girl hung up the phone that Sunday and ran out the door, answering "Chuy"—Jimenez's nickname—when asked who had called her. That was the last time Maria Diaz saw her daughter alive.

Court records show Jimenez took Marisol into a bedroom to give her some candy, then strangled her until she went limp. When Marisol's brother and sister came to the door looking for her, Jimenez stuffed Marisol under the bed and went to tell her siblings she was not there. While talking to the children, Jimenez heard cries coming from the bedroom. He hustled his visitors away and returned to the room after getting a steak knife from the kitchen.

Jimenez dragged Marisol out from under the bed and strangled her again. Then he started stabbing her.

Dr. Heinz Karnitschnig, the county medical examiner who performed the autopsy on Marisol, said the little girl died from asphyxiation as a result of strangulation. All of the stab wounds were inflicted post-mortem, he said, including lacerations that cut her heart in two, crushed her liver, punctured one lung 13 times and mutilated her vaginal and rectal areas.

While there was no evidence the child had been molested or raped, Karnitschnig testified the motivation for the attack was sexual, a theory bolstered by the discovery of semen inside the pants Jimenez was wearing at the time of the slaying.

Jimenez finished the bloodbath by sticking the knife in the little girl's mouth. Then he cleaned up his mess, changed his clothes, placed Marisol in a black garbage bag, carried her in a plastic trash can into the backyard and deposited the body in the trunk of his uncle's broken-down Mustang.

Next door, Maria Diaz was growing more and more concerned. Ninety minutes after Marisol had run out the door and disappeared, the girl's mother called the police. A full-scale search for the child ensued, complete with helicopters and volunteers passing out fliers.

Jimenez told police he knew nothing about Marisol's disappearance, then joined in the attempt to find his little friend, passing out fliers as he scoured the neighborhood.

At about 9:30 p.m., a police sergeant became suspicious of fresh hand prints on the dusty car behind Jimenez's house. The vehicle's owner, Jimenez's uncle, Ramon Sarabia, had returned home by that time and had given permission to open the trunk. When Sarabia could not locate the keys (they usually were handing in the kitchen), the trunk was forced open.

Inside, police found Marisol's body wrapped in the garbage bag, the knife still protruding from her open mouth.

Jimenez, who hung his head in apparent grief at the grisly discovery, was taken to a Phoenix police station where he confessed to Detective Tony Morales.

At trial, court-appointed defense attorney, C. Kenneth Ray said the confession was forced out of a petrified Jesus Jimenez, and argued Jimenez did not murder Marisol Diaz. He discounted evidence Deputy County Attorney K.C. Scull called overwhelming—including the confession to police and others, blood found on Jimenez's clothing and in the room where Marisol was killed, Jimenez's palm prints found on the trunk and the garbage bag used to wrap the body, and plenty of other circumstantial evidence.

In an unusual strategy, Ray also used the insanity defense. After arguing primarily that his client did not kill Marisol Diaz, Ray told jurors that if he did, he was insane and not responsible for his actions.

But expert witnesses did not support that defense. Prosecution experts agreed that Jimenez was mentally ill, but said his problems did not rise to the level of insanity. Even the witnesses hired by Ray did not testify convincingly Jimenez was insane when he murdered the little girl.

Jimenez, a slight young man who kept his eyes downcast or fixed ahead during most of the trial, listened to the evidence and arguments via an interpreter whose translations he heard through a headset. During the particularly gruesome testimony by Karnitschnig, Jimenez pulled his earphones off. He did not testify.

Jurors convicted him of first-degree murder and kidnapping.

On Jan. 22, 1988, Judge Michael O'Melia ordered Jimenez put to death in Arizona's gas chamber and imposed the maximum sentence for the kidnapping charge—22 years to be served consecutive to time served for the murder conviction.

The 5-foot-10, 140-pound youth was the second juvenile ever sentenced to death in Arizona, where the classification is measured by the age of the defendant at the time the crime was committed.

Frank Valencia, the first juvenile to be given the death penalty, had his sentence commuted to life in 1982 by the Arizona Supreme Court. The Tucson boy was 16 when he shot and killed a girl whose purse he was trying to steal. Arizona's high court ruled his age should have been given great weight as a mitigating factor at the time of sentencing.

In his sentencing memorandum, Jimenez's prosecutor argued age was not a great mitigating factor in the case of the murder of Marisol Diaz, first because the crime Jimenez committed was cruel, heinous and depraved, and secondly because Jimenez's actions revealed a maturity that belied his age.

"Not only did he lure the victim over to his house, he convincingly denied her presence when the sister and brother came looking for her and quickly made them leave so that he returned to the bedroom to kill her. His cunning behavior of wrapping her body, cleaning any trace of blood from the murder scene and the subsequent secreting of the body also shows 'substantial judgment of a normal mind.' The fact he was able to dupe the police authorities again reflects his maturity," Scull told the judge.

The deputy county attorney said the murder revealed "an abandoned and malignant heart" and called it a cold-blooded execution: "The defendant cannot even claim to have been in a rage because he was interrupted and calmly misdirected the poor victim's brother and sister. He also cooly and calmly

PHOTO • R. GATES/THE PHOENIX GAZETTE

Jimenez listens to testimony translated through earphones. During a particularly grisly testimony, he yanked the headset from his ears.

lied to the police and the distraught mother."

Scull also noted Jimenez's lack of remorse, quoting from his taped confession to police in which the youth said he knew he had done something wrong but said, "I don't feel bad."

After struggling with the amount of weight to give Jimenez's age and mental condition, O'Melia decided those factors were not sufficient to call for leniency.

"The aggravating factors outweigh the mitigating circumstances," O'Melia said. "The five-year-old was completely helpless and it appears to be a completely premeditated, covered-up murder."

Jimenez took the witness stand for the first time before he was sentenced and gave conflicting answers to questions. Asked whether he killed the girl, Jimenez said, "That I know of, no. But maybe so."

**Judge
Michael
O'Melia
ordered
Jimenez
put to
death in
Arizona's
gas
chamber
and
imposed
the
maximum
sentence
for the
kidnapping
charge.**

Scull tried further to get him to admit he murdered Marisol.

"Maybe yes, maybe no," was Jimenez's response. In answering another query, Jimenez said he didn't necessarily plan to kill the child.

In a pre-sentence interview with a psychiatrist, Jimenez explained himself a bit more clearly. Fearing he would not be able to say anything to the judge before his sentence was pronounced, he asked the doctor to pass on this message to the judge, the state and the detectives who had interviewed him.

"I am still not sure yet that I killed the little girl," Jimenez said. "I do know that I do bad things and after, it's like waking up from a dream. First I hear the voices, then for a few days I go without eating, then afterwards I lose control and hurt someone and not realize what I was doing.."

These days, Jimenez is in little danger of hurting anyone else.

He lives alone in a seven-by-nine concrete cell at the Arizona State Prison complex in Florence. Six hours a week, he is taken outdoors for exercise. The rest of the time he lives quietly in a section of death row reserved for child killers. Jimenez and the other three condemned men in his pod are well-behaved, prison officials report. They are already so hated by their fellow prisoners they do not want to cause any further trouble.

Unlike other death row residents who immerse themselves in their appeals, Jimenez has not been very involved in post-sentencing legal efforts. The attorney handling the appeal, Deputy Public Defender John Rood III, said he has not met Jimenez, but has written him letters informing him of the status of the case. Because of the language barrier, communication is difficult, Rood said.

So far, Rood has barely scratched the surface in the lengthy and confusing death penalty appeal process.

He and a state prosecutor have filed briefs with the Arizona Supreme Court, which has indicated it will conduct oral arguments on the case, but has not set a date for that hearing.

"We are really just at the first stage," Rood said. "Undoubtedly this will take a considerable length of time"—an understatement in a state that has not executed anyone since 1963.

Complicating Jimenez's case are two crucial issues. One is the question of the constitutionality of Arizona's death penalty statutes. John Harvey Adamson, the confessed killer of newspaper reporter Don Bolles, won a Ninth U.S. Circuit Court of Appeals decision in November, 1988, which, if upheld, would strike down the state capital punishment laws. The federal judges ruled Arizona improperly allows trial judges to determine aggravating and mitigating circumstances in addition to sentencing defendants in capital cases, Jurors should be the ones to find the existence of such factors before the judge passes sentence, the court said.

That ruling, which Arizona Attorney General Bob Corbin called "asinine," has been appealed to the U.S. Supreme Court, which has not yet decided whether to accept the case. If it does, experts say, the justices could rule next summer at the earliest.

A second major issue—the constitutionality of executing juveniles—was resolved recently when the U.S. Supreme Court decided it was not cruel and unusual punishment to put to death convicts who were 16 and 17 years old when they committed capital crimes.

In a 5-4 vote on two cases, the justices said there was no national consensus against putting to death juvenile offenders. Their ruling in effect set the cutoff date for execution at 16, because it came a year after the high court struck down the death penalty for a 15-year-old in an Oklahoma case. In that decision, the justices declared execution cruel and unusual punishment in the absence of a law saying death is appropriate for an offender so young.

Another question that remains open-ended in the Jimenez case involves the role of the Mexican government. Of the three or four Mexican nationals on death rows across the United States, Rood said, two of them are in Arizona.

He said the officials of Jimenez's native country have expressed an interest in the status of his appeal. What they might do as the case progresses remains to be seen, Rood said. As is routine in cases involving Mexican citizens, the government has put an immigration hold on Jimenez, meaning if he ever were to be released from custody, he faces deportation.

This much is certain: Jesus Rodriguez Jimenez will not be visiting Arizona's gas chamber anytime soon. One of his neighbors in Florence, Willie Lee Richmond, has been awaiting execution nearly 16 years for a murder committed in 1972, longer than any other condemned prisoner in the United States.

Death penalty expert Crane McClennen of the Arizona Attorney General's Office said with the constitutionality of the state's capital punishment laws up in the air, Richmond can expect to wait at least another year in limbo.

The assistant attorney general cited the Richmond case in answer to a question about how long Jimenez may have to wait before his sentence is carried out.

"That's 17 years," he concluded after summarizing the Richmond case—a time period equal to the length of Jimenez's life before he telephoned Marisol Diaz, his favorite neighborhood buddy, and asked her to come over to his house one Sunday afternoon.

Laura Laughlin spent six years as a reporter for the Phoenix, Gazette, *covering Superior Court activities for five of those years. She has also covered the courts and education for the* Tucson Citizen *and the* Manteca (Calif.) Bulletin.

John J. Joubert

Jim Ivey

Joubert noticed blood on his hands as he entered a fast-food cafe for breakfast. He washed it off, then sat down to order. He ate and went back to the barracks. He went to sleep.

Late summer, 1983, presented itself pleasantly to metropolitan Omaha. The days were in the 80s, dry and warm. At night, the temperature dropped into the 60s.

The nation still buzzed about the Soviet downing of a Korean jetliner. Pete Rose was soon to become the second baseball player in history to get 4,000 major league hits. In downtown Omaha, the first River City Roundup—Johnny Cash and Alvin and the Chipmunks for the kids—was coming.

Those events were edged Sept. 18 by the pride of Nebraska, the university football team. That Saturday night, the team had rolled over Minnesota, 84 to 13, and Nebraskans wondered if a national championship would come with the fall.

It would be fall in a few days—and it looked good.

But what was coming for suburban parents was an autumn of terror.

At 5 a.m. Sept 18, the Sunday morning newspapers were loaded onto the big green stake-bed trucks. They pulled out through the night, over the cool pavement to a thousand waiting newspaper carriers.

PHOTOS • OMAHA WORLD HERALD

Former Eagle Scout and Airman, first class, John Joubert is now a resident of Nebraska's death row.

At 5 a.m., Danny Joe Eberle was getting up in his home at 113 Valley View Drive in Bellevue, an Omaha suburb. The 13-year-old eighth grader pulled on his light-blue corduroy trousers, the long-sleeved blue-denim shirt and the dark-blue sneakers. In minutes, the morning papers would be at the corner near the parking lot of an all-night grocery a few blocks away.

At 5 a.m., the alarm went off in Room 113, Barracks 400, at nearby Offutt Air Force Base, the headquarters of the Strategic Air Command. It aroused the sole occupant, John J. Joubert. Through his 20-year-old mind again went the thought:

Is this the day I will do it?

Kill.

That mind picture, psychiatrists said later, was the stimulus for his awakening from a string of fantasies he had been having since his childhood. In the next few days, he was to become the target of the biggest manhunt in Sarpy County history; in a few months, the biggest in metropolitan Omaha history. More than a hundred lawmen would be working full time searching for him.

In little more than a year, he was to be on Nebraska's death row, the admitted killer of two young boys and the accused killer of a third. Behind him would echo the testimony of one of those who had examined him:

"He would have killed again."

But all that was far away on the clear morning of Sept. 18. Joubert got up quickly, dressed and went to his car. Inside, he strapped the sheathed knife to his side. It was a knife for fileting fish—thin, razor sharp. He had purchased it a few days earlier at a shopping center near Bellevue expressly for what he was going to do. He brought with him a few loops of rope with colored strands and a roll of plain adhesive tape.

In his newly purchased 1979 tan Chevrolet Nova the radar technician began cruising, something he had done a lot of since arriving at Offutt two months earlier. He pulled up at the all-night market near Madison Street and Mission Avenue, where he had seen newspaper carriers gather in the past. One of them was a kind of skinny blond-haired kid.

Joubert purchased a soft drink in the grocery store, went back outside and leaned up against the car, swallowing the liquid, looking about. He noticed the same blond-haired boy, four or five inches shorter than himself. Danny Joe Eberle was fixing the papers for his route.

The airman knew the procedure. He had been a carrier in his hometown of Portland, Me. He finished off the pop, threw the container in a trash can, got into his car and drove south on Madison, pulling over into a parking lot. He grabbed some rope and tape and walked back up toward Mission, where the boy was crossing the street to make a delivery. The two said hello to each other.

Joubert crouched behind a tree while the boy continued his route. At 2302 Madison, Danny got off his bike to make a delivery. It was still dark when Joubert walked up to him again. The boy said pleasantly, "Hello."

"Hello," Joubert replied.

When the paper boy returned and started to get back onto his bike, Joubert grabbed him from behind and held the knife to his throat.

"Come with me and don't make any sounds," he commanded.

When they got to the Nova, Joubert ordered him again: "Lay on your stomach."

With the rope, he tied Danny's hands behind him and tied his legs. He ripped off a piece of the tape and placed it over the boy's mouth. Then he opened the car trunk, put the bound boy inside, started the car and drove.

South past the base he drove, to a dirt road leading east to a Missouri River community called Iske Park. A hundred yards off the paved road, he stopped and got out. He took Danny Joe from the trunk and laid him in the ditch at the side of the road. Danny had made no sound so far.

Danny had worked the tape from his mouth and now he pleaded, "Don't, please don't kill me."

Joubert untied the boy, made him take off all his clothing but his shorts, then re-tied him.

"He struggled a little bit then and I stabbed him in the back. When I done that, he told me that if I would take him to the hospital, he wouldn't say anything. I didn't believe him, so I stabbed him again a couple of times," Joubert said later.

Joubert also sliced the boy on the neck and legs.

"He didn't move or make any noise, so I assumed he was dead and I just got in the car and left," Joubert said.

Joubert noticed blood on his hands as he entered a fast-food cafe in Bellevue for breakfast that morning. He washed it off, then sat down to order. He ate and went back to the barracks. He went to sleep.

PHOTOS • OMAHA WORLD HERALD

Danny Joe Eberle was abducted, bound, stabbed and left in a ditch.

Later, he was surprised at how fast he had dropped off.

At about 8:30 a.m., Danny's supervisor, Ray Rowell became concerned when the telephone began ringing with calls from Danny's customers: Their Sunday newspapers hadn't been delivered. Danny was very reliable. He hadn't missed a paper since taking over the route months before.

Checking, he found the bike and the newspapers at 2302 Madison. He circled the area, discovered that possibly only as few as three papers had been delivered. Rowell called Danny's parents, the Leonard Eberles. The

According to an autopsy, the youth had been stabbed or slashed nine times. One leg bore what appeared to be a human bite. Death came many hours after the wounds were inflicted.

Eberles and Rowell began their search. They were very worried—Danny was proud of his bike and wouldn't leave it anywhere.

Bellevue police were called that morning. They circled the route. Only the three customers had received their newspapers. They broadened the search to include the entire city of 30,000 at the south edge of Omaha.

At the base, Joubert awoke early in the afternoon. His base duty tour was at night, with weekends off. Sunday night he attended an early-evening committee meeting with the parents of Boy Scouts with whom he worked. He felt uncomfortable when they began talking about the missing newspaper boy: he hadn't known the boy's name until then.

He left, attended a late movie in Omaha, then went to work at 11:30 p.m. Tuesday night, he had a Scout meeting. They worked on knot-tying, using rope with colored strands.

By that time, authorities were convinced this wasn't a runaway or lost boy incident. Monday morning, in light of Danny's reputation as a responsible youngster, Chief Warren Robinson was treating the matter as a possible abduction. John Evans, assistant director of the Iowa-Nebraska Federal Bureau of Investigation headquarters in Omaha, sent agents to work with local officers.

It was feared that this could be another Johnny Gosch case. That 13-year-old paper carrier had vanished in Des Moines, Ia., on Sept. 5, 1982, and no trace had been found of him.

Bellevue stretches east of Highway 75 from Omaha south of Offutt Air Force Base. To the southwest lay the Missouri River bottoms. Wednesday morning, the search was expanded to include those bottoms. Search directors laid out a 10-mile patch to be tramped, foot by foot, by 130 searchers from 22 law agencies. Divided into 10 teams, they headquartered at a pavilion at Offutt Base Lake, a recreation area east of the huge SAC center. The teams set out about 9:30 a.m. Sept. 21, three days after Danny's disappearance.

In Wahoo, Neb., Police Chief John Kolterman was working his way down the river road east of the Iske Park riverside community. With him was Saunders County Sheriff Ron Poskochil, two deputies and an FBI agent.

Barely 90 minutes after they began, Kolterman saw something in the marsh grass and weeds at the south edge of the dirt road, 30 feet off the road. It appeared that someone had tried to camouflage something by pulling the grass over it.

Checking closer, Kolterman found the body of a young boy, clad only in underwear, bound with unusual-looking rope. He had been stabbed several times. Kolterman knew at once it was Danny.

"It was obvious he was not alive at the time, so we just preserved the scene," he said.

Because the body was in Sarpy County, the case now became that of Sheriff Pat Thomas. The area was draped with the yellow bands of the sheriff's lines for several hundred yards. Local and federal agents scoured the field for several hours.

The boy's clothing was nearby. There was the rope with the red-and-yellow strands, a couple of beer cans that had been hurled into the field, an old newspaper and nothing else.

Thomas, a former school teacher and juvenile probation officer, was always bothered by violence against youngsters. Determined and grim, he walked away from the scene late in the afternoon. As he approached the roped-off main road, he saw a familiar face among the reporters, a newsman he had known for years.

"How does it look?" he asked.

"It looks like there might be another one," the reporter replied.

Thomas nodded and his lips tightened as he walked on.

The crime was shattering to Sarpy County, a growing suburban county of 100,000 at the south edge of Omaha. Bellevue was the largest city in the county and about half of its residents were connected with Offutt, the base, and the SAC headquarters there. Most had young children. Most were trusting people.

"I never thought I would see anything like this in Bellevue. It's the kind of place where people leave their doors unlocked," said Mayor Joe Baldwin.

According to an autopsy, the youth had been stabbed or slashed nine times. One leg bore what appeared to be a human bite. Knife cuts and slashes had been made over it. Death came many hours after the wounds were inflicted. The victim "might well have been tortured," the pathologist said.

The 110 lawmen who began working the Eberle case battled against clock and calendar. They felt it was only a matter of time before another body might be found. But the leads were skimpy, the trail faint. All they had was the strange rope, which became a Gordian knot for the Federal Bureau of Investigation, with its far-flung services.

The FBI, with 400 agents in more than 50 United States and 13 foreign offices, agreed to take up the rope search. That task spanned the globe.

Special attention was given to rope manufacturers and wholesalers in Scotland and the Orient, where much of the world's rope is made.

Nothing.

The thorough agents went to a convention of the National Institute on Rope late in 1983. Government and military outlets for rope were checked.

Nothing.

No one had ever seen that kind of rope or knew where it might be obtained.

Back with the Nebraska task force, investigators went over the nearly 200,000 autos registered in the region, following tips they received. They questioned more than 2,000 child-crime suspects in Eastern Nebraska. Special teams went out into the field and searched through every vacant farm building in the Omaha area. They also tramped all remote, little-traveled regions, on the possibility the victim might have been taken elsewhere before he was dragged into the marsh reeds.

The shocked community acted with typical human concern. The officers went over many groundless complaints, answered many false calls. By the end of October, they were frustrated. By the end of November, they were pessimistic.

* * * * *

Meanwhile, the life of John Joubert went on as it had before—the secrets of the slight, dark-haired airman remained concealed within him.

Joubert was born on July 2, 1963, near Lawrence, Mass., and spent the first eight years of his life there. When his parents were divorced, Joubert went with his mother, an accountant, to live in Portland, Me.

He was a loner, spending his time jogging, riding his 10-speed bicycle and involving himself in the Boy Scouts. He had learned to read by the time he was 5 years old, and loved reading. He made balsa wood models.

Joubert received all As and Bs in elementary school. He was concerned about the use of drugs and alcohol in the public high schools—a watchful mother discouraged him from hanging out on the street corners with other kids—and he worked his way through Cheverus, an all-boy parochial school in Portland, by carrying newspapers.

He did well in his studies and he enjoyed track. Joubert turned the quarter mile in 54 seconds and finished third in the regional meet in the 600-yard dash one year. He spent his summers scouting, working, and bicycling through New England.

A standard American boy. He was never arrested, never in trouble.

But there were the fantasies, running through his mind since he was 6 years old, he later told psychiatrists. In the beginning, he fantasized about killing his baby sitter, a 13-year-old girl who lived in his neighborhood. In some, he cannibalized her. All the images were of violence and killing, sometimes strangling, sometimes stabbing, but never shooting.

In his fantasies, the victims were sometimes women, sometimes young males.

He never felt he was acceptable to women. His only date came in his high school senior year, when he took a girl to a prom. The next year, he enrolled at Norwich University, a military school.

He sought an education in civil engineering. But with his first taste of freedom, he partied too much his freshman year. He dropped out of Norwich in 1982, after his freshman year, with low grades and little money. That summer, he worked in a Portland warehouse. He stayed in scouting and spent much of his spare time riding his 10-speed around his neighborhood in Portland.

On Aug. 23, 1982, residents of Portland were jolted when a motorist found the body of a young boy near Tukey's Bridge at Interstate 295. It was laying in a grassy strip by a pedestrian foot bridge.

Joubert put his hands on the boy's shoulder and directed him to the car. Christopher started to cry and Joubert thought about freeing him. He hated to see kids cry.

"I stabbed him in the back a couple of times and then I sliced his throat... It looked like he was dead so I sliced his stomach a couple of times just to make sure."

The boy was Richard Stetson, 11, reported missing the night before. His family had last seen him jogging around Back Cove in Portland early in the evening.

His jogging suit was in disarray, as if someone had tried to pull it off, but failed. The boy had been stabbed and strangled to death. One of the cutting marks, forensic dentists said, was found to have been made over a human bite.

A short time later, John Joubert joined the Air Force.

Joubert had his basic training at Lackland Air Force Base at San Antonio, Tex., then went to a technical service school in Kessler Air Force Base at Biloxi, Miss. He was assigned to Offutt in Bellevue in July, 1983.

In Bellevue, he bought a car and again took up scouting. Already an Eagle Scout, he became an assistant scoutmaster in Troop 499. He was unfailing in his conscientious duty to the troop and to all its projects.

"While John was here, the troop got going again," a young scout said.

As the searchers groped through mountains of reports, records and registrations through the fall, life went on for Joubert. He and the scouts made several camping trips. With the scouts, he was introduced to city officials at a city council meeting late in the fall.

Mayor Baldwin was impressed by the young scout leader.

"It's good to see a fine young man like you moving into the community," he told Joubert.

He still frequently set his alarm for an early hour. Generally, he shut it off and turned back to sleep. He bought detective magazines with lurid covers, and he dream-dwelt on the incidents depicted on the covers.

Once in a while, he got up and cruised around the community. Once he saw a young girl on a corner and circled the block but she was gone. Another time, he saw a boy but lost track of him at a shopping center.

On Dec. 2, 1983, the alarm sounded and he responded. It was still dark when he left the barracks. He was dressed in a green jacket of Norwich and wore a service pull-down winter cap. He took with him the same sharp knife.

Again cruising, Joubert went around the bus stops. He saw no single kids, only groups of youngsters on their way to school. Joubert worked his way west out of Bellevue to the area of Pawnee Grade School at 7310 S. 48th Street. There he saw 12-year-old Christopher Paul Walden walking alone along 48th Street toward the school.

"Something said he's going to die," Joubert recalled later.

Christopher was the only child of Lt. Col. and Mrs. Steven Walden, assigned to Offutt and the Strategic Air Command from Florida in July, the same month Joubert came to the area. They were living at 4558 Holly St., in the Faulkland Heights subdivision west of Bellevue. His mother had set Christopher off for Pawnee school about 8:20 a.m. that Friday, dressed in his parka, carrying his books in his knapsack.

Joubert pulled into a side street, figuring the boy was bound for the school. He waited until the boy crossed to his side of the street. He walked up behind Christopher and called, "Stop."

He showed the boy the knife.

"Come with me and be quiet or I'll kill you," he said.

Joubert put his hands on the boy's shoulder and directed him to the car. He ordered the boy on the floor on the passenger side and started away. Christopher started to cry and Joubert thought about freeing him. He hated to see kids cry.

"I just figured that if I did let him go, he would probably tell someone and then what would happen to me?" he said.

On west they drove, Joubert knowing little of the winter-frozen country they passed. Northwest of a suburb called Papillion, the car rumbled over some railroad tracks on a remote farm road and Joubert spotted a wild plum grove. Joubert pulled the car over to the roadside, up under the scant, bare tree limbs and ordered the boy out. There was snow on the ground and it was very cold. They turned into the grove and walked about 100 feet. Joubert stopped the boy.

"If you do everything I tell you, nothing will happen," he said.

Joubert told the boy to remove everything but his underwear. It was all by command, by ritual he had conceived before, he told psychiatrists. The youth obeyed, laying his clothes neatly on top of his books. Joubert made the boy lay on his back and started to strangle him. The boy started to struggle.

"I didn't want to see him suffering too much so I took out my knife and stabbed him," Joubert said.

"I stabbed him in the back a couple of times and then I sliced his throat...It looked like he was dead so I sliced his stomach a couple of times just to make sure."

Joubert went to his car and drove straight back to the barracks. This time, he noticed, he had no blood on his hands. He threw the knife in a trash can, went to his room, where he drifted off to sleep.

At 4 p.m., Mrs. Walden became worried because Christopher hadn't returned home. She called Sheriff Thomas' office. Deputies and police searched and interviewed. They found witnesses who had seen a young man, dark-haired, in a tan car in the area that day, but nothing to connect him with an abduction. Just a young man in a tan car.

Officers had been uncertain what they would find when they began looking for Danny Joe Eberle: This time, just 75 days later, they were afraid of what they would find.

Late the next Monday evening, two hunters working along the road northwest of Papillion downed a pheasant in the plum grove. There they discovered the body in the snow. He had been stabbed seven times. From the circumstances, investigators felt there was no doubt the same person killed both Danny Joe Eberly and Christopher Walden. Now near-panic gripped Omaha and its suburbs.

Streets around schools were jammed morning and evening with parents taking youngsters to class. Large Omaha firms found their switchboards jammed about 4 p.m. every day: Parents were calling home to see if their children were there. Few pre-teenage children were seen in shopping centers, alone, that Christmas.

Still there were no leads for the investigative task force. By Jan. 10, 1984, about a month after the Walden killing, they had interviewed more than 3,400 persons. It was, Thomas recalled, the "lowest day in the morale" of the investigation. Three new leads had fizzled.

They had devised Code 17, a method whereby in a reported abduction, they could close off all major streets, bridges and highways in the county. By prearrangement with commanders of more than 10 local, state and

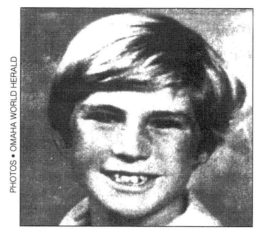

PHOTOS • OMAHA WORLD HERALD

federal agencies, more than 500 men could be thrown into the field immediately.

In one false run, the sealing of the area was done in 11 minutes.

The call was regarding an uncle, newly arrived in the area, who had picked up his nephew at school and had been reported by teachers.

* * * * *

Barbara Weaver is a religious woman. Every day during the Eberle-Walden investigation, while she was directing the pre-school at Aldersgate United Methodist Church, she and her children prayed for the capture of the man who had killed Danny Joe and Christopher. Every day, at lunch, even at the bus stops, where she now walked with the children. Every day, the same prayer. But in the early morning of Jan. 11, 1983, she felt a sudden compulsion.

"I prayed to the Lord that He would use me in a special way that day to witness for Him and give Him glory."

At 8:20 a.m. that day, she was preparing to receive the 22 children at Aldersgate at 3617 Greene Ave., not far from where Christopher had been abducted. She looked through the ground-level window into the slowly brightening winter gloom and saw a young man in a car next to the patio at the pre-school. When the young man saw her looking at him, he drove off. Minutes later, he returned to the same place and stopped, just

On his way to school, Christopher Paul Walden was forced at knife point into Joubert's car.

watching. Mrs. Weaver walked over and noted the license number. She memorized it, repeating it to herself, over and over.

"Something strange is going on," she thought.

She got her coat but when she returned to the window, the man had driven away. Her

Two hunters discovered Christopher's body in a remote, snowy grove.

PHOTOS • OMAHA WORLD HERALD

relief was short-lived. The man returned to the same place, got out and walked to the main entrance. Mrs. Weaver kept staring at the license plates, remembering them.

"I kept saying it over and over," she recalled.

"May I help you?" she asked as the man entered the pre-school. He asked directions to a street but when she responded, "he just shook his head like he didn't know where he was." Then he asked for a telephone and Mrs. Weaver, now fully alarmed, said there was none. They stood eye to eye, she at 5 feet, 5 inches, he at 5 feet, 6 inches. He suddenly pushed at her and shouted:

"Get in there or I'm going to kill you."

She saw no weapon, but Mrs. Weaver threw her hands forward and darted past him: "I never looked back."

She ran next door to the home of Pastor David Kelly and shouted, "Call the police.

Someone just tried to kill me."

"That's the guy, that's the guy," she cried when the Kellys came out.

Her call shortly after 9 a.m. looked "awful good," said Thomas and the case's coordinator, Lt. James Sanderson, now a captain. The combination of despair galvanized by new hope spurred investigators. The license was registered to Beardmore Chevrolet, a large new-and-used car firm at the west edge of Bellevue. The license was issued to a 1983 white Chevrolet Citation. An airman had rented it Jan. 4 while the firm worked on his Nova, which had a blown engine. The young man who rented the car was an airman first class at Offutt Air Force Base.

John J. Joubert was his name.

Early in the afternoon, the investigators got search warrants and went onto the base. They found the Chevy, a trailer belonging to the scout troop, and a knife. Joubert was taken into custody at the base about 4 p.m., in connection with the Aldersgate incident. Chief Deputy County Attorney Michael Wellman and other officials had instructed the officers: keep the scope of examination to the Aldersgate case. If something else comes up, return, get new search warrants.

Sanderson, FBI agent Charles Kempf and Offutt Office of Special Investigations officers went to Joubert's barracks. Sanderson, the civilian detective remained outside while the others looked around. Suddenly Air Force security man Greg Thurn called: "I think you better look at this."

In Joubert's duffel bag, they found an unusual rope. Sanderson's heart leaped. He seen it only once before: tightly binding Danny Joe Eberle. He thought: "This is the man."

Shortly after 11 p.m., Joubert admitted the Eberle and Walden killings to Sanderson, Bellevue Police Capt. Don Carlson and FBI agent Charles W. Kempf. Carlson asked if he might have killed more young boys.

"If I wasn't picked up today, yes. I'm glad I was picked up today," he said. "That's my big worry."

After finding the rope and hearing the confession, issues moved fast. Joubert was charged with two counts of first-degree murder, a capital offense in Nebraska, and two counts each of using knives in felonies and kidnapping.

Public Defender James Miller and an assistant, Owen Giles, began to prepare a defense as the stones of justice turned. Hearing after hearing was held before district Judge Ronald Reagan. Outside the courtroom, the strings pulled tighter and tighter.

Deputies David Krecklow and Ray Paulsen had picked up a single hair from Joubert's tan Chevrolet Nova when they vacuumed it the day after Joubert's arrest. As a prelude to the trial, Sanderson went to the microscopic analysis unit of the FBI labs in Washington for a pre-trial briefing. There it was determined that the hair found in Joubert's car came from Danny Joe Eberle's head.

"Like they say, in every crime somebody leaves something behind," said Thomas.

While in jail, awaiting trial, Joubert was visited several times by young scouts. During one visit, he informed one of the shocked young boys that he had committed the Eberle-Walden crimes, but he didn't know why.

Five psychiatrists examined him, at the request of both Miller and Wellman. All explored his lifetime of fantasies, with their themes of violence and death. They found him to be obsessive, compulsive, perhaps with no control over actions at times. Ritualistically, he had planned the crimes in advance.

But none could call him legally insane under Nebraska law: He knew right from wrong at the times of the crimes and he could participate in his own defense. In fact, he was termed very bright.

The case had drawn the attention of Portland, Me., authorities, who got the Sarpy County reports as a matter of course. They were interested in the age and sex of the victims, in the method of killing and in the circumstances. They were interested in the bite marks: Joubert told psychiatrists he bit Eberle, he didn't know why, then tried to conceal the bite with knife marks.

That, too, had been the forensic report on young Stetson. Joubert had lived in that area when Stetson was killed. He was known to ride his 10-speed bicycle along Marginal Way, where the victim was jogging.

Portland police found six witnesses who had seen a young jogger followed by a dark-haired youth on a 10-speed bicycle the day before Stetson was killed. They also had some hair, and the teeth marks found in the victim's right calf. Armed with affidavits, Portland police came to Sarpy County and took samples of Joubert's hair and casts of his teeth marks.

He was later indicted by a grand jury in Portland for murder in the Stetson case.

In the Sarpy jail shortly before the 1984 July 4th holiday, Joubert told his lawyers he had killed the Stetson youth nearly two years before. Both Miller and Giles were to testify about the statement months later, when they were no longer his attorneys and were under court order in a hearing to determine if Joubert had competent lawyers.

For that time, however, the two men kept the secret locked within. They faced a long trial, up to three weeks of prosecution testimony. Wellman planned to call more than 60 witnesses. There was the rope, the hair and the statements to both police and Joubert's youthful companion.

After a finding of guilty in a Nebraska capital case, another hearing is held by a panel of judges to determine a sentence of either life

Carlson asked if he might have killed more young boys. "I'm glad I was picked up today," Joubert answered. "That's the only thing I'm afraid of, yes. That's my big worry."

imprisonment or death in the electric chair. The judges consider aggravating and mitigating circumstances. Wellman planned to bring up what was now called "the Maine case" at this hearing.

On July 3, a day after Joubert's 21st birthday, he pleaded guilty to two counts of first-degree murder. Under sanctioned agreements between Miller and Wellman, the weapons and kidnapping charges were dropped.

At the penalty hearing, Wellman agreed not to ask for the death penalty, and not to bring up the Maine case.

Miller said that by pleading guilty—a show of remorse and a savings of trial costs—they hoped to avoid the death penalty. Both Miller and Wellman felt the state's case now was strong enough to warrant convictions.

"It was really our only option based on the number of statements he had made," said Miller.

PHOTOS • OMAHA WORLD HERALD

Joubert has given one interview while on Nebraska's death row. His sentence is on appeal to the Nebraska Supreme Court.

The secret world of John Joubert was examined at length. The serial-killing aspects of the case came out through psychiatrists. He wanted to know what it was like to see people die, they said. Mrs. Weaver, at Aldersgate, would have been his next victim, they felt.

"I do not believe Mr. Joubert was able to stop," one said.

The 22-page decision which sentenced Joubert to die called the crimes "totally and senselessly bereft of any regard for human life." The three judges noted the fear the killings caused in the community: "The children were held hostage by his conduct."

Today Joubert's battle against Nebraska's electric chair involves two legal fronts. His court-appointed attorney, J. Joseph McQuillan of Omaha, has applied for help under the state's post-conviction procedures. This permits defendants, after a failed appeal, to attack early convictions and sentences, generally on the grounds that new evidence has been found or that the defendant didn't have good legal advise.

McQuillan maintains Joubert had ineffective legal counsel at the time of the pleading and he has asked that the plea and sentence be set aside. Judge Reagan has denied the motion and it now is on appeal to the Nebraska Supreme Court.

Wellman also has asked the courts to halt the appointment, at public expense, of an attorney for Joubert. Wellman has cited a June United States Supreme Court ruling in a Virginia case. It stated that in capital cases, the states were not compelled to provide free attorney service beyond the level of the first appeal.

Sheriff Thomas' office today has moved into a new law enforcement center with a sophisticated computer system. In a test several months ago, the computer was given the meager description of the young man in the tan car that witnesses saw in the area of the Walden kidnapping in 1983.

In 28 minutes, the computer from more than 10,000 records had kicked out about 300 such autos driven by young men. The name of John J. Joubert was among them.

Thomas was among the earliest to believe that investigators were seeing what might be the start of a string of serial killings. Does he still believe so?

"Oh, yes. I felt it right away. There was no money involved, no prestige. No one kills like that just for the sake of killing one small child," he said.

Joubert has killed several times, he said, and of the confrontation that day at Aldersgate he added, "He would have killed her, too, but she got out too quickly."

From death row, Joubert has consented to only one interview, with a television reporter in the spring of 1987. He found that incident objectionable and wrote about it to a newspaper reporter who had covered the case from the beginning.

The television reporter, he said, "suggested that there could be others in the Omaha area who had thoughts of killing, yet believed that they would remain just that—thoughts. I was told that I might be able to help them, or at least convince them to go seek help on their own."

Joubert said this was the only reason he consented to the interview. However, he said, only one question which concerned that issue was asked and it didn't appear in the airing of the program on May 24, 1987.

Joubert said during the interview he was given the chance to express his sorrow and remorse but the reporter "negated this by having a psychiatrist state that my only sorrow was for getting caught."

"I will say once again that I am sorry for the hurt I have caused to my victims, to their families, and to those who have been touched by my actions," he wrote.

James Ivey has spent 30 years with the Omaha World Herald *covering the courts, crime, politics and energy. In 1984, he won the Nebraska State Press Association award for continuing coverage of the Joubert case.*

Vern & Lester Killsontop

Rita Munzenrider

Marty Etchemendy was 23 years old, a white man connected with the Miles City, Mont. business and political establishments, and the son-in-law of an FBI agent, when he was beaten to death late in 1987.

Two Cheyenne Indian brothers named Killsontop, one a self-proclaimed alcoholic, now await execution on Montana's death row for the kidnap-torture slaying of Etchemendy.

Marty Etchemendy was beaten to death during the course of a 13-hour drive, part of which he spent in the trunk of a black Dodge Duster, which carried him and his assailants from Miles City in the early morning hours of Oct. 17 to an abandoned community hall 155 miles away in Gillette, Wyo.

That is where his body was found at 7 a.m. on Oct. 19. Kelly Hemmert, one of team of FBI agents from Montana and Wyoming on the scene to assist in the investigation identified

the body. Hemmert was Etchemendy's father-in-law.

Separate juries convicted the Killsontop brothers of the same charges: deliberate homicide, aggravated kidnapping and robbery. Different judges imposed identical sentences: 40 years for robbery, and death for aggravated kidnapping and murder.

Lester Killsontop, 27, arrived on death row in July 1988, two months before his older brother, Vern, 31.

The brothers had no significant involvement with the law until 2 a.m. on Saturday, Nov. 17, 1987, when they coaxed Etchemendy into their car outside a Miles City bar. An intoxicated Etchemendy believed the brothers

Vern and Lester Killsontop await their executions on Montana's death row. The last execution in that state was in 1943.

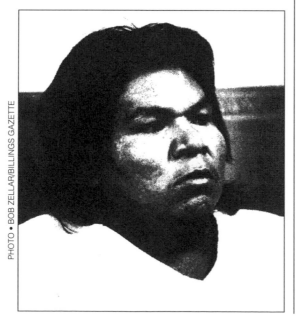

PHOTO • BOB ZELLAR/BILLINGS GAZETTE

PHOTO •JAMES WOODCOCK/BILLINGS GAZETTE

and their two female companions were giving him a ride to his home a mile away.

Thirteen hours later, Etchemendy lay dead in the abandoned community hall near Gillette, Wyo., the victim of a brutal beating.

Two days later, law officers had five people in custody in connection with Etchemendy's death. Charged were the Killsontop brothers; Diane Bullcoming, 32, and Lavonne Quiroz, 21, both Cheyenne Indians; and Doretta Four Bear, 32, a member of the Sioux Tribe of South Dakota.

Bullcoming and Four Bear were with the Killsontops and Etchemendy when the car left Miles City. Three hours later, the group stopped in the tiny town of Ashland on the Northern Cheyenne Indian Reservation to pick up Quiroz.

A frightened Four Bear left the car at Rabbit Town near Ashland and went to a friend's home. She later told friends that the Killsontop brothers were holding a white man from Miles City against his will, and that they had severely beaten him.

Each of the three women drove the car at some point during the long trip from Miles City across the reservation and eventually to Gillette.

The car had stopped repeatedly along the route, and Etchemendy had been dragged to the side of the road and beaten. After the first three assaults, the brothers ordered the blood-covered Etchemendy to strip and get in the car's trunk.

Etchemendy was conscious most of the time.

Meanwhile, back in Miles City, Etchemendy's wife, Colleen, waited for him to return home. At noon on Saturday, when Etchemendy did not show up for work at his father's sanitation business, his wife called the Miles City Police Department.

Police officers who investigated the report found that Etchemendy had left the bar with four Indians in a black Dodge Duster. An all-points bulletin was issued for the car. Custer County sheriff's deputies, as well as deputies from neighboring counties, joined the search.

Investigators wondered why Etchemendy had climbed into the vehicle that night, but still, no one worried too much about his welfare. After all, they reasoned, Etchemendy

was sensible and could take care of himself.

Marty was well known and liked by most residents of Miles City, where he grew up, one of four children of John and Julie Etchemendy.

He recently had graduated with honors and a degree in petroleum engineering from Montana College of Mineral Science and Technology at Butte. There, he met and married Colleen, the daughter of Special Agent Kelly Hemmert, a supervisor in the FBI's Montana-Idaho division at Butte.

The decline of the oil business brought the athletic, blond-haired, blue-eyed father of two young sons back home to manage the family business, Miles City Sanitation Service. He was a responsible young man, but occasionally, he liked to party, friends remembered.

Etchemendy had too much to drink that early morning of Oct. 17, and he couldn't find his car. Later, his wife and a family friend located the car in a parking lot across the street from the bar where Etchemendy was last seen.

It wasn't until the following day that Miles City authorities began to piece together what had happened to him. On the afternoon of Oct. 18, a woman called the Northern Cheyenne Tribal Police dispatcher to report that Four Bear had arrived at her home, afraid of the Killsontop brothers and what they had done to a white man they had picked up outside the Golden West Lounge on the outskirts of Miles City.

The woman said Four Bear told her that the Miles City man was being held against his will and had been severely beaten by the Killsontop brothers, who had been drinking heavily. The caller said the beatings occurred in Custer County, along the Tongue River Road.

Four Bear was arrested and questioned further.

A massive manhunt began. It involved a dozen local, state and federal agencies before it ended a day later.

The Custer County Search and Rescue team first was dispatched to the Tongue River Road, where members scoured the roadside for any clues to Etchemendy's disappearance. They found a beer carton smeared with blood.

That afternoon, Yellowstone County sheriff's deputies spotted the black Dodge Duster

Bullcoming testified that she and Lester started drinking rum at 8 a.m. Vern joined them about midday, and the three drank hard liquor and beer almost incessantly for the rest of the day and night.

on a street in downtown Billings, Montana's largest city, 150 miles west of Miles City. A teletype from Custer County had advised Yellowstone County law officers that Four Bear had told investigators Etchemendy was in the trunk of the car the last time she saw him.

After opening the trunk of the car and finding what appeared to be blood, Yellowstone County deputies arrested Vern Killsontop and Quiroz, 21. They impounded the black Dodge.

Deputies found Etchemendy's driver's license in Vern's coat pocket when they booked him into jail. But Etchemendy still hadn't been found.

By nightfall, Custer County Search and Rescue President Marty Lawrenz had found a pair of bloody boxer shorts in a sparsely populated area along the Tongue River Road. Colleen Etchemendy identified them as her husband's, and the hope that Marty was still alive quickly began to dwindle.

The focus of the investigation turned toward the Gillette area after law officers interviewed Four Bear. She told them the others had planned to go that direction.

PHOTO • JAMES WOODCOCK/BILLINGS GAZETTE

A Wyoming crime lab technician examines the exterior of the Killsontops' vehicle for traces of Etchemendy's blood.

On the evening of Oct. 18, Quiroz also told FBI agents that the Killsontop brothers had dumped Etchemendy's body somewhere south of Gillette.

After receiving word from Montana law officers, Campbell County Wyoming sheriff's deputies began a search for the body at daybreak on Oct. 19. On a hunch, a deputy who routinely patrolled the area made the abandoned community hall one of his first stops that morning. The hunch paid off.

At 7 a.m., the deputy found Etchemendy's partially clothed body sprawled beneath a door that had been ripped from its hinges in the deserted building.

A team of FBI agents from Montana and Wyoming arrived at the scene to assist in the investigation. It was Hemmert who identified his son-in-law's battered body.

Some veteran federal agents described Etchemendy's killing as one of the most heinous crimes they had seen.

"It was a vicious, brutal, senseless act," said FBI special agent Elson J. Leavitt of the Billings, Mont., office. "He was beaten savagely about the head."

Investigators now had the body. They also had three of their suspects. But Lester Killsontop and Bullcoming remained free.

The pair's freedom lasted only a few more hours. FBI agents and Billings police arrested them without incident at a mobile home owned by Bullcoming's friend, Lorraine Four Colors.

Bullcoming immediately volunteered information to investigators implicating the Killsontop brothers in the kidnapping and killing. The woman minimized her involvement.

For the next two days, FBI agents retraced the route taken by the Killsontop brothers, combing the countryside. They found a long trail of bloody evidence.

The case was falling together, but authorities then faced the complex decision of jurisdiction for filing charges.

All five suspects first appeared in U.S. District Court in Billings, where they were charged with kidnapping and aiding and abetting in the crimes. The federal government had jurisdiction since the defendants crossed state lines and most of the beatings occurred on the Northern Cheyenne Reservation.

Meanwhile, Custer County prosecutors filed kidnapping and aggravated assault charges in Miles City.

Less than two weeks after the killing, Montana's U.S. Attorney Pete Dunbar dismissed the federal charges in favor of state charges. Prosecutors from both Custer and Campbell counties met in Billings with Dunbar to decide who should file homicide charges.

The ominous responsibility of piecing together the 155-mile trail of evidence ultimately fell on Custer County Attorney Keith Haker, who prosecuted four of the five defendants in state district court at Miles City.

Vern and Lester were charged with robbery, aggravated kidnapping and deliberate homicide. Bullcoming was charged with aggravated kidnapping and robbery, while Four Bear was charged with aggravated kidnapping.

Quiroz, who wasn't in Miles City when the crimes began, was charged in U.S. District Court at Billings with aiding and abetting in the kidnapping.

The decision to try the others at the Montana district court level was based on several factors, Haker remembers.

Montana's maximum penalty for aggravated kidnapping and murder is death. The federal government has no capital punishment statute. Prosecutors knew they had to seek the death penalty upon conviction.

"None of the parties had any contact with Wyoming," Haker said. "The victim and defendants were all Montanans. Wyoming viewed it as more of a Montana problem, even though the death took place there."

Wyoming offered the use of its state-of-the-art crime lab for analysis of all evidence, including what was collected in Montana. Lab scientists traveled from Cheyenne, to Billings to process the black Dodge, which essentially was the crime scene, for evidence.

Campbell County, Wyo., sheriff's deputies also completed the necessary investigation in Gillette.

"We had to pull all the evidence together from all the different agencies," Haker recalls.

With jurisdiction determined, the next hurdle was venue. It became immediately clear that the defendants couldn't be tried in the small, tightly knit community of Miles City, a town of about 10,000 people.

Most of the town's residents knew the Etchemendy name. Emotions ran high and talk of the brutal murder was rampant.

Finding a judge to preside over the trials also was an immediate problem. Custer County is headquarters for Montana's 16th Judicial District, which employs two district judges to preside over seven rural counties.

Both judges promptly withdrew from the cases because of their longtime friendships with the Etchemendy family.

District Judge H.R. Obert of the neighboring Seventh Judicial District assumed jurisdiction over Lester Killsontop's case. Charles B. Sande, a retired district judge in Billings, was appointed to preside over the cases of Vern Killsontop, Four Bear and Bullcoming.

Obert moved Lester's trial to Baker, a small oil town near the North Dakota border and about 80 miles east of Miles City. The trial was set for June 6, 1988.

In early May, Bullcoming entered a plea bargain agreement with the Custer County attorney's office. Prosecutors agreed to drop the aggravated kidnapping charge against her in exchange for her guilty plea to robbery, and most importantly, her testimony against the Killsontop brothers in their trials.

Bullcoming became the state's star witness. After testifying at Lester's trial, Bullcoming was sentenced to the maximum 40 years as a nondangerous offender at the Montana Women's Correctional Facility at Warm Springs.

Quiroz also admitted the federal charge and agreed to testify against the brothers. She was serving a three-year sentence at the federal women's prison at Alderson, W.Va., when she was returned to Montana for the trials.

Custer County prosecutors made no deals with Four Bear in advance of her testimony. After the Killsontops were convicted, Custer County dropped its charge against her in favor of refiling of charges in U.S. District Court in Billings. In October 1988, Four Bear was placed on probation for five years after admitting a felony charge, which said she did not attempt to stop the crime or report it to authorities.

Lester's trial began as scheduled, with attorneys taking most of the first week to select a jury in Fallon County, which has a population of about 2,300.

Three weeks later, the Fallon County jury of

Bullcoming approached the car and saw Lester trying to cut the beaten, bleeding man's throat with fingernail clippers. She went back into the bar.

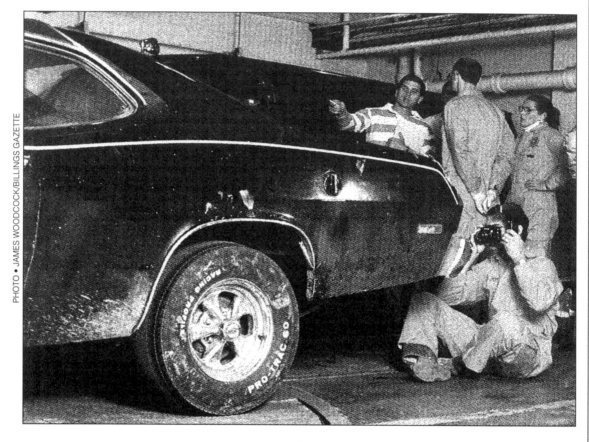

PHOTO • JAMES WOODCOCK/BILLINGS GAZETTE

The black Dodge Duster was the most important piece of physical evidence in the case. It was the car in which Etchemendy was kidnapped, tortured and killed.

six men and six women deliberated only two and a half hours before convicting him of robbery, aggravated kidnapping and deliberate homicide. Lester did not testify in his own defense.

Judge Sande decided to try Vern in Yellowstone County, which has a population of 80,000. On July 25, Vern's trial began in Billings. When the trial ended two weeks later, the Yellowstone County jurors had reached the same verdict as their counterparts in Fallon County.

Bullcoming, Quiroz and Four Bear told their stories at Lester's trial in Baker, and repeated them without variation at Vern's trial a month later.

Bullcoming testified that she and Lester began drinking rum at 8 a.m. Oct. 16. Vern joined them about midday, and the three drank hard liquor and beer almost incessantly for the rest of the day and night. After picking up Four Bear about midnight, the four went to the Golden West Lounge.

Four Bear and Bullcoming described how Vern and Lester approached Etchemendy in

the parking lot when the Miles City bar closed on Oct. 17, 1987. Etchemendy accepted an invitation for a ride and willingly climbed into the black Dodge Duster for the last ride he'd ever take.

After Vern and Lester conversed in Cheyenne, Vern turned the car around and headed away from Miles City.

The fighting apparently started shortly after the car reached the highway. Lester tried to force pills down Etchemendy's throat and asked him if he liked raping Indian women.

Etchemendy asked to go home. Lester began fighting with him in the back seat as the car headed south. The car stopped on the highway, supposedly so the victim could urinate. But once outside, Etchemendy, apparently sensing that he was in trouble, tried to run away.

Lester caught Etchemendy and forced him back into the car, then yelled at his brother, Vern, for letting Etchemendy get away.

Lester and Etchemendy continued struggling in the backseat as the car turned off the highway and onto the dark and deserted Tongue River Road, a back route between Miles

City and the reservation.

The car stopped again and the three men got out. Etchemendy offered to give his captors money if they would let him go unharmed. Instead, they put him back in the car and took his wallet.

Etchemendy again was taken from the car and hit and kicked by the Killsontops. This time, the victim cried, screamed and pleaded for his life.

The brothers climbed in the backseat with Etchemendy and Vern's hands closed around the victim's throat, causing him to choke.

At the next stop, they made him strip and forced him to get into the trunk. The temperature that clear fall night dipped to the low 30s.

Etchemendy bled heavily from wounds to the head.

When daylight broke, the group stopped in the tiny towns of Broadus and Biddle to cash two payroll checks—one for $179.31 and the other for $75—that had been taken from Etchemendy's wallet. They used some of the money to buy more liquor. Vern blindfolded Etchemendy so he wouldn't be able to identify them later if they let him go.

They used his credit cards along the way to buy gas.

The group drove on to Wyoming, stopping again when Etchemendy had to urinate. He also told his captors that he was thirsty, and they forced him to drink Everclear.

The blindfold was removed and Etchemendy saw his captors in daylight. He was stuffed back into the trunk and the group drove on to Gillette.

The four used Etchemendy's credit cards to buy new clothing at two Gillette stores, while Etchemendy, still locked in the trunk, pounded on the lid and screamed for help.

No one heard him.

The brothers then ordered Quiroz to move the car to a more remote spot so their hostage wouldn't be discovered. The four then went into a bar, where Vern and Lester agreed that Etchemendy would have to die.

At about 2 p.m. on Oct. 17, Bullcoming and Lester Killsontop left the bar and drove to a remote area outside Gillette. Vern and Quiroz were left at the bar.

Bullcoming said Lester opened the trunk and told her to look away. When she heard a "thump," she turned toward the trunk and saw Lester hitting Etchemendy in the head first with a metal pipe, then a tire iron, then a rock.

"Mr. Etchemendy had blood all over him," Bullcoming said on the witness stand at Lester's trial. "He kept saying 'Oh, God, no,' but Lester wouldn't quit."

Etchemendy was still alive and again pleaded for his life. But Lester just closed the trunk lid.

Bullcoming drove the car to another rural road nearby, where Lester tried to shoot Etchemendy in the head with a .22-caliber shell grasped in a ViseGrips and detonated with a rock. The bullet missed its target.

Again they closed the trunk lid and drove to another bar on the outskirts of Gillette at about 4 p.m.

Bullcoming called Vern and Quiroz and told them to meet her at the new bar. Lester continued to try to end Etchemendy's life. Bullcoming approached the car and saw Lester trying to cut Etchemendy's throat with fingernail clippers. She went back into the bar.

Finally, Lester came into the bar and told her: "I did it. He's gone. He's dead now."

When Vern and Quiroz arrived, the four drove to the abandoned community hall about 12 miles south of Gillette, where they dumped Etchemendy's body. Afterward, Lester was "happy" and "laughing," according to Quiroz.

The black Dodge and its occupants continued on to Sheridan, Wyo., and stopped at a motel. While Lester and Bullcoming were registering for the room, Vern and Quiroz left them and headed toward Montana.

Quiroz said she and Vern disposed of blood-covered items from the car on their way back to Busby, a town on the Northern Cheyenne Reservation. They went to the home of James and Sylvia Barragan, where Quiroz washed the clothes that she and Vern had been wearing.

They also hosed out the car's trunk, which "had a lot of blood in it," Quiroz testified.

FBI agents who later searched the Barragan's home recovered the laundry from the clothes line, and a bloody rock from the yard. Lab tests showed that the rock was stained with Etchemendy's blood.

Investigators also found two shirts along the Tongue River Road with Etchemendy's blood on them. The women said that Vern and Lester

Lester tried to shoot Etchemendy in the head with a .22-caliber shell grasped in a ViseGrips and detonated with a rock. The bullet missed its target.

had worn those shirts, but had taken them off when they stopped to wash themselves at a water trough on the Tongue River Road.

Attorneys appointed to represent Vern and Lester centered their defense cases on Bullcoming, arguing throughout each trial that she was responsible for the crimes.

Stephen Moses, a Billings lawyer who defended Lester, argued that Bullcoming was a strong, manipulative woman who can get violent if she doesn't get her own way. Moses said Bullcoming had beaten Lester up at the Golden West Lounge in Miles City shortly before Etchemendy left with the group.

Lester didn't testify in his own defense, but he did take the stand on his older brother's behalf and blamed events leading to Etchemendy's slaying on Bullcoming.

Lester claimed that Bullcoming told him at the Miles City bar that she wanted the "white guy" in the car and told him to go get Etchemendy from the bar's parking lot. He said Bullcoming spoke in Cheyenne and told them she wanted to mug Etchemendy.

Lester said he and Vern insisted that they didn't want to mug the man, but "she just stayed on our case." Lester said he was drunk and didn't know what was going on. He did what Bullcoming told him to do because he was afraid she was "going to hit me again."

Vern wasn't fighting with Etchemendy, Lester said, because "he can't fight." Lester said his brother has a bad arm and bad back from a car accident.

He told jurors that Vern never did anything to hurt Etchemendy.

Finally, Lester said that he and Vern tried to take Etchemendy back to Miles City to let him go while Bullcoming was asleep. But she woke up and told them to turn around and go to Gillette, he said.

At Vern's trial, Forsythe also attacked Bullcoming's character. He called her a "rough, tough fist-fighter, not the sweet, demure Diane" that jurors saw on the witness stand.

Forsythe described Vern's involvement in the whole scenario as "very minor."

His argument didn't work. The jury deliberated seven and a half hours before convicting Vern as charged.

Jurors determined that, although Vern wasn't present when the final blows to Etchemendy were inflicted, he was still legally accountable for Etchemendy's death because it occurred during the aggravated kidnapping or flight from it.

Recently, prosecutor Corbin reflected on Vern's and Bullcoming's involvement.

FBI agents and crime lab technicians go over every inch of the car, trying to piece together the 155-mile trail of evidence.

PHOTO • JAMES WOODCOCK/BILLINGS GAZETTE

"The hardest thing to do was to not prosecute Diane Bullcoming for the same charges as Vern" Corbin said. "To this day, I don't know. I just don't believe that Diane was as lily-white as she makes herself out to be, but I can't believe she was as involved as Lester wants us to believe. Yet, she was still as involved as Vern was."

During separate sentencing hearings that followed the convictions, defense attorneys pleaded for mercy for Vern and Lester.

The Killsontops' sister, Darlene Soldierwolf, testified that Vern and Lester were always obedient and easily manipulated while they were growing up. She said her two brothers were abused and neglected much of their lives by alcoholic parents.

Vern had been through alcoholism treatment three times since 1983, with the most recent treatment completed in August 1987. He remained sober for almost two months, until the week before the Etchemendy slaying.

Sheila Rebich, an adult probation-parole officer in Custer County, outlined a record of offenses charged against the Killsontops in Northern Cheyenne Tribal Court.

Lester's record involved only misdemeanor offenses, most of which were alcohol-related. In an interview with Rebich, he had described himself as an alcoholic.

Vern's record showed consistent involvement with the law between 1983 and 1987, but the charges were relatively minor.

His record included charges of intoxication, drunken driving and assault and battery. Vern's 5-year-old daughter was the victim of one assault, and the woman who raised him after his mother died was the victim of another.

Ministers, claiming that Vern and Lester had found God while in jail, argued that the brothers deserved to be spared from execution.

An angry Haker responded: "We're dealing with the laws of man, not the laws of God... Marty Etchemendy, during the 12 hours after being kidnapped, beaten, stripped and placed in the trunk, knows more about God than most of us."

Haker pleaded with the judges to sentence Vern and Lester to death.

Each judge concluded that there was no evidence that Vern and Lester were dominated by anyone. The judges found the following aggravating factors: The aggravated kidnapping of Etchemendy resulted in his death, and the killing of Etchemendy was committed by means of torture.

Neither Killsontops had significant criminal histories. However, the judges ruled that this single mitigating factor wasn't sufficiently substantial to call for leniency, considering the enormity of the crimes and the aggravating circumstances.

In documents filed to support the death sentences, the judges called Vern's and Lester's actions so depraved that "any leniency would be an injustice."

Today, the Killsontops live among five other men who await a date with the executioner at Montana State Prison in Deer Lodge.

Although the Killsontops are the only brothers on Montana's death row, they are among a half-dozen sets of brothers facing execution nationwide, according to the Colored People Legal Defense Fund in New York.

The last execution in Montana took place in 1943.

Montana law allows for death by lethal injection or hanging. Only Montana and Washington still having hanging on the books.

It isn't likely that either Killsontop brother will have to choose between the needle and the noose for years to come.

The first of the present condemned men arrived on death row in 1975. Each man's case has been tied up in years of costly appeals. None is near the end.

Appeals for the Killsontop brothers are only beginning. Both are awaiting their automatic appeal to the Montana Supreme Court.

Montana Assistant Attorney General Clay Smith, who is handling the appeals for Custer County, said it will be October or November 1989 before either case is argued before the state's high court.

In the meantime, the brothers are kept in separate cells, but are allowed to visit three hours daily in the death row unit's dayroom, according to Prison Warden Jack McCormick.

Rita Munzenrider is a reporter with The Billings Gazette *in Montana.*

Willie Mak

Mike Merrit

It was a rainy night in February 1983 when three young Chinese men slipped through the heavily barred entrance to the Wah Mee club, on Seattle's Maynard Alley. Willie Mak and his friends had no problem getting inside, since Mak was well-known as a gambler himself.

Mak, Benjamin Ng and Tony Ng left the Wah Mee club with $15,000 and 14 people left for dead inside.

It was to be a crime that was simple but bloody in its execution. There was an old saying: When one man sneezes in Chinatown, somebody else catches cold. You had to be known to gain admission to a gambling club. To successfully rob a club, there could be no witnesses left to identify you. This was a plain fact of life that Mak had talked over many times with his friends in coffee shops for years. No one could be left alive.

But for Wai Chin they might have gotten away with it.

Kwan Fai "Willie" Mak is escorted from the King County courtroom where he was sentenced to be executed.

Chin, a Wah Mee dealer who had served as a cook on U.S. ships during World War II, survived the massacre with two bullet wounds. His doctors called it miraculous. He not only survived the shootings, but he was able to stumble out of the Wah Mee Club, into the rain-slick alley, and call for help.

The names he gave Seattle police at Harborview Hospital were Mak and Ng.

Willie Mak today remains a somewhat shadowy figure. Like thousands of other Chinese in Seattle, Mak came to America from Hong Kong in 1975 with his parents, the youngest of three children. They naturally gravitated to the city's traditionally Asian enclaves just south of the booming downtown business district.

Skyscrapers loom over Chinatown's three- and four-story brick buildings, many of which were constructed and built at the turn of the century and still bear their builders' names. By day, the district was a favorite lunch and dinner spot for tourists and downtown workers. Chinese grocers, insurance brokers and herbal-medicine purveyors still do good business here.

But like many other Chinatowns in many other port cities, the old customs and traditional neighborhood and family Tongs still exist. The spectre of gangs, young toughs parading their drug money in flashy cars with guns under the seats, was just beginning to cast a shadow over the city.

Far more than a few city blocks, there was a immensely wide gulf separating Chinatown from the rest of the city. Although traditionally a tolerant city, Seattle had walled off its Chinese, Fillipino and Vietnamese communities. Only rarely did the two worlds meet.

Seattle police considered Chinatown a good beat to work. "There's not a lot of serious

PHOTO • ALAN BERNER/THE SEATTLE TIMES

crime," said one officer. "It's the best part of town...There's not much to do except try to keep the winos from killing each other in Hing Hay Park."

Mak arrived in Seattle when he was 15, and was enrolled in Cleveland High School. Speaking little English, he dropped out in his junior year. Like many new Chinese immigrants, he faced difficulties merging into the western culture. Mak was considered bright but quiet. In school he picked up the nickname Willie, which means "wolf" in Chinese.

Mak found refuge working in restaurants and in gambling clubs where the language was familiar. He went on to earn a high-school equivalency degree at a community college.

Mak worked off and on in other Chinese restaurants in the town of Blaine on the Washington-Canadian border, in Wenatchee in the dry orchard country of Eastern Washington, and in Seattle suburbs. He also worked briefly at a computer company on the assembly line and did heavy labor in a Seattle steelyard.

He thought of becoming a cook, maybe buying himself a restaurant some day.

But it was the gambling clubs of Chinatown where Willie Mak began spending more and more of his time. He returned to Seattle to stay in 1980. It wasn't long, according to court testimony and court documents, before Willie Mak and his friend, Benjamin Ng, began to graduate to robbery and murder.

The two young men had taken part in the burglary of a Blaine restaurant where a safe was stolen. As they tried to dump the 300-pound safe into Lake Washington after the burglary, they were surprised by an elderly man taking his regular walk. Ng, Mak said, shot Franklin Leach to death in cold blood.

In 1980 Mak took part in the gunpoint robbery of Hong Chin, the wealthy owner of seven Chinese restaurants, taking $52,000 in jewelry and $8,000 in cash from Hong's home. Just a few weeks prior, Mak had been at the house helping to move furniture, and Chin's wife had saved Mak from drowning when he fell into their pool.

In 1982, according to prosecutors' documents, Mak and Ng were the prime suspects in the shooting deaths of two Chinese women, Lai Kuen Lau and Lau Ling Chung, on Seattle's Beacon Hill. Mak handed a small-caliber gun to Ng, who shot the women, the prosecutors said. One of the women, Lau Ling Chung, 75, was found on her stomach, her hands bound behind her back in a fashion chillingly similar to the hog-tied Wah Mee Club victims just a year later.

Charges were never filed against Mak in any of the previous murders.

Mak liked to think of himself as a professional gambler. He bragged about winning hundreds of dollars a night. But, according to police, he lost a great deal more. One friend said Mak lost $20,000 or $30,000 playing cards in the weeks before the Wah Mee Club was robbed.

Wherever there was Willie Mak, the slight, boyish Benjamin Ng was never far away.

Like Mak Benji Ng was a Hong Kong immigrant and had dropped out of Cleveland High School. But unlike Mak, he couldn't seem to keep out of trouble with the law.

His record was littered with arrests for shoplifting, assault and strong-armed robbery. Ng had trouble keeping out of trouble—he performed well in school but too often became involved with the wrong people. In 1981 he was arrested in connection with the shooting of four young Chinese men in a dispute over money and slashed tires.

"Benjamin was always respectful to me," one high school counselor later said. "From the relationship we established, it was always a good one." Tony Ng—no relation to Benjamin—had no notable police record. According to police, Tony was another of the young men who floated through the city's underworld without visible means of support, looking for a quick way to make some money.

Mak had an idea, an idea to rob a gambling club. But everybody knew there was only one way to rob a Chinatown gambling club and get away with it, because everybody's family knew everyone else's family.

Gambling was one of the oldest forms of recreation for Chinese immigrants in Chinatown Each group of families had its own clubs—in a way, a re-creation of the village life they had known in their native land.

Wah Mee meant "Beautiful China," and it was one of the city's oldest gambling clubs.

Gambling and drug dealing, Mak's attor-

In 1980 Mak took part in the gunpoint robbery of Hong Chin, the wealthy owner of seven Chinese restaurants, taking $52,000 in jewelry and $8,000 in cash from Hong's home.

neys would later claim, "was not deviant or evil according to traditional Chinese values."

Young men like Mak were drawn to Tong activities "because organized crime is tolerated in Hong Kong and it is common practice for young men to make contacts and earn a nest egg through organized crime activities which later evolve into legitimate business careers."

Not until the carnage inside the Wah Mee Club was discovered did police know the long-closed Wah Mee Club had re-opened. In earlier years, city officials knew gambling took place in Chinatown—and throughout Seattle—but choose to look the other way.

Seattle, like other cities with large Chinese populations had experienced Tong wars. Seattle's last was in 1949, when the Bing Kung members robbed the Hop Sing Tong's Macao Club of $20,000. The outcome was much different then: The Hop Sing Tong demanded restitution plus interest.

At the time of the Wah Mee killings, police once again had a free hand to pursue gambling violations, but were hampered by the closed world of the Chinese community and the legal difficulties of obtaining warrants.

"The club was obviously set up for high-stakes gambling, but we did not know that before the shootings," said Maj. Dean Olson, the veteran commander of the Seattle Police Department's vice and narcotics unit. "We had no information it was even open."

Gambling club members were screened, and admission was strictly limited. In other instances where club operations were know, Olson said, police were frustrated by their inability to place informants inside in order to obtain search warrants and make arrests.

Doorkeepers kept a close watch on the street outside. If a police car approached, the peepholes would be quickly slammed shut.

Ruby Chow, a King County Councilwoman who owned a well-known Chinese restaurant famous as a meeting place for politicians and the city administrators, said the high-stakes gaming in the Wah Mee Club was the exception. Mostly the clubs catered to the cooks and waiters of the district's restaurants, who would come to unwind after a hard night's work.

"They sit and play Mah Jongg. That is their only recreation," Chow said. "A lot of them can't afford to go hunting or fishing. I think they are entitled to their privacy and their own recreation after working the whole day."

The game played most often at the Wah Mee was Pa Gow, a complicated domino-like game.

When Olson took over the vice unit in 1981, he found investigators had no current cases underway on Chinatown gambling. City officials said no tolerance policy existed, but they were also sensitive to charges of harassment in the minority community.

In the end, police acknowledged they believed the games inside the clubs were not much to get concerned about. One ranking officer said he thought the gambling was limited to a "bunch of older gents playing nickel-and-dime games."

Said Paul Woo, who owned the building housing the Wah Mee Club: "I assumed it was a social club, like the Elks."

At his trial later, Willie Mak would attempt to portray himself as simply a good soldier in a Tong rivalry, sent to the Wah Mee Club by one Tong chieftain to rough up another Tong leader. But, according to prosecutors, the reality was much simpler. Mak's claims of a Tong war was a last-ditch effort to shift the blame elsewhere and an appeal to the stereotypes of the Chinese community, said King County Deputy Prosecutor James Lasnik.

The FBI became involved in the investigation in part because of the potential for racketeering violations. But both the FBI and Seattle police said their investigations turned up nothing more than robbery for a motive. A March 1983 FBI report concluded, "there is no indication that the Wah Mee robbery-homicides were an orchestration motivated by other than those actually present and responsible for this most hideous crime."

The picture painted by police and prosecutors was one of escalating violence by Willie Mak and Benjamin Ng, first with burglaries, moving to the killings of the elderly woman and her daughter in a robbery and then to the cold-blooded shooting of Leach as the two dumped the stolen safe into Lake Washington.

Mak and his friends talked constantly about robbing gambling clubs and killing the players.

"It was basically a very simple, straight-forward pattern. If you eliminated the witnesses you didn't get caught," Lasnik said. The Wah Mee killings were "an extension to an unbelievable degree of that simple philosophy."

"Willie and Benjamin were a good team, in the Wild West sense," Lasnik said. "Willie liked the action. He liked shooting people," he said. Although police and prosecutors still don't know all the details of the Chung robbery and murders, Lasnik said, "I'd be surprised if Wah Mee was the first time Mak shot anybody."

According to later trial testimony, Willie Mak, Benjamin Ng, Wai Chung "Danny" Tam and another friend met in a Denny's Restaurant just before the Wah Mee shooting, where Mak talked about robbing the Wah Mee and another Chinatown club, the Bing Kung. They talked of using guns, Tam said, "because they know a lot of people in Chinatown."

Tam claimed that Mak had lost $20,000 or $30,000 gambling at the Wah Mee Club in the weeks leading up to the shooting.

Other friends, Yen Yin Lau and Bon Chin, would later tell jurors that Mak talked incessantly about robbery when he was losing lots of money playing cards. Guns and shooting were always a part of Mak's plans, they said. "Just go in there, tie them up and get their money and shoot them," Lau testified, describing Mak's murderously simple plan. Mak said he would use a .22-caliber gun because it would make little noise. Asked why Mak planned to shoot the victims, Lau answered in two words: "No witness."

But both Lau and Chin said they turned down Mak's invitation to take part in a robbery. "I said I don't want to go," Lau said. "I don't need the money. In Chinatown, everyone knows me."

Ng, in a prison interview with a Seattle newspaper following his conviction, said robbery was only a steppingstone for Mak.

"He had all kinds of plans. He would say, well, when we get this money, I'm going to deal drugs. After I deal drugs, I'm going to get a restaurant," Ng said. "My only regret is that if I would have thought through everything real thoroughly, I wouldn't be in here."

Why Tony Ng, the third member of Mak's trio, took part in Wah Mee isn't clear today. He testified that Mak threatened to shoot him and burn down his house if he didn't take part, and he insisted that Mak had told him nothing about shooting the gambling club patrons.

On the night of the shootings, Benjamin Ng was with his girlfriend, Kennis Izumi, at her parent's house. From about 8:30 p.m. until 11 p.m. they watched television. Then Ng, who had been ill with the flu, told Kennis he was leaving to go to his mother's home to get some medicine. When she kissed him goodbye, she noticed Ng was carrying two guns.

Ng often carried one gun, she said. Two was unusual.

The subsequent events are still not completely clear. The three young men gained entry into the club, one by one.

After entering the Wah Mee Club, Mak, Benji Ng and Tony Chin flashed their pistols and told everybody to lie on the floor.

They walked around the room, hog-tying the 14 people playing cards that midnight.

They emptied their victims' pockets and cleared the tables, picking up $15,000.

Then the shooting started. Who fired which of two guns used in the murders is still a matter of dispute. The card players and club employees were all methodically shot, execution-style, in the head.

The only person to survive, Wai Chin, said he was forced to lie on the floor while he was tied, his hands behind his back. He saw the three men stand together, putting on gloves.

Mak, Chin said, "act like a leader," watching the other two men tie up the club patrons with white nylon cord pre-tied with loops.

Chin said he told Tony Ng, who was wrapping rope around his hands and legs, not to bind him so tightly. "I am an old man, Why tie me up so tight?" he asked. Prosecutors said the request likely saved Chin's life and was the undoing of the three killers. Tony Ng tied only one of Chin's legs, making it possible for Chin to free himself and stagger out the club and summon help.

"I turned my head up. I watch because I wonder why they don't leave. I saw the guns pointing. Bap, bap, bap—like a firecracker, and I saw the fire come out of the guns," Chin said. "Bullets were flying all out. I get a bullet in the jaw and one in the neck and blood was coming out of my mouth. I heard, 'Is that all the bullets?'"

Then he passed out.

In all, 32 bullets were fired. Shell casings from a .22 caliber handgun and a Ruger automatic were found, but the weapons them-

The picture painted by police and prosecutors was one of escalating violence by Willie Mak and Benjamin Ng, first with burglaries, moving to the killings of the elderly woman and her daughter in a robbery and then to the cold-blooded shooting of Leach.

PHOTO • MATT McVAY/ THE SEATTLE TIMES

Homicide detectives and a medical examiner remove the last body from the Wah Mee Club.

selves were never recovered. Police believe only two guns were fired, although there is slim possibility the shattered remnants of one recovered slug were fired from a third weapon.

Chin awoke to the carnage of 12 murders. The 13th victim, still alive when medics arrived, later died at Harborview Medical Center.

Physicians would testify Chin could have literally drowned in his own blood had he not slipped out of his bonds. He made his way out of the double-barred doors of the club out into the alley, where he pleaded with a passerby for help.

Benjamin and Tony went to a Rainier Valley bowling alley after the shootings. Mak, according to court documents, returned to Chinatown "to watch the goings-on there." What he didn't know was that already police were looking for him and Benjamin Ng.

Kennis Izumi, Ng's girlfriend, said she became worried when her boyfriend didn't return, as he had told her he would, from his mother's home. She had called the house but got no answer. When he came home at about 1:10 a.m., Kennis testified she thought Ng might have been out with another girl.

She said Benjamin was uncommunicative with her. They watched television until 2:30

a.m. "He was laying there, gazing at the ceiling," she said. "He normally didn't do that."

Shortly thereafter Seattle police officers arrived to arrest Benjamin Ng. Mak, knowing he was being sought by police, turned himself in. Tony Ng, the third man, had fled the city. He wouldn't be found for 19 months.

But even with the eyewitness testimony of Wai Chin, and the two suspects in jail, the Seattle Police Department's investigation of the crime was far from over. A blizzard of rumors and tips flooded the city, as the curtain of privacy that had been drawn for so many years around Chinatown was ripped aside. The full glare of media attention spotlighted Seattle, the quiet city in the rainy Northwest where one of the nation's worst mass murders had taken place.

Seattle Police Chief Patrick Fitzsimons, a former top New York cop, assembled a team of 40 officers for the investigation. Soon the police realized how much information they lacked about Chinatown. The FBI lent a Chinese-speaking officer to the force to aid the investigation. Mayor Charles Royer and community leaders asked Chinatown for its help.

The team descended on Chinatown looking for friends of the three men in an effort to piece together the motives and movements to explain the grisly crime. The Washington State Patrol crime laboratory put its best forensic researchers to work examining the scraps of physical evidence left behind in the shootings.

King County Prosecutor Norm Maleng assigned two of his top deputy prosecutors, Chief of Staff Bob Lasnik and Senior Deputy Bill Downing, to the case.

Perhaps most importantly, Wai Chin was put under heavy round-the-clock guard, with two officers assigned to watch over him constantly. They would play cards with the elderly man, go out occasionally to the Longacres Race Track, and just talk. The frail man's testimony at trial, under the pressure of the best cross-examination the defense could offer, would be essential to winning convictions.

It was no mistake that a veteran homicide detective, Joe Sanford, was the man to first interview Willie Mak the day after the shootings.

Mak told Sanford he'd been bowling at the Imperial Lanes in Rainier Valley that night. But the cool facade crumbled when Sanford told him somebody survived Wah Mee.

Mak wanted to make a deal. Mak told Sanford that he alone did the shootings. But it was just the first of a patchwork of lies that Mak would tell authorities in the coming months, police believed.

Within a few days of the arrests, King County Prosecutor Norm Maleng filed charges of aggravated murder and assault against Ng and Mak, the first step under Washington law in seeking the death penalty. It didn't come as a major surprise when Maleng, a month later, filed for the death penalty.

Legal maneuvering began almost immediately. The team of Willie Mak and Benjamin Ng, strong enough to commit murder, broke up when their own lives were at stake. Ng's lawyers claimed he was nothing more than an unwitting accomplice under Mak's spell. Mak would assert that he intended only to go to the Wah Mee Club to carry out an order to beat up a rival Tong leader. Mak's line of defense was that he slipped outside the club, fearing Ng would do something crazy, and never saw the shootings.

Prosecutors tried to put both Mak and Ng on trial at the same time. But after weeks of hearings through the summer of 1983,

Superior Court Judge Frank Howard agreed with Ng's lawyers' arguments that their defenses to the charges would be antagonistic to Mak's—that Mak was attempting to pin the blame for all the killings on Ng.

After hearing defense counsel John Henry Browne assert that Mak was "literally trying to save his own neck," Howard severed the trials of the two and scheduled Ng's trial first.

The stage was set for what one lawyer called "high theater," a death-penalty case that featured some of the city's best prosecutors, defense lawyers, police officers and a respected veteran judge, Frank Howard. Everybody knew that the outcome of the first trial was crucial. A conviction against Ng, the henchman, would almost certainly toll heavily for Mak.

Browne headed Ng's defense team. One of the city's most successful defense lawyers, the tall and handsome Browne favored the dramatic appeal, the carefully timed gesture. He wore expensive suits but a cheap Timex watch.

He chose his opposite for his co-counsel. David Wohl was an appellate attorney with a skilled grasp of the lawbooks, but halting and uneasy when it came to the histrionics of the courtroom, the play acted out for an audience of 12 jurors and a judge.

Howard was the perfect foil for Browne. Browne's bluster could never pierce Howard's cool. His voice remained low and controlled even in the face of Browne's constant prodding.

On the eve of Ng's trial, after a day of pretrial hearings, Browne casually motioned to the courthouse press to look at a set of new court papers just unsealed. Among them was the report of Sanford's interview with Mak, in which he "confessed" to the murders, a document that several newspapers had gone to court to obtain earlier in the year without success. The next morning's papers were headlined with stories of Mak's admission of guilt.

In court the next day, Browne rose to appeal to Howard to dismiss the case, citing the impossibility of a fair trial given the enormous publicity the press was devoting to the trial.

Browne's legal attack was aimed at convincing jurors that Ng didn't know what Mak planned that night, in February. Ng took part in tying up and robbing the club's patron, Browne asserted, but never pulled the trigger. By law, an accomplice shares the guilt of mur-

Who fired which of two guns used in the murders is still a matter of dispute. The card players and club employees were all methodically shot, execution-style, in the head.

der, but Browne's goal from the start was to save his client from the death penalty even if it meant admitting to crimes serious enough to send him to prison for life.

"Benjamin was there. That's not going to be disputed in this case," Browne said. "The evidence will show that Benjamin premeditated robbery. But there is no evidence that Benjamin premeditated murder."

Daily the relatives of the dead sat quietly in the courtroom. Many never missed a day of the long trial. It was clear that they wanted nothing short of the death penalty for Ng.

The police department's dogged efforts to track down the often-unwilling friends of Mak and Ng paid off. The friends offered a consistent picture of Mak and Ng talking, plotting, arming themselves for a violent robbery.

The climax of the drama came when Wai Chin was led under heavy guard into the courtroom. His voice was shaky but he told his story plainly and compellingly. He had narrowly escaped death but there was no revenge in his voice. Shards of the bullets were still in his neck.

Of all those inside the Wah Mee Club who might have survived, Lasnik would say years later, Wai Chin was the best witness. His English was the best, and his service as a cook in the Navy and his years of plain living made him a believable figure for the jury. It wasn't certain that three guns were fired (as Chin thought he saw) but nevertheless he offered convincing testimony of the utter brutality of the crime.

"But for Mak the crime wouldn't have happened. But for Wai Chin the crime would never have been solved," Lasnik told jurors in his closing arguments.

Swiftly, the jury returned with a guilty verdict. But, everyone knew, the trial phase was only the prologue. The real test would come in the penalty phase, where the jury would decide whether sufficient mitigating factors existed to save Ng from death or to send him to prison for life without parole. It was a test less of legal skills than it was the power of persuasion and the particular chemistry of the jury.

Ng's mother, who spoke only Chinese, told the jury that her son had been beaten severely with a stick as a child in Hong Kong. His injury, a psychologist would later claim, could

have led to emotional instability, making it difficult for him to "hold back his impulses."

Finishing her testimony, Ng's mother stood and bowed deeply to the judge, jury, spectators and court personnel. Several jurors fought back tears as she left the witness stand.

"Eight months ago, Benjamin's family came to me and put Benjamin's life in my hands," said Browne. "His life is now in your hands."

The jury needed just three hours to decide it could not reach the unanimous decision needed for the death penalty.

Mak went on trial a month later. His defense pursued two lines of attack; shift the blame for the actual shootings to Ng's shoulders and raise the suggestion of gangland warfare and drug dealing in Chinatown, abetted by powerful community leaders and the police. He portrayed himself as a new member of the Hop Sing Tong anxious to make good, agreeing to rough up another Tong leader at the Wah Mee Club but planning no killings.

Seemingly taking his cue from Ng's trial and testimony about his head injury, Mak described what he called an "expressionless look" in Ng's eyes after they entered the Wah Mee Club.

"I was feeling a little bit scared. The way Ben was acting. He was acting strange, not normal," Mak said. "There was a lot going on in my mind. I had flashbacks to the past to how Ben acts. The expression from his eyes. I had the experience before. I sense something is not right. I try to decide what to do. What's he going to do? What's going to happen? I was really scared."

Mak claimed he put his gun away and slipped out of the club before the shooting started.

Lasnik, however, called Mak's defense "a transparent attempt to shift blame" that the jury refused to accept.

Mak's jurors quickly found him guilty. James Robinson, one of Mak's attorneys, pleaded for his client's life by arguing that Mak's sentence should be no harsher than Ng's. It took just two hours for the jury to return with a verdict of death.

"We were convinced he was the leader and we felt the evidence proved that," one juror said later. "Good or bad, he knew what he was doing."

Nearly two years after the shootings, Seattle police made the last arrest in the Wah Mee killings. Tony Ng, who had fled the country after the massacre, was found living an underground existence in Calgary, Alberta. Police said little about how they traced Ng, but investigators apparently got a tip about calls Ng placed to relatives in Seattle.

Returned for trial, Ng argued that he was an unwilling participant in the murders and claimed that Mak had threatened his life if he didn't take part. He pleaded that he didn't know shooting would take place, and the jury found him guilty on multiple counts of robbery. He was sentenced to seven life terms.

Willie Mak is one of six men on Washington's Death Row. The state has carried out no executions since Joseph Self was hanged at Walla Walla State Penitentiary on June 20, 1963 for the murder of a Seattle cab driver.

He lives under the constant eye of a television camera in the top tier of a cell block inside the penitentiary's Intensive Management Unit. He has no direct contact with other inmates, including his fellow death row prisoners. Each day he gets an hour of time out of his cell, an hour inside a large room, alternating every other day with an hour in an enclosed courtyard with a sliver of a view of the sky.

As his appeals drag on, he has never given interviews to the press.

His appeals have been twice rejected by the U.S. Supreme Court, but he is continuing to press his case before the Washington State Supreme Court and the federal Ninth Circuit Court of Appeals. He has claimed his defense was prejudiced by ineffective counsel and the failure of police to pursue evidence that the shootings were carried out by Benjamin Ng as part of a conspiracy by a Chinese businessman to take over Chinatown gambling—claims the trial court reviewed but rejected as unfounded.

There are few outward signs left today of the killings that took place in the Wah Mee Club. Maynard Alley remains barred. Souvenir hunters apparently ripped off the bell button from the wall outside. Relatives of the dead visit their graves at the Lakeside Cemetery on Seattle's Capitol Hill.

Six years later, police have new concerns about gangs—the Vietnamese, the Cubans and the suspected migration of Bloods and Crips from Los Angeles to Seattle.

Chinatown is perhaps more popular than it was in 1983. Restaurants are doing booming business. Chinese New Year's celebrations are happy times, occasions when families wish each other good luck for the coming year. Upscale shopping developments and a new high-speed bus tunnel station are planned nearby, which will likely make Chinatown even more attractive.

Chinatown has tried to bury the memory of Wah Mee.

Because of worries about his safety in prison, Benjamin Ng was transferred to the more secure state penitentiary in Walla Walla. In his only newspaper interview, Ng refused to speak in detail about the killings. Asked about Mak's attempts to hold him responsible for the killings, Ng replied, "What can I say? He was trying to save his own neck."

Ng is philosophical about the American dream and what it meant to Chinese coming to America.

"Back in my great-great-grandfather's age, they came here for gold. But in my stage, we didn't do that. We just wanted to come over here for a better life. For better stuff for the next generation. There is an old saying. When you look at the United States, go dig gold. ...Well, the gold rush was over 100 years ago. There isn't any gold rush here."

Six years later, Lasnik believes the difference in verdicts—life without parole for Ng and death for Mak—was due more to the vagaries of juries than to the evidence on trial.

"I felt we did as good a job of presenting the case of Benjamin as we did on Willie. I think the roles of the two [in the killings] were different, and the role of the jury was different in terms of capital punishment. The aggravated murder verdict was the top priority. The death penalty was the jury's call," he said.

"When we got the death penalty, I never really thought it would be carried out," Lasnik said. "We wanted to ensure that they spent the rest of their lives in jail."

Mike Merrit is a reporter with the Seattle Post Intelligencer.

Sean Richard Sellers

Don Mecoy

Sean felt good; he laughed. A great burden had been lifted from him. It had gone down without a hitch. But after all, it wasn't the first time the 16-year-old had committed murder.

Sean Sellers in custody, before being escorted to Oklahoma's death row.

Photo copyright 1987, the Oklahoma Publishing Company. From the July 19, 1987 issue of the Daily Oklahoman.

In Oklahoma, spring brings warmth and fear. A flat land of rich, red earth and oil, Oklahoma is the world's greatest breeding ground for tornados. When the wind comes sweeping down the plain, it often bumps headlong into the moist, warm air flowing northward from the Gulf of Mexico. The collision, five miles high, spawns deadly twisters that drop from the sky.

In 1986, spring arrived a couple of weeks early. Longtime residents of the Sooner state welcomed winter's departure, even as they kept an eye to the skies for the tell-tale wall of clouds that could foreshadow destruction. They know how quickly the dark, ominous clouds can obscure azure skies.

March 4 dawned clear and crisp; another balmly spring-like day. But as Vonda Bellofatto sat in her modest northwest Oklahoma City home, she was chilled to the bone. She feared for her troubled son, Sean Sellers.

Vonda and her second husband, Lee, were worried about the increasing distance between Sean and themselves. He seemed to be erecting an emotional barrier between himself and his parents. Vonda was concerned about the kids he ran around with, and the strange girls he was dating. She recently had forbid him to continue going out with a girl he met at a midnight movie. It wasn't the first time Sean had dated a girl of whom Vonda did not approve. Sean didn't like his mother's meddling.

On this day, she had found a poem written by her son that spoke of his attitude "causin' people to drift away," and told a story of a lover who "hurled himself over a cliff to be with his girl again." Vonda feared she had gone too far. The time had come to reach out to Sean.

By all accounts, Sean was doing well in his junior year at Putnam City North High School, a suburban school comprised mostly of white, middle-class kids like himself. An attractive and talented boy, Sean demonstrated an aptitude for drama and art and enjoyed writing poetry and song lyrics.

Privately, Sean's interests encompassed the martial arts and the occult, which led to one of his few bouts with trouble in school. A teacher discovered he had brought a Satanic bible to class with him, and notified Vonda and Lee. They were concerned, but talked to Sean about it and felt the situation was under control.

Sean's teachers described him as a loner, interacting with few students except in his drama class, where he excelled. He seemed to have conquered his earlier difficulties with adapting to his new surroundings in the two years he had been living in Oklahoma City. But then, he had had a lot of practice fitting into new environments.

From the time Vonda and Lee married in 1976, the family moved on an almost annual basis. After four years in Ravia, Okla., where they lived with Vonda's parents, the Bellofattos hopscotched across the West, touching down in Los Angeles, three different towns in Oklahoma, and twice in Greely, Colo. During their second stint in Greely, the family declared bankruptcy before packing their bags for Oklahoma City.

As an only child, Sean often stayed with his grandparents while Vonda and Lee worked as a team hauling big rigs from one side of the country to the other. As Sean grew older, Vonda and Lee permitted him to care for himself during their sometimes lengthy road trips. During those times, Sean grew accustomed to setting his own rules.

Now that Vonda and Lee had landed jobs with more conventional hours, Sean bristled under their authority and their attempts to set limits—at their very presence in the house. A few weeks earlier, Sean had run away from home after Vonda made known her feelings about his girlfriend.

Lee, a former Green Beret and a bull of a man, had a good relationship with Sean and expressed pride in Sean's accomplishments in the Civil Air Patrol. But Vonda, after her divorce from her first husband, had been thrust into the role of disciplinarian for Sean, who was only three when his parents split. Vonda was vocal and emotional in exerting her authority over Sean.

She and Sean often wrote to one another about their feelings and fears, and she felt they communicated best on paper. When writing, Vonda was able to tell Sean of her hope for him even as she expressed doubts about his lifestyle.

On this day, Vonda wrote to Sean about the pride she felt for him and the pain she knew he was feeling. She told of the deep maternal feelings that his birth had stirred within her, and her understanding of his troubled teen years.

In six emotional pages scripted in a disciplined hand, Vonda wrote to Sean of her love for him and how he could find his way back to his family.

" My dearest and most precious son,

I start this off with words that hopefully will tell you what you mean to me. Nothing in this world could ever mean more to me than you Sean. I love you so very much and would give my life for you without a second thought. Please believe that."

Tragically, Vonda never delivered her letter.

That evening, after Sean returned home from his part-time job at a pizzeria, he completed his homework and chatted aimlessly with his parents before Vonda and Lee went to bed. Sean had already decided what he was going to do. He went to his room and waited until he was certain Vonda and Lee were sleeping.

About 11:30 p.m., Sean, clad only his underwear and armed with a .44-caliber pistol taken from Lee's closet, crept into his parents bedroom. For a few moments, he stood motionless listening to their measured breathing. Then he walked to Lee's side of the bed.

Sean had planned what he would do. Knowing Lee was stronger than himself and fearing his stepfather's Green Beret training, Sean had determined to kill Lee first.

Sean placed the heavy pistol against the back of Lee's head and pulled the trigger. Lee died instantly. The blast was deafening, and Vonda, lying face-down, arose. Sean shot her in the face. She collapsed, but continued to breathe. Sean walked around to her side of the bed and fired another shot point-blank to the back of her head.

One of the rounds pierced the waterbed, which slowly began to drain into the plush bedroom carpet.

Startled by the noise of the big gun, Sean briefly crouched outside the house to make sure none of the residents of the quiet neighborhood was responding to the gunfire. Reassured, he returned to the house, showered, dressed and opened a sliding glass door to convince police that burglars had committed the act. He turned on the light in his parent's bedroom to survey the gruesome scene, then took the gun and drove away in his pickup.

Sean felt good: He laughed. A great burden had been lifted from him. It had gone down without a hitch. But after all, it wasn't the first time the 16-year-old had committed murder.

Sean entered the house, but moments later rushed frantically out the door, screaming that someone had killed his parents. Richard entered the house and saw the bodies, still poised as if in sleep.

Oklahoma County District Attorney Robert Macy, a man of stern countenance and silver hair, has spent almost his entire adult life in law enforcement. He earned his law degree while serving as an Oklahoma City police officer. Throughout the state, he is recognized for his trademark black string tie and his skill at trying murder cases.

Macy, whose determined arguments have put 33 individuals on Oklahoma's Death Row, is not widely perceived as a sentimental man.

Nevertheless, Macy says, "In my opinion, Vonda's letter is one of the most beautiful letters a mother has ever written to a child." Police found the letter the next day on a clipboard in the Bellofatto's house.

To this day, Macy carries a copy of that letter in his briefcase.

Robert Paul Bower was a 36-year-old convenience store clerk whose life had been marked with few significant achievements. His crude tatoos, gold earring and thick mass of curly hair were trademarks of the rough crowd he ran with and the day-by-day lifestyle he maintained. But for Oklahoma City police, the way Bower lived did little to explain the manner in which he died on September 8, 1985.

For months, homicide detectives tried to understand why an armed assailant had chased Bower through the northside conve-nience store in the middle of the night. Bower's attacker fired shots at him and into him before leaving the clerk's body sprawled across the doorway of a bathroom splattered with his blood. Why would someone make such an effort to kill, and then leave without taking a dime from the cash register or a single piece of merchandise from the store? The only decent lead found at the scene were the remains of .357-caliber silver-tipped bullets taken from Bower's body and the store. Since such ammunition was popular among police officers at the time, this clue, just like every other clue in the case, led nowhere,

"That really had police baffled because we had no motive. We checked Bower out. We checked everything in the world to try to find a motive why anybody would kill him, and we could find none. Because there was none," Macy said. It was one of only a handful of cases the homicide unit failed to clear in 1985.

Sean couldn't wait to tell his best friend, Richard Howard, what he had done. Sean and Richard enjoyed a symbiotic relationship. Richard, a born follower, thrived while basking in the light of what he perceived to be Sean's radiance. Sean, the more intelligent of the two, could persuade Richard to believe or do almost anything.

It was a short jaunt from Sean's home to

PHOTO • OKLAHOMA CITY POLICE DEPARTMENT

Robert Paul Bower was Sellers first victim. The only motive for the murder was, according to detectives, "to find out how it felt."

Richard's in nearby Peidmont, a small, mostly rural community that borders Oklahoma City. Sean arrived just after midnight.

When Richard answered the knock on his door, he found Sean at his threshold, looking pale but excited.

"Richard, I did it."

"What the hell are you talking about?" Richard asked.

"I killed 'em," was Sean's reply.

Sean had discussed getting rid of his parents, but Richard was shocked to learn he had murdered them. But Sean had something for Richard to do, as well. Richard was to provide Sean's alibi, to tell authorities that Sean had spent the night at Richard's house. Sean also ordered Richard to dispose of the gun. Richard, ever the faithful disciple, did as he was told.

In the next few hours, Sean detailed for Richard how he had dispatched his burdensome parents. The pair also formulated a plan in which Sean would "discover" his parents' bodies the next morning on his way to school. Richard and his wife, Tracy, both of whom were teen-age dropouts, would drive Sean to school the next day, stopping at Sean's house so he could get a note explaining why he was late for class. Richard, believing his wife could not be trusted as an accomplice, told her nothing about what Sean had done or his own increasing involvement.

Tracy, who was anxious for herself and her husband to acquire their high school diplomas, thought she was on her way to the school to re-enroll. She had no inkling of the nightmare to come.

About 8 a.m., Robert, Sean and Tracy stopped at the pizza parlor where Vonda was scheduled to work a morning shift. They then drove to Sean's house, where Lee's construction company truck was still parked in the driveway. Sean, purely for Tracy's benefit, said he would be in trouble for allowing his parents to oversleep.

Sean entered the house, but moments later rushed frantically out the door, screaming that someone has killed his parents. Richard entered the house and saw the bodies, still poised as if in sleep, Vonda face down and Lee on his right side facing his wife.

A neighbor drawn by Sean's lamentations comforted him and told him police would soon arrive. Sean, drawing on his acting talent and high-school drama class experience, performed convincingly. However, he had never tested his thespian skills on homicide detectives, and they can be the harshest of critics.

About 9 a.m., Oklahoma City Homicide Detective Ron Mitchell arrived and was briefed on the preliminary investigation of the scene. Detective Sam Sealy told Mitchell that Sean claimed burglars must have murdered his mom and dad. But Sealy pointed out that there was no forced entry into the house. A broom handle that prevented opening the patio door could only have been removed from the inside, and there were numerous valuables in plain sight.

"Besides, burglars don't kill people in bed. So he doesn't have a good feeling about it at all at that point," Mitchell recalls. Mitchell, a veteran of the force attached to the homicide unit for more than two years, was assigned to interview Sean, whose dramatic performance began to deteriorate under the detective's questioning.

"It's kind of hard to put into words, but just watching him—I've seen people when they're upset, when they've gone through something that traumatic and I've seen the way they react. With Sean, my impression at the time was, 'This guy's trying to make me think that he's really upset about this. But something's not right. It just doesn't look right,'" Mitchell said.

Sean recounted his actions of the previous night, saying he left home about 11:30 p.m. en route to Richard's house. At this point, Mitchell was already skeptical.

"Now that doesn't make any sense to me. I've got a daughter his age, and I know what I would have said if she came to me and asked to go to a friend's house at 11:30 on a school night. She never would've gotten out of the damn house."

When Sean began to describe his discovery of the bodies, he balked, claiming he was unable to talk about it. More alarms sounded in the detective's head.

"It's a horrible thing if you were to ever find anybody that you loved murdered. That's terrible. But I've never run across anybody that

"It's a horrible thing if you were to ever find anybody that you loved murdered. But I've never run across anybody that doesn't want to tell me what they saw. They want me to do whatever I can to find the son of a bitch who did it."

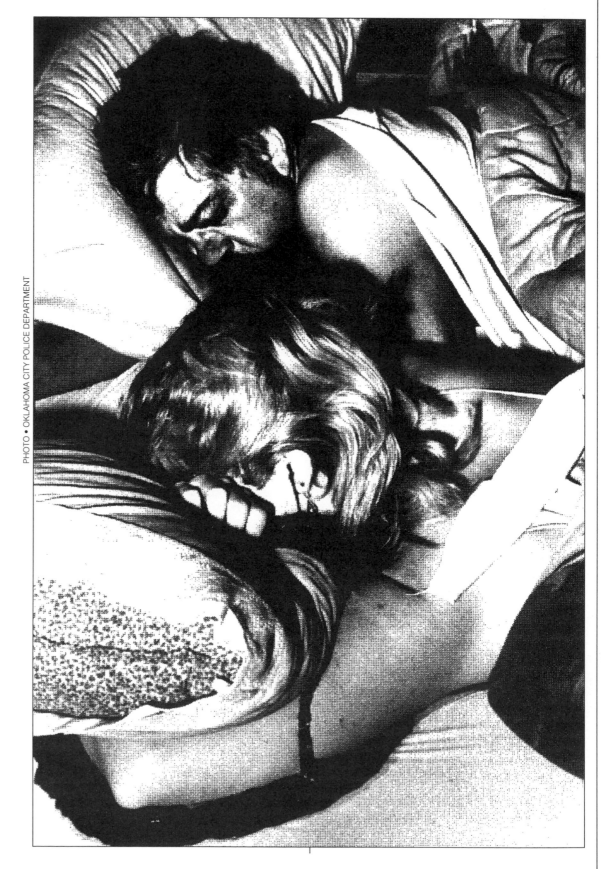

PHOTO • OKLAHOMA CITY POLICE DEPARTMENT

Sean claimed that burglars broke in and shot his parents as they slept.

doesn't want to tell me what they saw. They want me to do whatever I can to find the son of a bitch who did it."

Mitchell completed the initial interview, and although there were no gaping holes in Sean's alibi, the detective harbored nagging suspicions.

"It was really strange. After he got out of my cruiser, his whole attitude changed. I was no longer Detective Mitchell, now I was Ron. I've seen that before. It's almost like, "Well, I fooled you. Now we can be friends."

Richard's interview proceeded smoothly and, despite his nervousness, he confirmed Sean's story. In fact, Mitchell felt Richard's sense of remorse was more sincere than Sean's. Richard genuinely liked Vonda and admired Lee. He was having trouble coping with their deaths and his role in the coverup.

Sean told investigators he didn't know how to contact his grandparents, and asked if he could stay with Richard and Tracy until his grandparents were notified. Lacking any reasonable alternative, Mitchell approved.

Later that day, Sean boasted to Richard about his performance with the detectives. In the afternoon, Sean rode horses with his girlfriend.

"You couldn't help but be suspicious of Sean, but not to the point you're going to arrest him. It's easy now to look back and say that it was obvious. At that time, it wasn't obvious. It was just something you filed away in the back of your mind."

That night, the detectives gathered in the homicide office and discussed their suspicions of Sean. They decided to re-interview Sean and Richard the next day, but this time with greater intensity.

The next morning Vonda's father, James Blackwell, who recognized his daughter's house in televised reports of the murders, stopped by the downtown police station to talk to Mitchell.

Blackwell told Mitchell Sean knew exactly where he lived and how to reach him.

"If he told you he didn't know my phone number, he lied," Blackwell said.

As the two walked side by side, a subdued Blackwell inquired about the investigation.

"I just want to know if you have a suspect," Blackwell said.

"Yes sir, I think we do," Mitchell replied.

"Is it close to home?"

"Yes."

"I was afraid you were going to say that."

Later, Mitchell again listened to Richard recount the scripted sequence of events. But Richard was still too nervous, unable to meet the detective's eyes. Mitchell wasn't buying the act anymore and let Richard know it.

"I want you to look at me when I tell you this. We know who killed Lee and Vonda. We know Sean did it, but now we need to prove it."

Richard's head dropped and he stared at the floor. Mitchell pointed out that Sean had already killed two people and had no reason not to deal the same fate to anyone who could expose him.

Richard said, "You're right. He'll kill me and he'll kill Tracy. I know it,"

Richard began to tell of Sean's confession to him and the scenario they had devised for Sean.

In another interview room, Detective Eric Mullenix heard Sean repeat his alibi. Like Mitchell, Mullenix braced Sean with investigators' knowledge of his actions. However, he got a very different reaction.

"He was playing very cooperative," Mullenix said. "And then when I told him that we thought that he had done it, he totally changed."

Sean glanced around the room with wide eyes. His gaze finally settled on Mullenix

"Where am I at?" Sean asked.

The interview was over. Mullinex immediately went next door to the Oklahoma City Jail and booked Sean Richard Sellers on two counts of first-degree murder.

Richard, whose loyalty to Sean had always been unquestioning, was looking for a new leader. Ron Mitchell was happy to oblige. The two were in a race with local garbage men to Richard's trash can, where he had dumped the gun Sean used to kill his parents.

On the way, Mitchell decided to play a hunch. Earlier that morning, a 13-year-old girl had called the office and told a detective that Sean had killed Robert Paul Bower, the 36-year-old convenience store clerk, six months earlier.

The information was dubious, at best. The girl said Sean had told her he stabbed Bower

Richard told officers that Sean gunned down Bower as he waited outside the store. Sean wanted to see what it felt like to kill, Richard said. "He said it was a rush."

"He's just another damn, cold-blooded, murderer. He's one of the coldest ones down there. It takes a special kind of person to blow the brains out of the woman who gave birth to him just because he doesn't want to do what she tells him to."

to death. But Bower had been shot.

"You know what we heard today, Richard? We heard ol' Sean was involved in that convenience store killing up there," Mitchell said.

In his rearview mirror, Mitchell saw Richard's head drop.

"Yes, sir, he was. I was there," Richard said.

Mitchell was shocked. After retrieving the .44, Mitchell listened intently as Richard told how Sean gunned down Bower with Richard's grandfather's pistol.

Richard's grandfather was a State Capitol Patrolman. Detectives finally understood the mystery of the silver-tipped bullets that took Bower's life.

Richard told officers that Sean gunned down Bower as he waited outside the store. Sean wanted to see what it felt like to kill, Richard said.

"He said it was a rush," Richard said.

The trial promised to be a media circus. Macy opted to try Sellers for all three murders at once. Because there were two separate homicidal acts, Macy would seek the death penalty. It wasn't a difficult decision, Macy said.

"He's somebody who can extinguish a human life like you and I swat a fly," Macy said.

In 1986, any death penalty case attracted heavy local media coverage. But Sean's youth and, more importantly, his defense that he was influenced by Satanism drew nationwide attention.

Richard was the state's star witness in exchange for having a first-degree murder charge against him dropped. He later pleaded guilty to accessory to murder and received a five-year suspended sentence. His testimony was devastating.

Sean's memory, which disappeared in the police interview room, still had not returned. He said he didn't recall killing anyone. Each day, Sean sat quietly at the defense table, a Bible on the table in front of him. Sean had renounced Satan and found God behind bars.

Macy had seen jailhouse conversions before.

"There's an expression to the effect that Jesus Christ lives on the 11th floor of the Oklahoma County Courthouse," Macy said.

Public defender Bob Ravitz put several of

Sean's former friends on the stand to testify about Sean's fascination with the occult. Jurors heard that Sean attended covens where Satanic blood rituals were performed, that Sean cut himself and drank blood. Expert witnesses told how youngsters' morals could be warped by the game Dungeons and Dragons, which Sean played.

Ravitz said Sean was "a mixed-up kid."

However, Richard told the court that Sean mentioned nothing about a Satanic influence or ritual when he described the murders of his parents immediately after killing them.

Teachers called by the defense testified that Sean's behavior did not change in the period after he killed Robert Paul Bower. During that semester, Sean received mostly A's in his classes.

In his only display of emotion during the trial, Sean sobbed as Ravitz read Vonda's letter into the record.

Mitchell, who witnessed the entire trial, said he thought the Satanic argument worked against the defense.

"One juror had made the comment that if the trial had ended after the prosecution's part and the defense had done nothing, they would have convicted him. But based on that information alone, they would have given him three life sentences. After they heard everything they felt like they had absolutely no choice. This was a dangerous, dangerous kid, and he deserved a death penalty for what he'd done," Mitchell said.

"They [the defense] painted a picture of a monster."

Macy said jurors simply didn't believe the Satanic defense.

"I think the jury may have been a little bit offended and felt like this was a bogus defense, that it was flimsy," Macy said.

The jury brought back guilty verdicts on all three counts. In the penalty phase of the trial, the jurors returned after two hours and 45 minutes with three death penalty recommendations.

Ravitz called the penalty barbaric.

One juror remarked after the trial that although it was obvious that Sean was involved in Satanic activity, the jury believed he still knew right from wrong.

"All I can say is, if God will take his soul,

let Sean go up there to where Lee and Vonda are now and they can deal with it there," the juror said.

After receiving his sentence, Sean approached the District Attorney.

"Mr. Macy, do you really hate me?" Sean said.

"No, Sean, I don't hate you. But I really hate what you did," Macy said.

After receiving his guilty verdict, Sean, teary-eyed, held his first press conference to warn teens of the dangers of Satanism.

"It's not the way. It's not the way. Jesus is the only answer that's out there ... and it's time teenagers got serious about Jesus here in America. It's time now," Sean said.

It wasn't a great performance, but Sean improved with practice. He has since appeared with Geraldo, Oprah and on the CBS news show "48 Hours." He can be seen occasionally on late-night cable religious programs warning of the evils of Satan and praising the redemption of Jesus Christ.

Several months after his trial, Sean's memory of the killings returned during an interview with "People Weekly" magazine.

Oklahoma's favorite son, Will Rogers, could have been talking about the state's most troubled child when he said, "We don't give our criminals much punishment, but we sure give 'em plenty of publicity."

Sean's televised appearances infuriate law enforcement personnel.

Since the trial, Macy's feelings about the young killer have changed.

"I've got to where I really don't like him now because he's making a mockery of the system. He thinks he's some kind of big-shot. He's just another damn, cold-blooded, murderer. He's one of the coldest ones down there. It takes a special kind of person to blow the brains out of the woman who gave birth to him just because he doesn't want to do what she tells him to," Macy said.

"He really needs to die. I might have been better off to get him three consecutive life sentences so that I wouldn't have made a national hero out of him."

Sean, now 20, is one of 101 men and three women on Oklahoma's death row. He is in the midst of the automatic appeal of his death penalty to the Oklahoma Court of Criminal Appeals. It is only the second step in a nine-step appeal process, but already he has suffered a major setback.

On June 26, the U.S. Supreme Court, in a 5-4 decision, ruled that states are free to impose the death penalty for murderers who committed their crime when they were 16 or 17. Of the 2,200 convicted murderers on death rows in America, at least 32 committed their crimes while under the age of 18.

Oklahoma Assistant Attorney General Robert Nance said "I think we're pleased from the attorney general on down."

Despite the ruling, Sean won't face a lethal injection for many years, Nance said. Oklahoma hasn't imposed a death penalty for 23 years.

"Some attorney probably yet unborn will be sitting in this seat before Sean Sellers is executed," Nance said.

Macy also applauded the ruling.

"I think now there's a good chance he'll be executed. He had a fair trial." The memories of Vonda and Lee Bellofatto are still vivid to those who reside in the neighborhood where the couple lived and died. But few still think of Robert Paul Bower.

Ron Mitchell calls him "the forgotten man."

"If Sean Sellers is ever executed, in my mind it will be for Robert Bower. That's who I will be thinking of," Mitchell says.

Macy echoes that sentiment.

"That was the first one he committed. And he did it for the worst of all reasons: to find out how it felt. I can't think of a worse reason to take a human life. That's bizarre."

Don Mecoy has been a reporter with the Daily Oklahomian *in Oklahoma City for three years. Mecoy covers the police beat and state desk, which includes the Corrections Department.*

Roy Bruce Smith

Christine Riedel

Roy Smith didn't know what to do with the glass of wine in his hand. A computer technician who had just begun a two-year business assignment in Asia, he stood in a dining room in Taipei, Taiwan as a group of prominent businessmen rose to toast him.

The wine was a problem because Smith was an alcoholic. He hadn't taken a drink in seven years, a resolve he made following a string of alcohol-related arrests in 1978. The blond, plain-looking man had started drinking nearly two decades earlier with classmates at his Falls Church, Va. high school.

Like many teenagers, he began drinking just to feel drunk. But as he grew older, Smith, an intelligent, soft-spoken man, used the bottle more and more often to cope with rocky relationships and the feeling that he was merely mediocre at most things in life. Now, a few dozen important people watched as he decided what to do with the fateful glass of wine.

"I kind of thought real quick, 'How do I refuse this? I don't want to embarrass them,'" Smith recalled. "We had presidents of companies, chairmen of the board. I didn't want to say, 'Gee, I'm an alcoholic, I can't drink.'"

So Smith drank the wine. And he didn't get drunk or feel much of anything because of it. It made him believe he could handle drinking again. In the following days, weeks and months, Smith went back to the bottle again and again, embarking on a three-year bout with alcohol abuse that would end when he blew away a police officer with an assault rifle.

Smith spent two years in Asia teaching others how to install computers supplied by his employer, National Advance Systems, based in Lanham, Md. He came home to Manassas in Oct., 1987 to a place that seemed strange.

His wife, Carol, seemed distant and angry, a sharp contrast to Young Ae, the sweet, undemanding lover he had taken in Korea. And Manassas was undergoing explosive growth. Although Smith owned a townhouse on a quiet city street, much around him had changed. Shopping centers and housing developments had sprung up everywhere in the quaint, historic city, which lies

PHOTOS • TOM SUFLITA

Roy Smith, convicted cop killer, awaits his electrocution on Virginia's death row in the Mecklenburg Correctional Center.

about 30 miles southwest of Washington, D.C. On their way into work each morning, commuters inch to the nation's capital on clogged roads that cross Civil War battlefields.

"I came home to a home that wasn't my home anymore," Smith said later. "I should never have come back to the United States."

Just as adjusting to Korea had been difficult, so was readjusting to life at home. In the months following his return, Smith continued to drink, sinking deeper into depression. When he drank, the normally reserved man lost his inhibitions and sometimes became violent. Arrests followed. On Feb. 5, 1988, Smith was arrested in a Waltham, Mass. hotel after employees complained he was drinking from a bottle in the lobby. Less than a month later, on March 3, he was charged with drunk driving and later that month, on a trip to Santa Clara, Calif., a drunken Smith sat in an restaurant and exposed himself. In all three arrests, he either threatened or assaulted his arresting officers.

Smith was falling apart. At work, he talked of hijacking and crashing airplanes into buildings in cities along the East Coast. The 42-year-old man decided to seek help, and set up an appointment with a psychologist for July 21, 1988, a Thursday. At the last minute, however, the psychologist postponed the appointment for a week. Smith went home to pass another weekend.

Sunday, July 24 promised to be one of those rare, perfect days made for picnics and swimming. Smith awoke at 8 a.m., glanced over at his sleeping wife, and went downstairs to the kitchen to brew some coffee. Today was Carol's annual work picnic, and he looked forward to accompanying her. Smith watched the news and weather and then went back to the bedroom to see when Carol planned to leave for the picnic.

Carol, who was less enthused about the idea, shrugged in answer to her husband's questions. The couple had seen some hard times since his return home, especially with all his drinking and his talk of flying Young Ae to the United States to live with him—them—in Manassas. Carol didn't feel like spending the afternoon with the man.

Getting no answers from Carol, Smith went into his back yard and ran his hands through the grass. It still held the morning dew, so he decided to wait awhile before cutting it. He sat in the back yard and drank more coffee as the sun dried the grass. Two hours passed and he started up the lawn mower, breaking through the quiet that usually surrounded his row of townhouses on Laurelwood Court.

By the time Carol came downstairs and announced that she was leaving for the picnic, Smith was just finishing the lawn. His wife did not extend an invitation. Smith, trying to swallow his disappointment, busied himself with trimming some stray blades of grass he'd missed. He spent the better part of the noon hour drinking some more coffee in his yard and stewing about his marriage.

"I just sat around thinking about what was going on. I was thinking about why I came home from Korea. I guess I felt pretty lost," Smith recalled. His thoughts then turned to some beer he had stashed in a shed behind the house. He knew he didn't want to drink it, but after a brief battle with his conscience, he went to the shed. For next three hours, Smith, who hadn't bothered with breakfast or lunch, guzzled the beers.

After polishing them off, he changed from his T-shirt and shorts into trousers and a button-down shirt and went to grab a bite at Nobles, a restaurant and bar about a mile from his house.

By the time he arrived at Nobles, Smith was in an ugly, ranting mood, said manager Pat Davis, who recognized Smith from his weekly visits to the establishment.

"He started talking about his Korean girlfriend and he started talking about suicide," she said. "He wanted to move her here to Manassas, except his wife wouldn't allow it. He said that if he couldn't have his girlfriend he would commit suicide."

Although it wasn't the first time Smith had ranted and raved at the restaurant, his behavior that night was too much for Davis to tolerate. Before he could even finish his first beer, she told him to pay his tab and leave. As he walked out, Davis noticed Smith had something tucked into his pants pocket. It appeared to be a gun.

Smith was falling apart. At work, he talked of hijacking and crashing airplanes into buildings in cities along the East Coast.

Smith returned to an empty house at approximately 8:30 p.m. Although Carol had pulled into the driveway just as he left for the restaurant, she was gone again by the time her husband came back. Her absence upset Smith even more. Smith changed back

PHOTO • SAM ELLIS

Smith's victim, John Conner, was a popular man in the Manassas Police Department. He had been promoted to sergeant just two weeks earlier.

into his shorts and T-shirt and did something he hadn't done in some time—he went to his weapons collection, which consisted of an array of swords and guns, including an AR-15 semi-automatic rifle. He had bought the rifle nine years earlier because it was a favorite of his while in the U.S. Army. Smith had been drafted in 1966 and had served until 1969. Although he'd been trained for combat, he never had to fight in Vietnam. But his training had taught him to shoot to kill.

In his bedroom, Smith took a .357 Magnum from its case and tucked it into his belt. He then went to a spare bedroom, where he retrieved a .44 Magnum and the AR-15, plus a web belt and some ammunition. The .44 and the ammunition went into the belt, while he put a scope and bayonet on the already fierce-looking rifle. The drunken warrior posted himself on his front stoop.

Emmett Cottrell, a folksy, talkative man, lived at 9194 Laurelwood Court, next door to Smith. Since Smith's return from Korea, the two men had shared conversation over cups of coffee while sitting on their front stoops.

In the dusk of July 24, Cottrell came out to his stoop to find Smith sitting with the AR-15 jutting up into the air from between his knees. His friend was in no mood for a chat.

"He said, 'I'm not gonna make it through the night,'" Cottrell recalled. Smith then fired a round from the AR-15 into the air. A neighbor passing by warned Smith that firing the gun could lead to trouble. "You ain't seen nothing yet—wait until I start shooting people," Smith replied.

Smith told Cottrell he hoped the shots would bring the police.

"He said, 'I hope someone calls the police because I'll shoot the first one that arrives and I hope they shoot me in return,'" Cottrell said.

While Roy Smith's anger was exploding on Laurelwood Court, Manassas Police Sgt. John Conner was spending his dinner break less than a mile away at the home of his mother, Bertha. Conner, a 37-year-old father of four, had brought the latest portraits of his infant daughter, Elizabeth. As mother and son looked over the photos, Conner heard a police dispatcher radio that a man was firing shots on Laurelwood Court.

"I'd better see what's going on. I'll see you tomorrow, Mom," said Conner as he bent over to kiss his mother. Bertha watched her son close the sliding glass door behind him and walk toward his unmarked cruiser. Suddenly, he stopped and went back to the door.

"He pressed his face against the glass, made a face at me like he was a little kid," Bertha Conner remembered. "He then did something he'd never done before—he unlocked the door, ran inside, put his arms around me and said 'I'll see you tomorrow.'"

Bertha Conner watched her son speed off into the night to calm the unrest on Laurelwood Court.

John Conner was a popular man in the Manassas Police Department. In his seven years with the force, he had earned the friendship and respect of the men and women in the department, which traditionally attracts young officers. Connor, a shift supervisor and firearms instructor, had been promoted to sergeant just two weeks earlier.

When the first police officers arrived at 9196 Laurelwood Court, they saw Roy Smith on his front stoop, rifle in hand. He ran into his townhouse. In the meantime, John Conner ran to the back of the row of homes. Moments later, he radioed, "I've got him in sight. He's coming out the back door."

Conner was the first person to make it to the fence that separated Smith's yard from that of a neighbor's. Suddenly, a series of shots sounded from behind Smith's house. In the chaotic moments that followed, police filled the yard and found Smith squatting on the ground, trying to jam ammunition into his rifle. Conner was lying face down on the blood-stained grass near the fence. He was still alive, but the back of his skull had been shattered, and a portion of his brain was visible. Other bullets had hit him in the right arm and thigh and the back. As he fell to the ground, his right arm, which held his service revolver, had been pinned beneath him. It fired as he lay there, hitting his left hip. Roy Smith had been shot once in the right heel. There were no witnesses to the shooting.

Officers closed in around Smith and ordered him to drop the rifle. As they wrestled him to the ground, he began screaming, "I'm sorry. Shoot me, shoot me please." Officer Jeff Plum tended to his fallen colleague and told him they'd captured his assailant. "Good," Conner answered.

An ambulance whisked Conner to a nearby hospital, where a helicopter crew took him to a medical unit in Fairfax, Va. He died there later that night.

The 115-year-old Manassas Police Department had never lost an officer until Roy Bruce Smith entered the picture. Murders are a rarity in that quiet city, making Conner's death a particularly hard blow. News of the death spread quickly. Who was Roy Smith? How could he have shot an officer?

The police were trying to answer the same questions. Officers from the Prince William County Police Department grilled Smith for about 90 minutes after his arrest. As nurses tended to his injured foot, Smith tearfully told Investigator Robert Zinn that he shot Conner, that the death was his fault. But he insisted Conner fired first, triggering an automatic response he had learned in combat training. Smith said he fired back, not knowing he was shooting an officer.

"There was muzzle flash, muzzle flash... it's, it's enemy, that's all I know," Smith told his interviewer. He said he had been drunk and angry that evening, but had never intended to kill anyone.

After the interview, Smith recovered from his gunshot wound in a heavily guarded room at Prince William Hospital in Manassas. The next day, he refused to speak to anyone. Instead he cried and pulled his bedcovers over his head. On July 26, he finally spoke to a hospital employee. "I want to die by lethal injection," he said. The behavior prompted the hospital to place him on suicide watch. To prevent him from

PHOTOS • TOM SUFLITA

"Smith told the psychiatrist that the tragic events of July 24 unfolded because of "bad karma" from previous lives."

Conner was lying face down on the blood-stained grass near the fence. He was still alive, but the back of his skull had been shattered, and a portion of his brain was visible.

harming himself, his waist and left arm and leg were shackled to the hospital bed. He was later transferred to jail in neighboring Fairfax County, where he spent the next eight months awaiting trial. Authorities decided against the customary procedure of jailing him in Manassas because Conner's widow, Christine, worked at the facility as a classifications officer.

The Commonwealth's attorney, Paul Ebert charged Smith with capital murder, alleging he shot the Conner with the intent of interfering with his duties as a police officer. He also charged the computer technician with using a firearm in the commission of a felony, which carries a mandatory two-year sentence.

A big, blocky man with a country drawl, Ebert appears to be a laid-back southern gentleman. But he is a fearsome opponent in the courtroom. Ebert had been the Prince Williams Commonwealth's attorney for 20 years and had yet to lose a capital case. Smith became the fifth man Ebert prosecuted for capital murder.

The financially shaky Smith couldn't afford to hire his own legal counsel, so a judge appointed Edward Mann and Paul Maslakowski, two private attorneys, to defend him. Between the two of them, the short, mild-mannered Mann and the lanky, more aggressive Maslakowski, they had accumulated fewer than ten years' experience.

In the following months, Smith made several pretrial court appearances. Although he seldom had to take the stand in those appearances, he wept every time.

As the trial date drew near, Ebert disclosed details about Smith's history and his attitudes toward police. As it turned out, Smith had accumulated a lengthy criminal record, although he'd never been convicted of anything more serious than a misdemeanor. While stationed in West Germany in 1969, Smith was found guilty of being drunk and disorderly on one occasion, and was convicted of disorderly conduct for another incident six months later. Other arrests, which spanned a period from 1971 to 1978 and then began again in early 1988, were for offenses including assault and battery, indecent exposure and drunk driving. Although

the offenses differed, two threads connected them: alcohol and violent threats or acts against police officers.

In April 1971, Fairfax County Police Officer Albert Richter went to Smith's home to calm a domestic dispute. Richter was greeted at the door with the barrel of a rifle. Smith appeared intoxicated and threatened to kill Richter, who talked to the man until a back-up unit arrived. The officers had to wrestle the gun away from him.

"That was the only time in the 22 years at this point that I've been confronted with weapons," said Richter, now an investigator with the department.

Two weeks later, Smith had a run-in with another man in uniform. This time, it was Doug Guernsey, a security officer at George Washington University who was heading home from work shortly after midnight on March 1, 1971. On the road ahead of him, Guernsey saw a car sitting at a green light. As he drew closer the driver pulled into his lane, suddenly hitting the brakes. Guernsey swerved to avoid hitting the driver, but the man caught up to him and pulled the stunt again. Guernsey couldn't avoid rear-ending him this time. After the collision, the security guard, still in his work clothes, went to check the man ahead of him. Receiving no reply from a drunken Roy Smith, he surveyed the damage to the cars and suddenly felt a sharp pain slicing through his body.

"The next think I knew, I'd been stabbed with a bayonet," Guernsey said. Smith stabbed the guard three times in the side and the chest, injuring a rib and puncturing a lung. He then beat his victim in the face with the butt of the bayonet. Police charged Smith with assault with the intent to commit murder, but he later pleaded guilty to assault and battery. Smith never served any time for the attack.

Other arrests followed, including one for a late-night burglary of a Manassas home. In that incident, Smith, drunk and nude, beat a man as he and his wife lay in bed. Smith later told police he had wanted to rape the woman because he observed her earlier that day as she mowed the lawn in cut-off shorts.

In an effort to establish an insanity defense, Mann and Maslakowski submitted

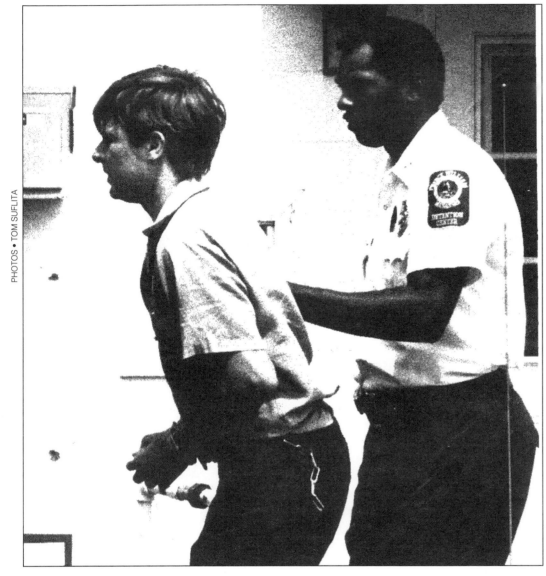

PHOTOS • TOM SUFLITA

Smith, handcuffed and chained is led away by an officer of the Manassas Detention Center.

Smith to two psychiatric evaluations. Neither psychiatrist deemed the computer technician insane, but one found he suffered from a condition known as a borderline personality disorder. Charlottesville, Va. psychiatrist Joseph David said the disorder is characterized by unstable moods and relationships and difficulty in dealing with stress or change. While those with the ailment can distinguish right from wrong, David said, they cannot always control or reflect upon their actions. Alcohol worsens the disorder.

David's interviews with Smith revealed a strange side of his personality. Smith told the psychiatrist that the tragic events of July

24 unfolded because of "bad karma" from previous lives. He also told David of a suicide attempt in which he held a gun to his head and pulled the trigger several times. Nothing happened. Smith then pointed the gun at a telephone and it fired, blowing the phone to pieces.

Smith's capital murder trial began on March 20, 1988 with Ebert telling the jury that Smith was a cold-blooded killer who loathed authority figures, especially police. Smith armed himself for battle and then lured police to his home, hoping to kill them and get himself killed, Ebert said. The prosecutor stalked around the courtroom and told the jury that Smith was a cunning, intelli-

DEATH ROW   117

gent man who would concoct any story, play any game, to get off the hook. Added to that was Roy Smith's cowardice—he didn't have the guts to kill himself and hoped the police would do it for him.

The case against Smith centered around one chilling element: spatters of blood on the opening of the barrel on Smith's .357 Magnum. Smith denied firing it July 24, but Ebert constructed a scenario which indicated Smith used it to shoot John Conner in the head. The evidence indicated that Smith wounded Conner with the AR-15 and then ran to the disabled officer's body. Holding the .357 within six inches of the man's head, Smith fired a bullet that shattered Conner's skull.

Smith took the stand on the fourth day of his eight-day trial and denied this. Under direct examination by Maslakowski, Smith cried and reiterated the story he had told police eight months ago: He never saw the police arrive, he was startled by Conner's gunfire, he fired back blindly. With his wounded heel, Smith claimed, he never could have run to Conner's body, shot him in the head, and run back into his yard, where other officers found him seconds later.

When Ebert began cross-examination, Smith's demeanor changed. He was calm, assertive and dry-eyed. Smith denied talking about killing cops July 24, and called Ebert's version of the shooting "absurd." When Ebert quizzed him about his past record with policemen, Smith said he couldn't remember beating, threatening or even hating a man in uniform.

A day later, the jury made its decision. Roy Bruce Smith knew what he was doing the night of July 24. He had shot John Conner with the full knowledge that he was a police officer.

The jury heard more evidence in the sentencing phase of the trial. Guernsey and Richter told of their run-ins with Smith in the 1970s, while David testified that Smith's drinking had impaired his mental capacity on July 24. But the most telling description of Smith came in the guilt phase of the trial.

Craig Sala, an officer in Santa Clara, Calif., encountered Smith on March 24, 1988 at the Korea House Restaurant, where he arrested Smith for indecent exposure. Smith apologized for the act, Sala said, and was polite and cooperative. Sala told Smith he'd help him if he could, and would get him through the arrest process as quickly as possible. Smith was told he probably wouldn't spend the night in jail.

But Sala's attempts to give him a break failed, and Smith was suddenly transformed.

"I told him he was going to the county jail, Sala said. "He stood back, he gritted his teeth, he squinted his eyes and clenched his fists. He looked at me and said if circumstances were different, he'd blow me away with his gun."

The jury recommended the death sentence. This decision was confirmed May 26 by Prince William Circuit Court Judge Frank Hoss, but not before Smith made an impassioned plea for justice. At his sentencing, Smith read a prepared statement that said his trial two months earlier had been based on "perjury, conspiracy and outright lies." Police charged him with the murder to cover up a scandal in the department, Smith asserted.

"I killed no one. Sgt. Conner was accidentally shot and killed by one of his own men," Smith said. As he finished reading the statement, he broke down crying and said he was telling the truth, "So help me, God."

Roy Smith is now sitting in the Mecklenberg Correctional Center, Virginia's death row. In the months since the trial, he has taken less and less responsibility for the shooting. Now, he theorizes Conner may have accidentally shot himself in the head.

In a recent death-row interview, Smith said he has changed his story because he did not learn of all the circumstances of the shooting until his trial. He believes that even his own attorneys failed to tell him all the facts, or to use them in his favor.

"There was a lot of pressure for a conviction. I'm sure they were under duress," said Smith, who recently notified the court he would appeal his sentence and conviction because he had ineffective legal counsel. Smith's case will come under an automatic review by the Virginia Supreme Court. He will probably be moving through the appeals process for the next seven or eight years.

In the meantime, Smith has become part of an unusual statistic, one that any prosecutor would envy. He is one of five death row inmates from Prince William County, making it the jurisdiction with more men on death row than any other in Virginia.

Although he faces electrocution, Smith insists his mental state has been "perfect" since his conviction. The quiet, smart kid, the eldest of three children in a middle-class family, has strayed far from what he expected his life to be. But, as he passes the days in prison, he tries to be upbeat. He reads the Bible every day and has faith that the "truth" about Conner's death will be revealed someday.

"I know the truth will eventually come out. I did not fire the shot that killed the sergeant," Smith said. "I've lost my faith in the system, but I truly have faith in God."

And if that "truth" never comes out, he will face death fearlessly.

"If it's God's will that I go to the electric chair, I'll go peacefully. It's important to ease the souls of the people who hate me."

Christine Riedel is a reporter for the Manassas Virginia Journal Messenger.

David Franklin Young

Mike Carter

I told you I'd kill you if you yelled for help," David Franklin Young told the pleading woman. "Now I'm going to."

Sixto Gonzales Amador was standing in the front yard of his home in the Salt Lake City, Utah suburb of Kearns when he heard the yell. He thought perhaps it had come from the house across the street where the young nurse lived, but he couldn't be sure.

Amador was moving from his house, a cookie-cutter replica of others on the street quaintly named Dew Drop Drive. The blue-collar subdivision is home to workers who make rocket motors at nearby Hercules, or dig copper ore from the huge open-pit mine of Kennecott that scars the foothills to the west. When Brigham Young entered the high desert basin in 1847 and pronounced "This is the place," to his Mormon pioneers, the arid flatlands that would become Kearns would have been almost out of sight.

Amador stood squinting at the high granite teeth of the Wasatch Mountains far to the east, and strained to hear the noise again, but he heard nothing. He couldn't even be sure what he had heard was human. After a few minutes, he went back inside. It was almost noon on Aug. 19, 1987

Across the street, at 6262 Dew Drop Drive,

PHOTO • SALT LAKE COUNTY SHERIFF'S OFFICE

A flier distributed by the Illinois State Police states that Young should be considered a suspect in any unsolved homicides in the states he has traveled.

Ember Kimberly Mars, 27, was screaming for her life.

"I told you that I'd kill you if you yelled for help," David Franklin Young told the pleading woman. "Now I'm going to."

Young, 27, had blown into Salt Lake City three days earlier with the hot western winds that sometimes fill the valley with the fetid odor of the Great Salt Lake—the briny inland sea straddling the alkali desert and salt flats along the Utah-Nevada border. He had hitched a ride with a trucker from Reno, thought briefly about robbing and killing the man, but decided not to because he couldn't get him alone.

The trucker had let Young spend the night at his home and then dropped him off at a popular truck stop, the Flying J, on the morning of the 17th.

A truck stop is a good place for David Young; he looks and talks country. That morning, he was a hulking 6-footer weighing close to 250 pounds, his muscles developed religiously a decade earlier at the weight machines of Red Hills High School in his hometown of Sumner, Ill. Although a beer belly protruded over the front of his jeans, the massive cords still bulged in his chest and wide shoulders, and his arms strained the seams of his western-styled shirt.

Country girls might find him attractive in that big, bluff "Howdy Ma'am" sort of way common to urban cowboys who spend weekends drinking in roadhouses and taverns, or sipping coffee at all-night cafes like the Flying J . His corn-silk blond hair and soft drawling tenor, with just a trace of a lisp, made him seem every bit a gentleman.

David Young was neither gentle nor a man. Inside his powerful adult body existed a mentally and emotionally retarded boy. Hidden was an inner cauldron of hatred and anger that had been simmering since childhood. There brewed a vat of pathological indignation that had twice in four years boiled over into innocent lives around him.

Both times, a woman had died.

Young would erupt again within the day. But this time, the explosion would come not at the whim of whirlwind emotional forces that had blown the simple-minded Young to and fro throughout his life. This time, he would savor the rage, letting a little bit out at a time. This time his anger would fuse with lust and meld into sadism. Ember Kimberly Mars would witness this metamorphosis, and she would die a horrible death

Three weeks before his arrival in Salt Lake City, on July 27, 1987, Young walked up to the door of his inlaws' home in Loogootee, Ind., and asked to talk to his estranged wife, Teresa Ann Rascio-Young.

She had left him after he had beaten her and stabbed her in the throat. He asked her if they could talk, maybe go for a walk. She agreed. Her mother, Betty, watched them walk off down the road of the sleepy southern Indiana town. A few minutes later Young returned alone, got into his truck and sped off.

Three days later, Rascio-Young's decomposing body was found in a vacant lot about a quarter of a mile from her home. She had been beaten to death with a set of rusty bicycle forks found lying nearby.

At the time of his wife's murder, Young was on parole. He had served 37 months in an Illinois prison after pleading guilty to voluntary manslaughter in the 1982 murder of his fiance, Teresa Schmittler, in Mt. Carmel, Ind. In a rage following a fight with his father, Young had held a tire iron across Schmittler's throat and then crushed her skull.

In Salt Lake City, sitting in the Flying J lounge with his suitcase, Young had one thing on his mind. He needed money and transportation to get back to Indiana and finish the job he started when he murdered his wife. Now he wanted to kill her parents.

Having convinced the manager that he was a driver whose rig needed work, Young spent the night of August 17th sleeping in the lounge. The next morning, he made a quick $75 moving furniture for some men who stopped at the truck stop for breakfast. That evening he bought a .38 from a trucker for $65. Equipped with the necessary tools for the job ahead, Young sat at a table drinking iced tea and coffee waiting for a victim.

Ember Mars was bored. The slender, part-time nurse had agreed to go barhopping with her friend, Angela Johnson, even though she had been feeling depressed and listless. They went dancing at several country bars and had a great time until they ran into Johnson's boyfriend, Gene Butcher. The two of them got drunk and fell to arguing, so that by the time they got to the Flying J, just after 1 a.m. on Aug. 19, Mars was tired of their bickering and was looking for a diversion.

PHOTO • SALT LAKE COUNTY SHERIFF'S OFFICE

6262 Dew Drop Drive, where Ember Mars spent her last agonized hours at the hands of her murderer, David Young.

He threatened to kill her roommate. He threatened to kill store clerks or policemen if she let her plight be known. He threatened to shoot the movers across the street if she tried to get their attention.

She turned in the booth and struck up a conversation with the husky blond man sitting alone behind her. He said his name was John Green, and that he was a trucker without a truck. She asked if maybe he'd like to join them—anything to break up the monotony of Gene and Angie's quarreling. He said he'd be happy to oblige.

Mars and "John Green" shared a piece of cantaloupe and made small talk with their companions until Butcher suggested that they continue the party at his apartment. Young readily agreed, secretly hoping to get the trio alone so he could rob them and steal Mars' truck.

Deep in the recesses of Young's troubled mind, the cauldron began to seeth. Early on, perhaps while sipping coffee and joking with her friends, a part of David Young was stoking a rage in preparation to rape and murder Ember Mars.

The 15-minute ride to Butcher's apartment in Mars' truck was uneventful, if cramped. Young had one bad moment when he thought Mars was going to sit on his lap in the pickup's crowded cab and feel the gun tucked down the front of his jeans.

The foursome reconvened in the dining room of Butcher's two-bedroom apartment around 2 a.m. Young was disappointed. He had hoped that Butcher lived in a house where neighbors would be less likely to hear the gunfire if he was forced to shoot them during the robbery.

Gene let Young take a shower and put his suitcase in the rear bedroom. Then the four of them sat around the kitchen table drinking and talking until Johnson and Butcher stumbled off to bed about 4:30 a.m.

Young and Mars stayed up to talk for a while. Once, while she was in the bathroom, he rifled through her purse looking for money and credit cards. He took about $30 from her wallet. When she returned, he asked her if she would sleep with him. "No," she replied. "I don't do that kind of thing. I'm a Christian woman."

Around 6 a.m., Mars said she had to go. She told Young she would drop him off at the Flying J and stood to go wake Johnson for company on the drive. Young told her to stop. He pulled the gun.

"Don't scream," he told her. "Don't do nothin' stupid and I won't kill your friends." Young forced her to the truck at gunpoint, leaving his suitcase in the back bedroom. He told her to take him to her house, the tiny rambler at 6262 Dew Drop Drive.

It was the threat of harm to others that made Ember Mars obey Young.

He threatened to kill her roommate. He threatened to kill store clerks or policemen if she let her plight be known when they visited a supermarket later that morning to cash one of her checks. He threatened to shoot the movers across the street at Sixto Amador's house if she tried to get their attention.

For the five hours before his rage finally erupted, Young terrorized Ember Mars.

In a chilling confession to Salt Lake County Sheriff's homicide Detective Dick Judd, Young recalled he and his victim were sitting in her living room at about 11:15 a.m. Mars was begging him to let her go.

"She started talkin' this religious stuff again. She said it three or four times," Young told the detective. "She said, ah, 'I'll let ya have all my money, just please don't kill my friends or me.'

"[I] said, 'That's fine with me, just do what I say.' Then she got up real quick and I slammed her down. And that's when I grabbed hold of her, and that's when I finally raped her, too."

After the assault in the front room, Young, who earlier had grabbed a butcher knife from a kitchen drawer, walked Mars down the short hallway to her bedroom, where they were less likely to be heard by the neighbors. He forced himself on her again.

"She said, 'Don't do this,'" Young told Detective Judd. "I said, 'It's too late now,' and she yelled for help. That's all. She didn't yell and scream or nothin' like that. She just yelled 'Help!'

"So I grabbed the flower vase and hit her. I was right handed, so I hit her here. That'd be on the left side of her face. Pretty hard. Hard. About nine or 10 times," Young recalled.

"She's bleeding pretty heavy [and] I'm still trying to have sex with her a little bit," Young said. He was distracted when he thought he heard something outside. Naked and smeared with blood, he peeked out a window and then returned to his dazed victim.

He led her across the hall to the other bedroom that was further still from the people outside, and forced her to the floor. Then he tried to think up a scheme that would allow him to clean out her checking account—something he had been counting on before his rage took over.

"If I just fixed her up," he reasoned with the detective, "maybe I can still get her to the bank. I don't know, she's in pretty bad shape, but she wasn't dead or nothin' like that."

Then Mars interrupted his thoughts.

"Rape! Help me! My God! Rape!" she hollered. Young, who again was peeping through the blinds, ran back into the bedroom. He explained to her that her only hope to live was to be quiet and cooperate with his plan. In reality, she had no hope at all.

"I told you what'd happen if you make noise, what'd happen to your friends," he said. "I'll go ahead and fix ya up, try to get you to the bank. If you make one more noise I'm gonna kill ya. I ain't gonna mess around here."

Young left her again to try to find something with which to tie her up for the time being. He had found a heavy clothes iron in a closet.

Across the street, Sixto Amador paused, listening.

Young walked back into the bedroom, the iron clenched in his fist. "I told her, I said, 'I told you what I'd do if you do that again,'" Young recounted to Detective Judd. "I figured the neighbors probably heard her this time, ya know, so I hit her with [the iron] six or eight times. It hurt her pretty bad." The force of those blows shattered the iron's handle.

"Anyway, like I said, I had a knife on the bed, I grabbed it and stabbed her in the stomach first. All of her upper chest. I stabbed her in the throat and then, ah, went ahead and stabbed her some more in the chest. And I knew I stabbed her in the heart, 'cause I could hear her heart breathin'.

"I had to hold her down while I was doin' it 'cause she was kickin' her legs, do ya know what I mean?" Detective Judd assured Young that he did.

Young told him that Mars wasn't dead yet, so he pulled a sheet off the bed and held it over her face, finally suffocating her.

"She died about three minutes later," he said.

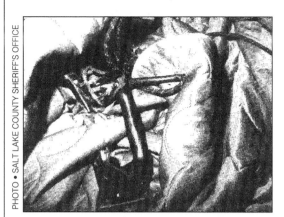

PHOTO • SALT LAKE COUNTY SHERIFF'S OFFICE

When Ember Mars defied Young's orders and called for help, he hit her six times with a clothes iron. The force of those blows shattered the iron's handle.

Young left Mars' brutalized body on the floor and went into the bathroom, where he took a shower to wash off the blood. Then he grabbed his gun and Mars' purse and keys and left. He used her credit card to gas up the Toyota truck, and headed toward Indiana and the unfinished business with his in-laws.

He never made it. On Aug. 27, eight days later, Young stopped two boys on the street of Russellville, Ind., and asked if they knew Betty Rascio, his dead wife's mother.

The youngsters recognized Young from the wanted posters plastered around the town. Utah authorities had identified Young through items found in his suitcase left at Gene Butcher's apartment. Utah lawmen also had been tracking Young's steady progress through his use of Mars' credit cards.

That afternoon, a Lawrence County deputy spotted a white pickup truck with Utah license plates. The ensuing chase stretched through two counties and involved eight police agencies. Nine shots were fired at the fleeing pickup as it ran two police roadblocks. Young fired at least once at lawmen from a shotgun he had stolen earlier that day.

Lawrence County Sheriff Eddie Ryan ended the pursuit when he fired through the rear window, showering Young with glass and causing him to run off the road. Young recognized the sheriff as he was surrounded by police. "Hi Eddie," he said. "I guess ya got me." Lawmen found two shotguns, a rifle, and Mars' purse in the truck.

Young was indicted in Washington County,

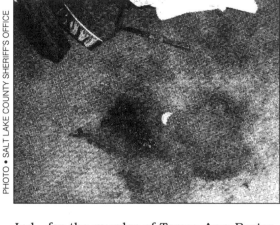

PHOTO • SALT LAKE COUNTY SHERIFF'S OFFICE

After beating and raping her, Young stabbed Ember Mars repeatedly with a knife taken from her kitchen.

"I had a knife on the bed, I grabbed it and stabbed her...In the stomach first...All of her upper chest... I stabbed her in the throat and then, ah, went ahead and stabbed her some more in the chest..."

Ind., for the murder of Teresa Ann Rasico-Young. Indiana authorities allowed him to plead guilty as charged and promised not to pursue a death penalty in the incident, after Young agreed to return to Utah to face capital homicide charges, which had been filed shortly after his arrest.

On Dec. 22, 1987, Young was sentenced to 35 years in prison for the murder of Teresa Ann Rasico-Young in Indiana. He remained in jail there until May, 1988, when he was flown to Utah aboard a federal prison transport. He was met by Detective Judd, who returned him to the Metropolitan Hall of Justice where he confessed to the murder of Ember Mars.

Young's case was assigned to the Salt Lake Legal Defender's Office, where a succession of defenders found Young uncooperative and a "client control" problem. Ultimately, two aggressive, experienced defense attorneys, Nancy Bergeson and co-counsel, Karen Stam, took the case to trial after almost 18 months of hard-fought pre-trial motions.

Bergeson and Stam prevented the prosecutors from admitting as evidence photographs of Mars' body, claiming the gruesome pictures would prejudice the panel against their client. They challenged and changed the county's entire jury selection process, claiming it discriminated against Hispanics and transient populations.

Young, however, was mostly oblivious to the need for the time-consuming procedures, many of which he did not understand. He once referred, in court, to a "change of menu"—rather than venue. And he wondered why, if Hispanics were discriminated against in the jury-selection process, his lawyers

didn't just go out and pull a few from the unemployment line and bring them to court.

The defense knew Young's simple-minded and peevish behavior were symptoms of much deeper mental and emotional disorders that they might use as mitigating conditions at trial. Early on, they had filed notice of their intent to rely on a defense of diminished mental capacity. They abandoned that strategy when a series of psychological examinations showed Young was not incompetent, insane or suffering from a mental illness that would impair his judgment of right and wrong.

Nonetheless, the mental health experts all found Young suffered from variety of illnesses that could be mitigating at trial.

The problems were so pervasive that the defense lawyers simply began saying that their client suffered from "a broken brain," which pumped destructive and violent behavior much as the heart pumps blood.

During trial, the defense introduced psychological and social history reports showing Young to have been severely developmentally handicapped from infancy. He was diagnosed as suffering from a "pervasive mental disorder" and an "organic personality syndrome" demonstrated by brain damage.

Young was born into a troubled middle-class family in the town of Sumner, Ill. His father, manager of the refinery that employed a majority of the townsfolk, was an abusive alcoholic who seldom spent time with his children. When he did, he expected perfection.

Young's oldest brother, Mike, recalled at trial that when David was 6 or 7 years old, he almost cut his ear off while climbing a fence. He ran home bleeding and terrified, only to be beaten by his father for hurting himself.

Young's mother was described as a nervous woman who abused prescription drugs and tried to kill herself twice before finally getting a divorce.

Throughout childhood, Young was a behaviorially disabled child. He had also been diagnosed as being of either borderline intelligence or mildly retarded. He was always in remedial classes and generally played with kids who were five or six years younger than himself.

Mike Young said his brother grew up lonely, fat, friendless and the brunt of cruel neighborhood jokes. He used to have to bribe other chlldren to play with him.

Once in high school however, Young garnered some acceptance through sports. He became a diligent weightlifter and played first-string linebacker on the football team.

In high school he also developed an explosive temper.

Friends said would slug trees until his hands bled. One neighbor recalled that he would beat the driveway with a piece of steel for hours after his mother would yell at him.

After high school, he took to manual-labor jobs, mostly on oil rigs. He began to abuse drugs and alcohol. One psychologist would later liken Young's substance abuse to "pouring gasoline on a fire."

Young married, but his first wife left him after he beat her. He became engaged to Teresa Schmittler shortly thereafter. He would kill her within months of meeting her.

In Utah, Young wanted no part of an insanity defense. He rejected testimony that showed him to be anything other than a cold, calculating killer.

His lawyers were constantly frustrated by his inability or unwillingness to acknowledge his illnesses, even when doing so might help his case. Young would rather face a death penalty than concede he was mentally ill.

He refused to attend the portions of his trial which dealt with his mental health. The only time he showed emotion during the trial was during opening statements, when he cried as Bergeson explained to the jury that he suffered from a broken brain. They were hot tears, not of remorse, but of embarrassment.

Afterwards, he complained to the court that his attorneys were lying about him and "trying to say I'm a fruitcake."

Third District Judge Timothy Hanson explained to Young that his lawyers were trying to help him, adding that further disruptions might lend credence to the argument that he was unaware of the stakes involved and possibly incompetent. It was the last thing the defendant wanted to hear.

The prosecutors saw no need to challenge the defense's psychiatric evidence. Young's mental defects were not severe enough to excuse his actions.

Two experienced deputy Salt Lake County attorneys, Glenn K. Iwasaki and Richard Shepherd, put on a no-frills case. Angela Johnson identified Young, who had put on more than 50 pounds while in jail. Randy Powell, Mars' roommate, recalled finding the

Shepherd argued that Young had planned to murder Mars from the beginning. "He cut her away from the herd like a pack of wolves attacking caribou."

PHOTO • MIKE CARTER

Young's attorneys tried to persuade Judge Hanson to set aside the death penalty because of Young's mental illness.

Young declined to choose between the Utah death penalty options of the firing squad or lethal injection. By law, Judge Hanson imposed the latter. "That's fine," Young told the court.

body that afternoon. The taped confession was introduced and played.

During closing arguments, Iwasaki reminded the jury that an organic brain disorder is not a defense to first-degree murder.

The nine-woman, three-man jury deliberated just four hours before convicting Young of capital homicide and theft on June 1, 1989.

At a penalty phase the following week, the defense presented more detailed psychiatric testimony. Dr. Breck LeBegue, director of forensic psychiatric services at the University of Utah Medical Center, presented a detailed view of Young's illnesses, which he said played a direct role in the homicides.

But the doctor also pointed out the shift in the method of homicide that marked Young's graduation into the more sophisticated pathology of a serial killer. In one paragraph, Dr. LeBegue gave the defense what it was looking for, only to snatch it away:

"A question may arise as to his capacity to conform his behavior to the requirements of law. He has a near-lifetime pattern of explosive outbursts...which has a clear organic and physiologic basis," he wrote. "I conclude that, due to his mental disorder, Mr Young lacked significant capacity to control his explosive rage in certain circumstances, but his physiologic explosiveness is overshadowed by his carefully calculated choice of victims, his method of sexual and sadistic assault and humiliation and the emerging pattern of serial murder....This explosive rage must be viewed in the larger context of a carefully planned murder, which was then rather chaotically carried out."

Bergeson, in closing arguments, said Young could not be held responsible for his rages. "If you kill him," she told the jury, "You will kill a child In a lethal body. If you kill him now, for a self he had no control in making, then you might as well have killed him when he was 3, or 7. He has the same brain."

Shepherd argued that Young had planned to murder Mars from the beginning. Young chose her as a victim of his rage and sadistically played with her before he killed her. "He cut her away from the herd like a pack of wolves attacking caribou," he said.

The jury returned a death verdict on June 14, after eight hours of deliberation. Young,

shackled and surrounded by bailiffs, turned and kicked a chair. "Shit," he said.

Young was formally sentenced on July 11. His attorneys failed to persuade Judge Hanson to set aside the death penalty because of Young's mental illness.

In denying the motion, the judge cited the recent U. S. Supreme Court ruling, Texas vs. Penry, that says the Eighth Amendment's ban on cruel and unusual punishment does not preclude executions of retarded persons.

Judge Hanson set Aug. 28 as the execution date, however that date will be automatically stayed to allow for a mandatory appeal of the case to the Utah Supreme Court.

Young declined to choose between the Utah death penalty options of the firing squad or lethal injection. Judge Hanson imposed the latter. "That's fine." Young told the court.

Young likely will be sent back to Indiana to begin serving the 35-year sentence for the murder of Teresa Young, even though he says he wants to stay in Utah to help with his appeal.

His lawyers don't want him in Utah, thinking that the further away he is from that state's death row, the better.

Regardless of where he is housed, the appeals will continue, and if his sentence is upheld, Utah authorities will ultimately ask the Indiana governor to commute the Indiana sentence so Young can be brought back to Utah and executed.

If Indiana refuses, which is unlikely, Young will have to serve his sentence in that state before Utah can claim him. The Indiana corrections system allows an inmate to be given one day of "good time" for every day served. If he's a model inmate, Young could be released in 17 and a half years, at which time he would be returned to Utah for execution.

His attorneys have said that should he be returned to Indiana, they will tell him not to be a model inmate.

_____

Mike Carter is a staff writer for The Salt Lake City Tribune, *where he has worked for the past 14 years. He has won numerous local and regional newswriting awards and has authored or reported stories for publications ranging from* The National Law Review *to* Time Magazine. *He is currently* The Tribune's *courts reporter.*

Death Row State Data

STATE CAPITAL	GOVERNOR	PARTY	POP.	METHOD	# OF INMATES	LAST EXEC	LAST NAME
Alabama Montgomery	Guy Hunt	R	3,894,025	Y Electrocution	94	8/28/87	Wayne Ritter
Alaska Juneau	Steve Cowper	D	401,851	None			
Arizona Phoenix	Rose Mofford	R	2,716,546	Y Gas Chamber	84		
Arkansas Little Rock	Bill Clinton	D	2,286,357	Y Injection Choice of Electrocution for those sentenced before 6/4/83	30		
California Sacramento	George Deukmejian	R	23,667,764	Y Gas Chamber	241		
Colorado Denver	Roy Romer	D	2,889,735	Y Injection	3		
Connecticut Hartford	William O'Neill	D	3,107,564	Y Electrocution	1		
Delaware Dover	Michael N. Castle	R	594,338	Y Injection Choice of Hanging those sentenced before 6/13/86	7		
Florida Tallahassee	Bob Martinez	R	9,746,961	Y Electrocution	290	1/24/89	Theodore Bundy
Georgia Atlanta	Joe Frank Harris	D	546,2982	Y Electrocution	107	7/28/88	James Messer
Hawaii Honolulu	John Waihee	D	964,961	None	0		
Idaho Boise	Cecil D. Andrus	D	944,127	Y Injection or Firing Squad	15		
Illinois Springfield	James R. Thompson	R	11427409	Y Injection	120		
Indiana Indianapolis	Evan Bayh	D	5,490,212	Y Electrocution	50	10/16/85	William Vandiver
Iowa Des Moines	Terry Branstad	R	2,913,808	None	0		
Kansas Topeka	Mike Hayden	R	2,364,236	None	0		

Death Row State Data

Kentucky
Frankfort   Wallace G. Wilkerson   D   3,660,324   Y Electrocution   30

Louisiana
Baton Rouge Charles Roemer   D   4,206,116   Y Electrocution   39   6/14/88   Edward Byrne

Maine
Augusta   John McKeman Jr.   R   1,125,043   None   0

Maryland
Annapolis   William Donald Schaefer D   4,216,933   Y Gas Chamber   18

Massachusetts
Boston   Michael S. Dukakis   D   5,737,093   None   0

Michigan
Lansing   James L. Blanchard   D   9,262,004   None   0

Minnesota
St. Paul   Rudy Perpich   D   4,075,970   None   0

Mississippi
Jackson   Ray Mabus   D   2,520,770   Y Gas Chamber   46   7/8/87   Connie Ray Evans

Missouri
Jefferson City John D. Ashcroft   R   4,916,762   Y Injection   71   1/6/89   George "Tiny" Mercer

Montana
Helena   Stan Stephens   R   786,690   Y Choice   7
                                                             Hanging or Injection

Nebraska
Lincoln   Kay Orr   R   1,569,825   Y Electrocution   13

Nevada
Carson City Richard Bryan   D   800,508   Y Injection   47   12/06/85   Carroll Cole

New Hampshire
Concord   Judd Gregg   R   920,610   None   0

New Jersey
Trenton   Thomas H. Kean   R   7,365,011   Y Injection   25

New Mexico
Santa Fe   Garrey E. Carruthers   R   1,303,302   Y Injection   2

New York
Albany   Mario M Cuomo   D   17,558,165   None   0

North Carolina
Raleigh   James G. Martin   R   5,880,415   Y Choice   82   9/19/86   John Rook
                                                             Gas Chamber or Lethal Injection

Death Row State Data

State / City	Governor	Party	Population	Death Penalty / Method	Death Row Inmates	Last Execution Date	Last Executed
North Dakota Bismarck	George A. Sinner	D	652,717	None	0		
Ohio Columbus	Richard F. Celeste	D	10,797,603	Y Electrocution	88		
Oklahoma Oklahoma City	Henry Bellman	R	3,025,487	Y Injection	98		
Oregon Salem	Neil Goldschmidt	D	2,633,156	Y Injection	15		
Pennsylvania Harrisburg	Robert Casey	D	11,864,720	Y Electrocution	115		
Rhode Island Providence	Edward DiPrete	R	947,154	None	0		
South Carolina Columbia	Carroll Campbell Jr.	R	3,120,730	Y Electrocution	42	1/10/86	James Terry Roach
South Dakota Pierre	George S. Mickelson	R	690,768	None	0		
Tennessee Nashville	Ned Ray McWkerter	D	4,591,023	Y Electrocution	70		
Texas Austin	Bill Clements	R	14,225,513	Y Injection	287	12/13/88	Raymond Landry
Utah Salt Lake City	Norman Bangerter	R	1,461,037	Y Choice Firing Squad or Lethal Injection	6	6/10/88	Arthur Bishop
Vermont Montpelier	Madeleine M. Kunin	D	511456	None	0		
Virginia Richmond	Gerald L. Baliles	D	5346797	Y Electrocution	40	4/14/88	Earl Clanton
Washington Olympia	Booth Gardner	D	4,132,353	Y Injection	7		
West Virginia Charleston	Gaston Caoerton	D	1,950,186	None	0		
Wisconsin Madison	Tommy G. Thompson	R	4,705,642	None	0		
Wyoming Cheyenne	Mike Sullivan	D	469,557	Y Injection	2		

Death Row Inmates

This list is complete and accurate as of March 1, 1989, according to information obtained from the NAACP Legal Defense Fund.

INMATE	STATE	SEX	RACE	NOTES/ EXECUTION DATES
Abram, Donald	Mississippi	M	B	1
Abu-Jamal, Mumia	Pennsylvania	M	B	
Adams, Sylvester	South Carolina	M	B	
Adams, Thomas	North Carolina	M	W	2
Adams, Larry	Nevada	M	W	
Adams, Aubrey	Florida	M	W	
Adams, James	Florida	M	B	5-10-81
Adamson, John	Arizona	M	W	1
Adcox, Keith	California	M	W	
Adkins, Carl Wayne	Tennessee	M	W	
Adkins, Ricky	Alabama	M	W	
Adrews, Jesse J.	California	M	B	
Agan, James	Florida	M	W	
Ainsworth, Steven	California	M	W	
Albanese, Charles	Illinois	M	W	
Albrecht, Alfred	Pennsylvania	M	W	
Alcala, Rodney	California	M	H	
Alderman, Jack	Georgia	M	W	
Aldrich, Leon	Florida	M	W	
Ali, El-Amin Ahmad	North Carolina	M	B	
Allen, Gary	Oklahoma	M	N	
Allen, Timothy	North Carolina	M	B	
Allen, Howard	Indiana	M	B	
Allen, Kenneth	Illinois	M	B	
Allen, William Horton	Georgia	M	W	
Allen, Stanley	Georgia	M	B	
Allen, Clarence R.	California	M	N	
Alley, Sedley	**Tennessee**	**M**	**B**	

●●●

SEDLEY ALLEY

FACTS

Alley was found guilty of the 1985 kidnapping, rape and murder of 19-year-old Suzanne Marie Collins, who at the time of her death was jogging in a Memphis area park. Collin's badly beaten body was discovered in the park the morning of the day she was to have been graduated from avionics training at the Memphis Naval Air Station. Alley, 33, was sentenced to death on the murder conviction and to consecutive 40-year terms on each of the other two convictions.

●●●

Allison, Watson	California	M	B	
Allridge, James	Texas	M	B	

Bold type identifies inmate for which there is extra related text about conviction etc.
1 indicates that either a new sentence proceeding is pending following a court order, or that a court ordered reversal of conviction or sentence is not yet final due to an appeal filed by the State.
2 These inmate were under the age of eighteen at the time of the offense.
3 Identifies inmates that are under death sentences in two or more states.
B Black; W white, H hispanic, A asian, N native american, U race unknown at press time.

Allridge, Ronald Keith	Texas	M	B	
Alvin, Eddie	Florida	M	B	
Alvord, Gary	Florida	M	W	
Amaya-Ruiz, Jose	**Arizona**	**M**	**H**	

• •

JOSE AMAYA-RUIZ

Race: Hispanic

Date of Birth: March 10, 1958

FACTS
Mark and Kimberly Lopez gave Amaya-Ruiz, a citizen of El Salvador, a job taking care of the stables at their ranch near Tucson. Mark and Kimberly had been married for a week and Kimberly was 4 months pregnant. On March 28, 1985, as Kimberly was talking to her sister on the phone, Amaya-Ruiz entered the house. He stabbed Kimberly 26 times with a kitchen knife while chasing her throughout the home. Finally, Amaya-Ruiz used Kimberly's handgun to shoot her in the ear. He fled in the Lopez' truck.

Start of Trial: November 26, 1985
Verdict: December 5, 1985
Sentencing: March 10, 1986

• •

Amos, Bernard	Texas	M	B	
Amos, Vernon	**Florida**	**M**	**B**	

• •

VERNON AMOS

FACTS
Amos' death sentence has been erased by a Florida Supreme Court ruling holding that Palm Beach County's jury selection process is racially biased.Amos, a black, was convicted in predominately white West Palm Beach. He will be retried on charges that he participated in a 1986 crime spree that included the murder of two men.

• •

Amrine, Joseph	Missouri	M	W	
Anderson, Johnny Ray	Texas	M	W	
Anderson, Larry	Texas	M	W	
Anderson, C. Michael	Nebraska	M	W	
Anderson, Richard	Florida	M	W	
Anderson, Stephen	California	M	W	
Anderson, James	California	M	B	1

Death Row Inmates

Andrews, William	Utah	M	B	
Andrews, Maurice	Texas	M	B	
Andrade, Richard	Texas	H	M	1-30-87
Anthony, Francis	North Carolina	M	B	
Antone, Anthony	Flordia	M	W	1-26-84
Antwine, Calvert	Missouri	M	B	
Apanovitch, Anthony	Ohio	M	W	
Appel, Martin	Pennsylvania	M	W	
Aranda, Arturo	Texas	M	H	
Arnett, James	**Arizona**	**M**	**W**	**1**

••

JAMES ALAN ARNETT

Date of Birth: May 26, 1944

FACTS

Arnett stole a car in California, abandoned it in Arizona, and walked to a construction site outside of Lake Havasu City in Mohave County. He spent his nights at this location in an abandoned camper shell. On the night of February 9, 1976, Elmer James Clary arrived at the site in his truck. The next morning, Arnett asked Clary for food, but Clary refused him. Clary also declined to drive Arnett into the nearest town. Arnett then offered to sell Clary some jewelry. Arnett walked to a shack where the jewelry supposedly was, and Clary followed him. Arnett entered the shack, got his rifle out of a pack, and shot Clary five times, killing him. Arnett drove Clary's pickup into California, where he was arrested.

Start of Trial: July 19, 1976
Verdict: July 22, 1976
Sentencing: September 10, 1976
Resentencing: November 17, 1978

•••

Arnold, John	South Carolina	M	W
Arthur, Thomas	Alabama	M	W
Artis, Roscoe	North Carolina	M	B
Asay, Marc	Florida	M	W
Ashford, James	Illinois	M	B
Ashmus, Troy	California	M	W
Askew, Robert	Kentucky	M	B
Atkins, Joseph	South Carolina	M	W
Atkins, Robert	Pennsylvania	M	B
Atkins, Phillip	Florida	M	W
Atwood, Frank	**Arizona**	**M**	**W**

•••

FRANK JARVIS ATWOOD

Race: Caucasian

Death Row Inmates

Date of Birth: December 9, 1956

FACTS

Atwood had been convicted of lewd and lascivious acts and kidnapping an 8-year-old boy in California. In May of 1984, he was paroled from the kidnapping sentence. Atwood came to Tucson in September of 1984 in violation of his Californiaparole. On September 17, 8-year-old Vicky Lynn Hoskinson was riding her bicycle home from mailing a letter. Atwood kidnapped the girl, molested her, and killed her. He left her body in the desert and fled to Texas, where he was apprehended. Vicky's body was not found until April of 1985.

Start of Trial: January 19, 1987
Verdict: March 26, 1987
Sentencing: May 8, 1987

Austin, Richard	Tennessee	M	W	
Avena, Carlos	California	M	H	
Averhart, Rufus	Indiana	M	B	
Baal, Thomas	Nevada	M	W	
Babbitt, Manuel	California	M	B	
Bacigalupo, Miguel	California	M	H	
Bacon, Robert Jr.	North Carolina	M	B	
Bailey, Billy	Delaware	M	W	
Baird, Arthur	Indiana	M	W	
Baker, Lee	Pennsylvania	M	B	
Baker, Herbert	Pennsylvania	M	B	
Baldree, Ernie	Texas	M	W	
Baldwin, Brian	Alabama	M	B	
Baldwin, Timothy	Louisiana	M	W	9-10-84
Bankhead, Grady	Alabama	M	W	
Banks, Delma	Texas	M	B	
Banks, George	Pennsylvania	M	B	
Banks, Anthony	Oklahoma	M	B	
Bannerman, Samuel	Pennsylvania	M	B	
Bannister, Alan	Missouri	M	W	
Barber, Danny Lee	Texas	M	W	
Barber, Terry	Tennessee	M	W	
Barefield, John Kennedy	Texas	M	B	
Barefoot, Thomas	Texas	M	W	10-30-84
Barfield, Velma	North Carolina	W	W	11- 2-54
Barnard, Harold	Texas	M	W	
Barnes, Herman	Virginia	M	B	
Barnes, Sterling	Ohio	M	B	
Barnes, Elwell	North Carolina	M	N	
Barnett, Larry	Oklahoma	M	W	
Barnett, Lee Max	California	M	W	

Death Row Inmates

Barney, Allen Jeffrey	Texas	M	W	4-16-86
Barrientes, Antonio	Texas	M	H	
Barrow, Ronald	Illinois	M	W	
Barwick, Darryl	Florida	M	W	
Basemore, William	Pennsylvania	M	B	
Bass, Charles William	Texas	M	W	3-12-86
Bassett, Herbert	Virginia	M	B	
Bates, Wayne Lee	Tennessee	M	W	
Bates, Wayne	Louisiana	M	W	
Bates, Kayle	Florida	M	B	
Battenfield, Billy	Oklahoma	M	W	
Battle, Thomas	Missouri	M	B	
Baxter, Norman	Georgia	M	W	
Beam, Albert Raymond	Idaho	M	W	
Bean, Harold	Illinois	M	W	
Bean, Anthony	California	M	B	
Beardslee, Donald	California	M	W	
Beasley, Raymond	Texas	M	W	1
Beasley, Leslie	Pennsylvania	M	B	
Beathard, James Lee	Texas	M	W	
Beaty, Donald	**Arizona**	**M**	**W**	

•••

DONALD EDWARD BEATY

Race: Caucasian

Date of Birth: February 7, 1955

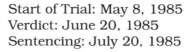

FACTS
On the evening of May 9, 1984, Christy Ann Fornoff, a 13-year-old news carrier, was collecting from her customers at the Rockpoint Apartments in Tempe. Beaty, who was the apartment custodian, abducted Christy and sexually assaulted and suffocated her in his apartment. Beaty kept the body in his apartment until the morning of May 11, 1984, when he placed it behind the apartment complex's trash dumpster.

Start of Trial: May 8, 1985
Verdict: June 20, 1985
Sentencing: July 20, 1985

•••

Beaver, Gregory	Virginia	M	W	
Beavers, Richard Lee	Texas	M	W	
Beck, Eli	Georgia	M	B	1
Bedford, Daniel	Ohio	M	W	
Bedford, Robert	Maryland	M	B	
Bedford, Michael	Florida	M	W	

Death Row Inmates

Beets, Betty Lou	Texas	F	W

....

BETTY LOU BEETS

Beets, 53 was sentenced to death in 1985 for killing her fifth husband, Dallas fire-fighter Jimmy Don Beets, for $100,000 in insurance benefits and burying him in their yard. She was also charged but not tried in the murder of a previous hus-band, Doyle Wayne Barker, who was found buried behind a tool shed. Beets was spared temporarily when the Texas Court of Criminal Appeals ruled in 1984 that her crime technically did not fit the capital offense of murder for remuneration, since no third party was hired to perform the killing. On rehearing, the state high court reversed itself.

....

Behringer, Earl	Texas	M	W
Bejarano, John	Nevada	M	H
Bell, Walter	Texas	M	B
Bell, Roger Morris	Tennessee	M	B
Bell, Larry Gene	South Carolina	M	W
Bell, Ronnie	California	M	B
Bell, Randy	Alabama	M	B
Bellmore, Larry	Indiana	M	W
Bello, Carlos	Florida	M	W
Belmontes, Fernando	California	M	H
Beltran-Lopez, Mauricio	Florida	M	H
Belyeu, Clifton	Texas	M	W
Benefiel, William	Indiana	M	W
Benner, Glen	Ohio	M	W
Bennett, Ronald	Virginia	M	B
Bennett, Baby Ray	**Texas**	**M**	**B**

....

BABY RAY BENNETT

FACTS

At 27, Bennett was convicted of shooting Coyte L. Green, 70, in a 1985 burglary of Green's house. Bennett told police he first shot Green's dog, then shot Green when he tried to run. Bennett, according to a psychologist, laughed when describing to him how hard Green had been to kill. Green's body was stuffed in a car trunk and dumped under a Louisiana bridge.

....

Bennett, Edward	Nevada	M	W
Benson, Richard Allan	California	M	W
Berget, Roger	Oklahoma	M	W
Bernischke, William	Indiana	M	W

Death Row Inmates

Berry, Benjamin	Louisiana	W	M	6-7-87
Berry, Earl	Mississippi	M	W	
Berryman, Rodney	California	M	B	
Bertolotti, Anthony	Florida	M	B	
Beuke, Michael	Ohio	M	W	
Bevill, Randy	Mississippi	M	W	
Bevins, William	Kentucky	M	W	
Brewer, John	**Arizona**	**M**	**W**	

●●

JOHN GEORGE BREWER

Race: Caucasian

Date of Birth: November 8, 1965

FACTS

Brewer and his girlfriend, Rita Brier, were living in a Flagstaff apartment. In the early morning hours of November 11, 1987, they argued about Brewer's excessive dependence on Brier. Later that day, Brier told Brewer that she was going to leave him to help him learn to live on his own. Brewer then locked the bedroom door and began to beat and strangle Brier. After a lengthy struggle during which Brewer bit Brier, tried to gouge her eyes out, and choked her with his hands, Brewer killed Brier by strangling her with a tie. Brier was 22 weeks pregnant at the time. After resting from his exertions, Brewer took a shower. He then had sexual intercourse with Brier's corpse. Brewer walked to a nearby bowling alley, called the police, and turned himself in Brewer pleaded guilty to first-degree murder.

Plea: July 18, 1988
Sentencing: August 26, 1988

●●

Bey, Marko	New Jersey	M	B	1
Biegenwald, Richard	New Jersey	M	W	
Bieghler, Marvin	Indiana	M	W	
Billa, Louis	Pennsylvania	M	H	
Billiot, James	Mississippi	M	W	
Bird, Jerry Joe	Texas	M	W	
Birt, Billy Sunday	Georgia	M	W	1
Bishop, Arthur	Utah	M	W	6-10-88
Bishop, Jesse	Nevada	M	W	10-22-79
Bishop, Ronald	**Arizona**	**M**	**W**	

●●

RONALD PAUL BISHOP

Race: Caucasian

Date of Birth: July 28, 1943

FACTS

On January 18, 1976, Bishop, Fred Van Haelst, Catherine Leckliter, and her 2-year-old daughter met each other and Norman Troxell at the Salvation Army Welfare Center in Phoenix. The group left Phoenix for Bumble Bee in Troxell's car on January 20, and began traveling around the desert. On January 22, Bishop instructed Van Haelst to tell Ms. Leckliter and her daughter to take a walk far from the camp. When they had gone, Bishop asked Troxell to help him fix the car. As Troxell stood at the rear of the car, Bishop hit him several times on the back of the head with a claw hammer. After Troxell fell, Bishop removed his watch, wallet, and shoes, and tied his legs together. He and Van Haelst then dragged the still living victim to an abandoned mine shaft and threw him in. Bishop threw rocks on top of the victim before the group left the area in the victim's car.

Start of Trial: May 17, 1976
Verdict: May 19, 1976
Sentencing: June 18, 1976
Resentencing: February 2, 1979

●●

Bittaker, Lawrence	California	M	W

●●

LAWRENCE BITTAKER

FACTS

Bittaker, 48, of Burbank, Calif., was convicted in March 1981 of murdering five girls ranging in age from 13 to 18, all residents of Los Angeles area communities. He was also found to have raped four of the victims, taking photographs of the sexual abuse and killing of several of the victims. Two of the victims were stabbed in the head with ice picks. In one case, a tape recording was made of 16-year-old Shirley Ledford's screams as she was assaulted, bludgeoned with a hammer and later strangled.

●●

Black, Robert	Texas	M	W	
Black, Robert	Georgia	M	U	
Blackmon, Ricky	Texas	M	W	
Blair, Walter	Missouri	M	B	
Blakley, Robert	Florida	M	W	
Blanco, Omar	Florida	M	H	1
Blankenship, Roy	Georgia	M	W	
Blanks, Kennith	Georgia	M	B	
Blazak, Mitchell	**Arizona**	**M**	**W**	

●●

MITCHELL THOMAS BLAZAK

Race: Caucasian

Date of Birth: November 14, 1946

FACTS

In the early morning hours of December 15, 1973, Blazak and another man, armed with pistols, entered the Brown Fox Tavern in north Tucson. Blazak, who was wearing a ski mask, went to the bar and demanded money. When the bartender, Elden Baker, did not comply, Blazak shot him four times and then shot and killed John Grimm, who was sitting nearby. A second patron was wounded.

Start of Trial: November 14, 1974
Verdict: November 20, 1974
Sentencing: December 17, 1974
Resentencing: September 11, 1980

Bloom, Robert S.	California	M	W	
Bloyd, Dale	California	M	W	1
Blystone, Scott	Pennsylvania	M	W	
Bobo, Tony L.	Tennessee	M	B	
Boclair, Stanley	Illinois	M	B	
Boggess, Holt	Texas	M	W	
Boggs, Richard	Virginia	M	W	1
Boggs, John	Florida	M	W	
Bolder, Martsay	Missouri	M	B	
Bolender, Bernard	Florida	M	W	
Boliek, William	Missouri	M	W	
Boltz, John	Oklahoma	M	W	
Bonham, Antonio	Texas	M	B	
Bonillas, Louis	California	M	H	
Bonin, William	**California**	**M**	**W**	

WILLIAM BONIN

FACTS

William Bonin was dubbed the Freeway Killer for his murder of 10 young men whose bodies were dumped alongside Southern California freeways. The victims, ranging in age from 12 to 19, were for the most part hitchhikers who were picked up by Bonin, sexually assaulted, tortured and strangled.

Bonnell, Melvin	Ohio	M	W	
Bonney, Thomas	North Carolina	M	W	
Booker, Winfred	Oklahoma	M	W	
Booker, John	Mississippi	M	B	
Booker, Stephen	Florida	M	B	1

Booth, John	Maryland	M	B	
Bottoson, Linroy	Florida	M	B	
Bouie, Johnnie	Florida	M	B	
Bowden, Jerome	Georgia	M	B	6-25-86
Bower, Lester L.	Texas	M	W	
Bowers, Marselle	Maryland	M	B	
Bowie, Benito	Oklahoma	M	B	
Boyd, Charles	Texas	M	B	
Boyd, Michael Joe	Tennessee	M	B	
Boyd, Ronald Lee	Oklahoma	M	B	
Boyd, Kenneth	North Carolina	M	W	
Boyd, Arthur Martin	North Carolina	M	W	
Boyd, Russell	Indiana	M	W	
Boyd, Juan	California	M	B	1
Boyd, William	Alabama	M	W	
Boyde, Richard	California	M	B	
Boyer, Richard Delmer	California	M	W	
Boyle, Benjamin	Texas	M	W	
Bracey, William	Illinois	M	B	
Bracey, William	**Arizona**	**M**	**B**	**3**

●●

WILLIAM BRACY

Race: Black

Date of Birth: August 23, 1941

FACTS

During the late months of 1980, Robert Cruz decided to have William Patrick Redmond murdered. Mr. Redmond owned a printing business in partnership with Ron Lukezic, and Cruz's ultimate goal was to take over the business. To carry out the murder, Cruz hired William Bracy and Murray Hooper from Chicago and Edward Lonzo McCall, a former Phoenix police officer. On the evening of December 31, 1980, Bracy, Hooper, and McCall went to the Redmond home in Phoenix. Mr. Redmond, his wife Marilyn, and his mother-in-law Helen Phelps were at home preparing for a New Year's Eve party. The men entered the house at gunpoint and forced the victims into the master bedroom. After taking jewelry and money, the killers bound and gagged the victims and made them lie face down on the bed. They then shot each victim in the head and also slashed Mr. Redmond's throat. Mr. Redmond and Mrs. Phelps died from their wounds, but Mrs. Redmond survived.

Cruz and McCall were convicted of the murders following a joint trial. Cruz' conviction was reversed on appeal, but he was again convicted after two mistrials. Mrs. Lukezic was convicted in a separate trial, but after obtaining a new trial, she was acquitted of all charges.

Start of Trial: November 4, 1982
Verdicts: December 24, 1982
Sentencing: February 11, 1983

●●

Bradford, Bill	California	M	W	
Bradley, William	Ohio	M	B	
Bradley, Danny Joe	Alabama	M	W	
Brandley, Clarence	Texas	M	B	
Breakiron, Mark	Pennsylvania	M	W	
Breaux, David	California	M	W	
Brecheen, Robert	Oklahoma	M	W	
Breedlove, McArthur	Florida	M	B	
Brennan, Mark Edward	Oklahoma	M	W	
Brewer, Benjamin	Oklahoma	M	B	
Brewer, David	Ohio	M	W	
Brewer, James	Indiana	M	B	
Bricker, Robert	Pennsylvania	M	W	
Briddle, James	Texas	M	W	
Bridge, Warren	Texas	M	W	
Bridges, Wilfred	North Carolina	M	B	
Briley, James	Virginia	M	B	4-18-85
Brimage, Richard	Texas	M	W	
Brisbon, Henry	Illinois	M	B	
Britz, Dewayne	Illinois	M	W	
Brock, Kenneth	Texas	M	W	6-18-89
Brode, Richard	Pennsylvania	M	W	
Brogdon, John	Louisiana	M	W	7-30-87
Brogie, Kirk	Oklahoma	M	W	1
Brooks, Charlie	Texas	M	B	12-7-82
Brooks, Reginald	Ohio	M	B	
Brooks, George	**Louisiana**	**M**	**W**	

••

GEORGE BROOKS

FACTS

Brooks, 47, and his co-defendant and one-time roommate, James Copeland, 29, were sentenced to die for the 1979 kidnapping, rape and murder of 11-year-old Joseph Cook Owen. Brooks and Copeland were accused of raping Owen at their home, then gagging him with a sheet and taking him to a site in Livingston Parish Louisiana, where they shot him in the back of the head as he knelt on the ground.

••

Broom, Romell	Ohio	M	B	
Brown, Cornelius	Oregon	M	B	
Brown, David	Oklahoma	M	W	
Brown, Debra	Ohio	F	B	
Brown, Duane	North Carolina	M	B	
Brown, Bobby Ray	North Carolina	M	W	
Brown, Thomas Jack	North Carolina	M	W	
Brown, Willie	North Carolina	M	B	
Brown, David Junior	North Carolina	M	B	1

Death Row Inmates

Brown, Vernon	Missouri	M	B	
Brown, Bryan	Louisiana	M	W	
Brown, John	Louisiana	M	W	
Brown, Debra	Indiana	F	B	
Brown, Nathan	Georgia	M	B	
Brown, Paul A.	Florida	M	W	
Brown, Walter	Florida	M	B	
Brown, Larry	Florida	M	B	
Brown, John	California	M	W	
Brown, Albert	California	M	B	
Brown, Raymond	Alabama	M	W	
Brown, Gary Leon	Alabama	M	W	
Browning, Paul Lewis	Nevada	M	B	
Brownlee, Virgil Lee	Alabama	M	B	
Bruno, Michael	Florida	M	W	
Bryan, Anthony	Florida	M	W	
Bryant, James	Pennsylvania	M	B	
Bryant, Robert Pernell	Pennsylvania	M	B	
Bryant, James A.	Florida	M	W	
Buchanan, Douglas	Virginia	M	W	
Buehl, Roger	Pennsylvania	M	W	
Buell, Robert	Ohio	M	W	
Buenoano, Judi	Florida	F	W	
Buford, Robert	Florida	M	B	1
Bui, Quaing	Alabama	M	A	
Bunch, Timothy	Virginia	M	W	
Bundy, Theodore	Flordia	M	W	1-24-89
Bunyard, Jerry	California	M	W	1
Burchette, Franklin	Illinois	M	B	1
Burden, Jimmy	Georgia	M	B	
Burdine, Calvin	Texas	M	W	
Burgener, Michael	California	M	W	1
Burger, Christopher	Georgia	M	W	2
Burns, Daniel	Florida	M	B	
Burr, Charlie	Florida	M	B	
Burrell, Albert Ronnie	Louisiana	M	W	
Burris, Gary	Indiana	M	B	
Burton, Andre	California	M	B	
Bush, John Earl	Florida	M	B	
Butler, Steven	Texas	M	B	
Butler, Jerome	Texas	M	B	
Butler, Horace	South Carolina	M	B	
Buttrum, Janice	Georgia	F	W	2
Buxton, Lawrence	Texas	M	B	
Byrd, John William	Ohio	M	W	
Byrd, Maurice	Missouri	M	B	
Byrd, Milford	Florida	M	W	
Byrne, Edwards	Louisiana	M	W	6-14-88

Death Row Inmates

Caballero, Juan	Illinois	M	H	
Cade, Clyde	Alabama	M	B	
Cage, Tommy	Louisiana	M	B	
Cain, Russell	South Carolina	M	W	
Cain, Tracy	California	M	B	
Caldwell, Richard	Tennessee	M	W	
Caldwell, Rickie Tim	South Carolina	M	W	
Calhoun, James	Maryland	M	B	1
Callahan, James	Alabama	M	W	
Campbell, Charles	**Washington**	**M**	**W**	

•••

CHARLES CAMPBELL

FACTS

Campbell was convicted of the 1982 murders of two women and a girl in Clearview, Wash. The victims, Renae Wicklund, 31, her daughter, Shanna, 8, and a neighbor, Barbara Hendrickson, 51, were stabbed to death. Campbell has been sentenced to be hanged, and the case has drawn some recent attention because a qualified hangman apparently could not be found in Washington state.

•••

Campbell, Kenneth	Tennessee	M	W	
Campbell, James	Florida	M	B	
Canaan, Keith	Indiana	M	W	
Cannon, Joseph J.	Texas	M	W	2
Cannon, Randy	Oklahoma	M	W	
Cantu, Domingo	Texas	M	H	
Cantu, Ruben	Texas	M	H	2
Card, James	Florida	M	W	
Cargill, David	Georgia	M	W	
Caro, Fernando	California	M	H	
Carpenter, James	Pennsylvania	M	B	
Carpenter, David	California	M	W	
Carrera, Constantino	California	M	H	
Carriger, Paris	**Arizona**	**M**	**W**	

•••

PARIS HOYT CARRIGER

Race: Caucasian

Date of Birth: March 17, 1945

FACTS

On March 13, 1978, Carriger entered a Phoenix jewelry store and forced the proprietor, Robert Gibson Shaw, into a back room. He tied Shaw's hands behind his back with adhesive tape. Carriger then killed Shaw by beating him over the head with a cast iron skillet and a ring sizer, and strangling him with his own necktie.

Death Row Inmates

Start of Trial: July 10, 1978
Verdict: July 25, 1978
Sentencing: October 27, 1978
Resentencing: October 27, 1982

●●

Carter, Douglas	Utah	M	B	
Carter, Johnny Ray	Texas	M	B	
Carter, Robert Anthony	Texas	M	B	2
Carter, James David	Tennessee	M	W	
Carter, Darryl	Pennsylvania	M	W	
Carter, Charles	Florida	M	W	
Carter, Antonio	Florida	M	B	
Cartwright, Timothy	Oklahoma	M	W	1
Caruso, Michael	Florida	M	W	
Caruthers, Walter	Tennessee	M	B	
Case, Jerry Douglas	North Carolina	M	W	
Cass, Mark R.	Texas	M	W	1
Casteel, Dee Dyne	Florida	F	W	4
Castell, James	Georgia	M	W	
Castillo, David Allen	Texas	M	H	
Castor, Marvin	Indiana	M	W	
Castro, John	Oklahoma	M	W	
Castro, Edward	Florida	M	H	
Cauthern, Ronnie	Tennessee	M	W	
Cavanaugh, Patrick	Nevada	M	B	
Cave, Alfonso	Florida	M	B	
Celestine, Willie	Louisiana	M	B	7-20-87
Ceja, Jose	**Arizona**	**M**	**H**	

●●

JOSE JESUS CEJA

Race: Mexican-American

Date of Birth: October 24, 1955

FACTS
On Sunday, June 30, 1974, Ceja went to the home of Randy and Linda Leon in Phoenix intending to steal a large shipment of marijuana. Upon entry, Ceja shot Linda (who apparently resisted him) twice in the chest, and then dragged her body from the living room to the bedroom where he shot her at least four more times in the head at close range. When Randy arrived home, Ceja shot him four times with his own gun, which Ceja had removed from a drawer in the house. Ceja loaded a suitcase he had brought with him with 12 kilos of marijuana. He removed the receiver from the phone and turned on the television to create an appearance that someone was home. He later attended the funeral of the victims, helped move furniture, and offered to help police find the murderer.

Start of Trial: November 8, 1974 (first trial) May 12, 1976 (second trial)
Verdicts: November 19, 1974 (first trial) May 18, 1976 (second trial)
Sentencing: December 19, 1974 (first trial) June 25, 1976 (second trial)
Resentencing: July 17, 1979

●●●

Chaffee, Jonathan	South Carolina	M	W	1
Chambers, Ronald	Texas	M	B	
Chambers, Karl	Pennsylvania	M	W	
Chambers, James	Missouri	M	W	
Champion, Steve	California	M	B	
Chandler, Mark	Illinois	M	W	
Chandler, James	Florida	M	W	
Chaney, Anthony	**Arizona**	**M**	**W**	

●●●

ANTHONY LEE CHANEY

Race: Caucasian

Date of Birth: April 4, 1954

FACTS

Chaney and Deanna Jo Saunders-Coleman were on the run from a string of burglaries in Texas and Colorado. They were driving a stolen pickup truck and were in possession of 11 stolen firearms. On September 6, 1982, Coconino County Sheriff's Deputy Robert Cline, on routine patrol, checked the campsite where Chaney and Saunders-Coleman were staying outside of Flagstaff. After requesting a check on the stolen truck, Cline got out of his car and began talking to Chaney. Chaney pulled a gun on the deputy, had Deanna disarm him, and handcuffed him to a tree. Chaney and Deanna got into the truck and started to leave. As they did, John Jamison, a reserve deputy who was also a medical doctor, arrived at the scene. Chaney jumped out of the truck and began firing at Jamison with an AR-15 rifle. Using a hail of fire to pin Jamison down inside his car, Chaney advanced to point blank range and fired three fatal shots into the deputy. In addition to the fatal 3 wounds, the deputy was struck by over 200 fragments of metal and glass from the shots fired into the vehicle.

Saunders-Coleman pled guilty to second-degree murder and received a 21-year prison sentence. She testified against Chaney.

Start of Trial: February 16, 1983
Verdict: March 17, 1983
Sentencing: April 20, 1983

●●●

Charo, Robert Phillip	Arizona	M	W
Chenault, Marcus	Georgia	M	B
Cherry, Roger	**Florida**	**M**	**B**

•••

ROGER CHERRY

FACTS

At 37, Roger Cherry was convicted of two murders during the course of a 1986 burglary at the home of an elderly Daytona Beach, Florida couple. Esther Wayne, 77 was killed by blows to the head, and her husband was found by the medical examiner to have succumbed to a heart attack as a consequence of the confrontation with Cherry. The Florida Supreme Court in April 1989 upheld the death sentence for the beating death of the woman, but set aside the same penalty in her husband's death.

•••

Chester, Frank	Pennsylvania	M	W

•••

FRANK CHESTER

FACTS

Frank Chester, 21, and Richard Laird, 25, were sentenced to die for the 1987 murder of Anthony Milano, a gay, who was tortured and whose throat was slashed. According to trial testimony, the two met Milano, 26, at a bar in December of 1987, insisted he take a ride with them, then attacked him because he was gay. Chester, who admitted pushing Milano to the ground, said it was Laird who repeatedly slit Milano's throat with a box-cutting knife.

•••

Childs, Johnny	Georgia	M	B	
Chmiel, David	Pennsylvania	M	W	
Christian, Doy	Florida	M	B	
Christianson, Edgar	Illinois	M	W	
Christopher, William	Florida	M	W	1
Christy, Lawrence	Pennsylvania	M	W	
Clabourne, Scott	**Arizona**	**M**	**B**	

•••

SCOTT DRAKE CLABOURNE

Race: Black

Date of Birth: September 6, 1960

FACTS

On the evening of September 18, 1980, Laura Webster, a University of Arizona student, was at the Green Dolphin Bar in Tucson with friends. She met Clabourne and Larry Langston at the bar and agreed to leave with them. Clabourne and Langston then took Webster to the house of a friend of Langston. Ms. Webster was repeatedly raped and sodomized, then strangled and stabbed in the heart three times. Her body was dumped in an arroyo, where it was found the next morning. Langston pleaded guilty to murder and received a life sentence.

Start of Trial: November 16, 1982
Verdict: November 23, 1982
Sentencing: January 24, 1983

Clair, Kenneth	California	M	B	
Clanton, Earl	Virginia	M	B	4-14-88
Clark, David M.	Texas	M	W	
Clark, Herman Robert	Texas	M	B	
Clark, Joseph Lewis	Ohio	M	B	
Clark, Terry	New Mexico	M	W	
Clark, Michael	Kentucky	M	W	
Clark, Larry	Florida	M	B	
Clark, Raymond	Florida	M	W	
Clark, Richard	California	M	W	
Clark, John William	California	M	W	
Clark, Douglas	California	M	W	
Clark, Antonio	Arkansas	M	B	3
Clark, James Dean	**Arizona**	**M**	**W**	

JAMES DEAN CLARK

Race: Caucasian

Date of Birth: October 18, 1957

FACTS

For most of 1977, Clark worked as a wrangler at a dude ranch in Elfrida. In the early morning hours of December 4, 1977, Clark killed two other wranglers at the ranch, George Martin, Jr. and 17-year-old Gerald McFerron. Clark stabbed Martin numerous times in the chest and shot McFerron three times in the head. Both victims were asleep at the time of the attacks. Clark then took a .357 Magnum and walked to the house of the owners, Charles and Mildred Thumm. After shooting Mr. Thumm twice, Clark shot Mrs. Thumm through the head as she slept. He took jewelry, credit cards and money from the Thumms, stole their car and, after slashing the tires of all the vehicles at the ranch, drove to El Paso. To a friend, Clark gloated, "You should have seen Charley when I hit him with those cutters." When he was arrested, the police found on Clark a souvenir he retained from the murders: the bullet that had passed through the head of one of the victims with organic matter still on it.

Start of Trial: May 4, 1978
Verdict: June 23, 1978
Sentencing: July 28, 1978

Clausell, James	New Jersey	M	B	
Clayton, James	Texas	M	B	
Clayton, Willie	Pennsylvania	M	B	
Clayton, Robert W.	Oklahoma	M	W	
Claytor, Justin	Ohio	M	B	
Clemmons, Eric	Missouri	M	B	
Clemons, Chandler	Mississippi	M	B	
Clines, Hoyt	Arkansas	M	W	1
Clisby, Willie	Alabama	M	B	1
Clozza, Albert	Virginia	M	W	
Cochran, James	Alabama	M	B	
Cochrane, Guy	Florida	M	B	
Cockrum, John	Texas	M	W	
Coe, Glen	Tennessee	M	W	
Coffey, Fred	North Carolina	M	W	
Cohen, Michael Anthony	Georgia	M	B	
Coker, Rocky	Tennessee	M	W	
Cole, Carroll	Nevada	F	W	12-6-85
Cole, Ted Calvin	Texas	M	W	
Cole, West	Mississippi	M	B	
Coleman, Roger	Virginia	M	W	
Coleman, Michael	Tennessee	M	B	
Coleman, Charles	Oklahoma	M	W	
Coleman, Alton	Ohio	M	B	
Coleman, Dewey	Montana	M	B	
Coleman, Alton	Indiana	M	B	3
Coleman, Alton	Illinois	M	B	3
Coleman, Russell	California	M	B	
Coleman, Calvin	California	M	B	
Colina, Manuel	Florida	M	H	
Collier, Gregory	Nevada	M	W	
Collier, Robert	Georgia	M	B	
Collins, Kenneth	Maryland	M	B	
Collins, Roger	Illinois	M	B	
Collins, Roger	Georgia	M	B	
Colvin, Eugene	Maryland	M	B	1
Combs, Ronald	Ohio	M	W	
Comeaux, Adam	Louisiana	M	B	2
Comer, Robert	**Arizona**	**M**	**W**	

●●

ROBERT CHARLES COMER

Race: Caucasian

Date of Birth: December 14, 1956

FACTS
On February 23, 1987, Comer and his girlfriend, Juneva Willis, were at a camp-

ground near Apache Lake. They invited Larry Pritchard, who was at the campsite next to theirs, to have dinner and drinks with them. Around 9:00 p.m., Comer shot Pritchard in the head, killing him. He and Willis then stole Pritchard's belongings. Around 11:00 p.m., Comer and Willis went to a campsite occupied by Richard Brough and Tracy Andrews. Comer stole their property, hogtied Brough to a car fender, and then raped Andrews in front of Brough. Comer and Willis then left the area, taking Andrews with them, but leaving Brough behind. Andrews escaped the next morning and ran for 23 hours before finding help. Willis pleaded guilty to kidnapping and testified against Comer.

Start of Trial: January 6, 1988
Verdict: January 21, 1988
Sentencing: April 11, 1988

●●●

Cone, Gary	Tennessee	M	W
Conklin, Robert	Georgia	M	W
Conner, Kevin	Indiana	M	W
Connor, John Wayne	Georgia	M	W
Connor, Ronnie	**Arizona**	**M**	**W**

●●●

RONNIE LLOYD CONNER

Race: Caucasian

Date of Birth: July 5, 1961

FACTS
Ed Tinnerman, age 61, frequently stayed at the Arrowhead Motel in Las Vegas, where he got to know Emory (Amy) Marle Fisher, the manager of the motel. On several occasions Mr. Tinnerman got drunk and passed out and Ms. Fisher stole his traveler's checks and personal checks. Mr. Tinnerman eventually became suspicious, so Ms. Fisher decided to have him killed. She contacted Conner and promised him $500 and Tinnerman's pickup and money if Conner would kill Tinnerman. On January 19, 1982, Conner and Fisher drove to Dolan Springs, where Tinnerman lived. Conner dropped Fisher off at Tinnerman's house. At about midnight, Conner returned and Fisher let him in. He went into Tinnerman's bedroom, and tried to suffocate him as he slept. Tinnerman awoke and Conner began beating the victim in the head with a closed hunting knife. When Tinnerman lost consciousness, Conner suffocated him. Conner disposed of the body in a remote area off of Route 93. These events occurred in Mohave County.

Start of Trial: June 29, 1982
Verdict: July 1, 1982
Sentencing: August 6, 1982
Resentencing: September 3, 1985

●●●

Death Row Inmates

Cooey, Richard	Ohio	M	W
Cook, Anthony	Texas	M	W
Cook, Kerry Max	Texas	M	W
Cook, Robert	Pennsylvania	M	B
Cook, James	Georgia	M	B
Cook, David	Florida	M	B
Cook, Daniel Wayne	**Arizona**	**M**	**W**

••

DANIEL WAYNE COOK

Race: Caucasian

Date of Birth: July 23, 1961

FACTS
Cook, John Matzke, Kevin Swaney, and Carlos Froyan Cruz-Ramos worked at a restaurant in Lake Havasu City and shared an apartment. On July 19, 1987, Cook stole some money from Cruz-Ramos. When Cruz-Ramos began searching the apartment for the money, Cook and Matzke tied Cruz-Ramos to a chair and began beating him with their fists and a metal pipe. Cook also cut Cruz-Ramos with a knife, sodomized him, and burned his genitals with cigarettes. After several hours of this torture, Matzke and Cook crushed Cruz-Ramos' throat with the pipe. When Swaney arrived at the apartment, Cook forced him upstairs and showed him Cruz-Ramos' body. Cook and Matzke then tied Swaney to a chair. Matzke went to sleep while Cook sodomized Swaney. When Cook was finished, he woke Matzke and the two men strangled Swaney with a bed sheet. Cook received the death penalty for both murders. Matzke pled guilty to second-degree murder and testified against Cook.

Start of Trial: June 27, 1988
Verdict: July 7, 1988
Sentencing: August 8, 1988

••

Cooks, Vincent	Texas	M	B	
Cooks, Cornell	Oklahoma	M	B	
Cooper, Vernon Franklin	Tennessee	M	W	
Cooper, Paula	Indiana	F	B	
Cooper, Richard	Florida	M	W	
Cooper, Vernon	Florida	M	W	1
Cooper, Kevin	California	M	B	
Copeland, James	Louisiana	M	W	
Copeland, Johnny	Florida	M	B	
Coppola, Frank	Virginia	M	W	8-10-82
Cordova, Joseph Angel	Texas	M	H	
Corley, Edward	Texas	M	W	
Corn, Charles	Georgia	M	W	1
Correll, Walter	Virginia	M	W	
Correll, Jerry	Florida	M	W	

Correll, Michael	Arizona	M	W

•••

MICHAEL EMERSON CORRELL

Race: Caucasian

Date of Birth: January 8, 1960

FACTS

Correll and John Nabors decided to rob Guy Snelling of money and drugs. On the night of April 11, 1984, Correll and Nabors went to Snelling's trailer and tied up Snelling and his girlfriend, Debra Rosen. When Robin Cady and Shawn D'Brito arrived at the trailer a short time later, they were also bound and gagged. Rosen was killed at the trailer by strangulation with a heavy shoelace knotted around her neck. Correll and Nabors took Snelling, Cady and D'Brito to a desert area north of Phoenix where all three were shot in the head. Snelling survived and lived to testify against Correll. Nabors committed suicide when police were about to arrest him.

Start of Trial: October 15, 1984
Verdicts: October 23, 1984
Sentencing: November 23, 1984

•••

Cosby, Teddy Lee	Kentucky	M	B	
Coulter, David	Alabama	M	W	
County, Charles	Texas	M	B	
Cox, Russell	Pennsylvania	M	B	
Cox, Sue	North Carolina	F	W	
Cox, Robert Craig	Florida	M	W	
Cox, Tiequon A.	California	M	B	
Cox, Michael	California	M	W	
Coyle, Bryan	New Jersey	M	W	
Craig, Andrew	North Carolina	M	B	
Craig, Donny Gene	Florida	M	W	
Craig, Robert	Florida	M	W	1
Crandell, Kenneth	California	M	W	1
Crank, Denton Alan	Texas	M	W	
Cravatt, Darias Jr.	Oklahoma	M	N	
Crawford, Joseph	Oklahoma	M	B	
Crawford, Eddie	Georgia	M	W	
Crawley, Dewitt	Pennsylvania	M	B	
Creech, Thomas	Idaho	M	W	
Crews, William	Illinois	M	W	
Cross, Charles	Pennsylvania	M	W	
Crump, Thomas	Nevada	M	W	
Cudjo, Armenia	California	M	B	
Cuevas, Ignacio	Texas	M	H	
Culberson, Alvin	Mississippi	M	B	
Cumbo, Sam Edward	Texas	M	B	1

Cumings, Jerry Ray	North Carolina	M	N	
Cummings, Edward Lee	North Carolina	M	B	
Cummings, Raynard	California	M	B	
Cunningham, James	Georgia	M	B	
Curtis, Ronnie Allen	Federal	M	B	
Cyril, Wayne	Oklahoma	M	B	
Czubak, Walter	Florida	M	W	
Dailey, James	Florida	M	W	
Damon, Shellie	South Carolina	M	B	1
Daniel, Larry	Georgia	M	W	
Daniel, George	Alabama	M	B	1
Daniels, Michael	Indiana	M	B	
Daniels, Jackson	California	M	B	
Daniels, John R	Alabama	M	W	
Danielson, Robert	California	M	W	
Darden, Willie	Louisiana	M	W	3-15-88
Daughterty, Jeffrey	Florida	M	W	11-7-88
Davenport, John	California	M	W	1
Davis, James Carl Lee	Texas	M	B	
Davis, William Prince	Texas	M	B	
Davis, Charles	Oklahoma	M	W	
Davis, Raymond	Ohio	M	W	
Davis, Von Clark	Ohio	M	B	1
Davis, Eugene	North Carolina	M	B	
Davis, Steven Ray	**New Jersey**	**M**	**W**	

••

STEVEN RAY DAVIS

FACTS

Davis, 32, was convicted of the January 1983 murder of Barbara Blomberg. Blomberg, who had sold Davis a trailer in which he occasionally lived, was strangled with an electrical cord before being stabbed with a knife and screwdriver. At the time of the killing, Davis owed $1,800 on the trailer, and evidence produced at the trial indicated that payments were late and inconsistent. Davis has testified that on the day of the killing, he had been drinking beer, had taken two Quaaludes and had injected himself with methamphetamine. His death sentence has been set aside by the the New Jersey Supreme Court and a new penalty hearing ordered.

••

Davis, Gregory	Mississippi	M	B	
Davis, Greg	Indiana	M	B	
Davis, Frank	Indiana	M	W	
Davis, Girvies	Illinois	M	B	
Davis, John Michael	Georgia	M	W	
Davis, George	Georgia	M	B	
Davis, Curfew	Georgia	M	B	1
Davis, Mark	Florida	M	W	

Death Row Inmates

Davis, Allen	Florida	M	W	
Davis, Gary	Colorado	M	W	
Davis, Michael	**Arizona**	**M**	**W**	

••

MICHAEL WAYNE DAVIS

Race: Caucasian

Date of Birth: February 20, 1965

FACTS

On July 25, 1986, Davis and Alfonso Salazar pulled the wrought iron bars from a window and entered the Tucson home of Sarah Kaplan. Ms. Kaplan was 83 years old, weighed less than 90 pounds, was 5 feet tall, and wore a patch on one eye. They beat her and strangled her with the telephone cord. Fingerprints belonging to both men were found at the scene. One of Salazar's prints was in blood. In a separate trial, Salazar was convicted and sentenced to death.

Start of Trial: September 16, 1987
Verdict: September 23, 1987
Sentencing: December 22, 1987

••

Davis, Jimmy Wayne	Alabama	M	W	
Davis, Timothy	Alabama	M	W	2
Dawson, Henry	**Nevada**	**M**	**B**	

••

Henry Dawson

FACTS

Dawson, 45, was sentenced to death for the March 1985 slaying in Clark County Nevada of Leslie Gail Shepard, a convenience store clerk who resisted his sexual advances.

••

Dawson, David T.	**Montana**	**M**	**W**

••

DAVID T. DAWSON

FACTS.

Dawson was sentenced to die for the April 18, 1986 killings of three family members in a Billings, Mont. motel room he had rented. The victims, David and Monica Rodstein and their 11-year-old son, Andrew, were found in the room on April 19 by Billings police detectives. They had been bound, gagged and injected with an unknown substance, then strangled with a telephone cord. Amy Rodstein, then 15, a daughter of the couple, survived.

••

Death Row Inmates

Dawson, David	Delaware	M	W	
Day, Christopher	California	M	B	
De La Cruz, Jose	Texas	M	H	
DeBlanc, David Wayne	Texas	M	B	
DeBoue, Thomas	Louisiana	M	B	
DeLong, Wayne	Virginia	M	W	
DeMouchette, James	Texas	M	B	
DeSantis, Stephen	California	M	W	
Dean, Roy Wayne	Kentucky	M	W	
Deaton, Jason P.	Florida	M	W	
Debeler, Shelby	Missouri	M	W	
Deeb, Muneer M.	Texas	M	W	
Deere, Ronald	California	M	N	
Degarmo, Roger	Texas	M	W	
Dehart, Robert	Pennsylvania	M	W	
Delap, David	Florida	M	W	1
Delk, Monty Allen	Texas	M	W	
Deluna, Carlos	Texas	M	H	
Delvecchio, George	Illinois	M	W	
Demps, Bennie	Florida	M	B	
Dennis, William	California	M	W	
Deputy, Andre	Delaware	M	B	
Derrick, Mikel	Texas	M	W	
Derrick, Samuel	Florida	M	W	
Deshields, Kenneth	Delaware	M	B	
Deutscher, Henry	Nevada	M	W	
Devier, Darrell	Georgia	M	W	
Diaz, Angel	Florida	M	H	
Diaz, Robert R.	California	M	H	
Dickerson, Frederick	Ohio	M	B	
Dicks, Jeffrey	Tennessee	M	W	
Difrisco, Anthony	New Jersey	M	W	
Dixon, Philip	New Jersey	M	B	
Dobbert, Ernest	Florida	M	W	9-7-84
Dobbs, Wiley	Georgia	M	B	
Dock, Todd	Federal	M	W	1
Doering, Al Wayne	Maryland	M	W	1
Dolinsky, Raymond	Florida	M	W	
Dominick, Occhicone	Florida	M	W	
Douglas, Robert	Pennsylvania	M	B	
Douglas, Howard	Florida	M	W	
Douglas, Fred Berre	California	M	W	
Downs, Ernest	Florida	M	W	1
Doyle, Danny	Florida	M	W	
Draughon, Martin	Texas	M	W	
Drayton, Leroy	South Carolina	M	B	
Drew, Robert	Texas	M	W	
Drinkard, Richard	Texas	M	W	

Death Row Inmates

Driscoll, Robert	Missouri	M	W	
Duckett, James	Florida	M	W	
Dudley, Katsie	Florida	F	W	
Duest, Lloyd	Florida	M	W	
Duff-Smith, Markham	Texas	M	W	
Duffey, Steven	Pennsylvania	M	W	
Dufour, Donald	Mississippi	M	W	
Dufour, Donald	Florida	M	W	3
Dugar, Troy	Louisiana	M	B	2
Duhamel, Emile Pierre	Texas	M	W	
Duncan, David	Tennessee	M	B	
Duncan, Henry Earl	California	M	B	
Duncan, Joseph Cecil	Alabama	M	W	
Dunkins, Horace	Alabama	M	B	
Dunn, Kenneth D.	Texas	M	B	1
Duren, David	**Alabama**	**M**	**W**	

••

DAVID DUREN

FACTS.

In 1983, Duren and an accomplice abducted 16-year-old Nancy Kathleen Bedsole and her date, Charles Leonard and drove them to a deserted area, where they bound and shot them. Bedsole died as a result of her wounds, but Leonard survived.

••

Durr, Darryl	Ohio	M	B	
Duvalle, John	Oklahoma	M	W	
Dyer, Alfred	California	M	B	
D'Amato, Carmen	Pennsylvania	M	W	
D'Ambrosia, Joe	Ohio	M	W	
Earhart, James	Texas	M	W	
Earvin, Harvey	Texas	M	B	
Easley, Elbert	California	M	W	1
East, Wayne	Texas	M	B	
Eaton, Winthrop	Louisiana	M	B	
Eddmonds, Durlyn	Illinois	M	B	1
Edelbacher, Peter	California	M	W	1
Edmonds, Dana	Virginia	M	B	
Edwards, George	Pennsylvania	M	W	
Edwards, Leo	Mississippi	M	B	
Edwards, Daniel	Illinois	M	W	
Edwards, Thomas F.	California	M	W	
El-Mumit, Abdullah Hakim	Louisiana	M	B	
Eley, John	Ohio	M	B	
Ellason, Thomas	Texas	M	W	
Elledge, William	Florida	M	W	1
Elliott, John	Texas	M	H	

Ellis, Edward	Texas	M	W
Elmore, Edward Lee	South Carolina	M	B
Emerson, Dennis	Illinois	M	B
Emery, Jeff	Texas	M	W
Emil, Rodney	Nevada	M	W
Engberg, Roy	Wyoming	M	W
Engle, Gregory	Florida	M	W
Ennis, Tony	Illinois	M	B
Enoch, Willie	Illinois	M	B
Epperson, Roger Dale	Kentucky	M	W
Epperson, George	**Arizona**	**M**	**B**

••

GEORGE EPPERSON

Race: Black

Date of Birth: September 2, 1960

FACTS

Epperson's common law wife was Nancy Solomon, by whom he had two children. In the past, when she had tried to leave him, Epperson took her out in the desert, stripped her, and hit her on the head. Solomon survived this earlier beating. On November 14, 1986, Solomon was again planning to leave Epperson. This time he drove her out into the desert west of Phoenix. He hit her with a blunt instrument on the head. There were scuffle marks left on the ground in the area of the homicide. After she was probably dead from the trauma to the head, Epperson set her body on fire with gasoline.

Start of Trial: September 22, 1987
Verdict: October 14, 1987
Sentencing: December 11, 1987

•••

Erazo, Samuel	New Jersey	M	H	
Erickson, Paul	Illinois	M	W	
Esparza, Gregory	Ohio	M	H	
Espinosa, Henry	Florida	M	H	
Espinoza, Antonio	California	M	H	
Esquivel, Rudy	Texas	M	H	6-9-86
Eutzy, William	Florida	M	W	
Evans, Connie Ray	Massachusetts	F	B	7-8-87
Evans, Michael Wayne	Texas	M	B	12-4-86
Evans, Wilburt	Virginia	M	B	
Evans, John	Alabama	M	W	4-22-83
Evans, Derrick	Ohio	M	B	
Evans, Vernon	Maryland	M	B	
Evans, Charles	Indiana	M	B	
Evans, Johnnie Lee	Illinois	M	B	

Death Row Inmates

Evans, Larry	Arizona	M	W	1
Eyler, Larry	Illinois	M	W	
Fahy, Henry	Pennsylvania	M	W	
Fain, Charles	Idaho	M	W	1
Fairchild, Barry	Arkansas	M	B	
Farinas, Alberto	Florida	M	W	
Farmer, Robert	Nevada	M	W	
Farmer, Lee	California	M	W	1
Farrar, Stephen L.	Oregon	M	N	
Farrell, Dallas	South Carolina	M	W	1
Farris, Troy Dale	Texas	M	W	
Fauber, Curtis	California	M	W	
Faulder, Joseph	Texas	M	W	
Faulkner, Arthur	Pennsylvania	M	B	
Fearance, John	Texas	M	B	
Felde, Wayne	Louisiana	M	W	3-15-88
Felker, Ellis	Georgia	M	W	
Feltrop, Ralph	Missouri	M	W	
Feraga, Lazaro	Mississippi	M	H	
Ferguson, John	Florida	M	B	
Ferrell, Eric	Georgia	M	B	
Fetterly, Donald	Idaho	M	W	
Fields, Nathson	Illinois	M	B	
Fields, Stevie	California	M	B	
Fierro, Cesar	Texas	M	H	
Fierro, David	California	M	H	
Fierro, Jose	**Arizona**	**M**	**H**	

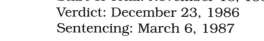

JOSE ABEL FIERRO

Race: Hispanic

Date of Birth: March 27, 1958

FACTS
On September 29, 1985, Merle Moseley and Anne Manross returned to their home to find Fierro burglarizing it. Moseley got out of the car and held a gun on Fierro while Manross sat in the car and called the police on a mobile phone. When Manross called to Moseley that the police were on the way, Fierro shot Moseley. Bullets hit the car's windshield, narrowly missing Manross. Fierro fled the scene in a brown pickup. He was apprehended that night, and several guns, jewelry from the victims' home, and a VCR were recovered from his car. Moseley died 2 months later.

Start of Trial: November 18, 1986
Verdict: December 23, 1986
Sentencing: March 6, 1987

Finney, Eddie	Georgia	M	W
First, Kenneth	Texas	M	W
Fisher, James	**Arizona**	**M**	**W**

••

JAMES CLIFFORD FISHER

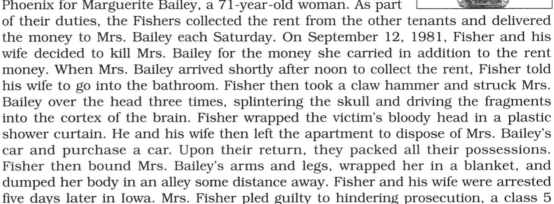

Race: Caucasian

Date of Birth: May 22, 1939

FACTS

Fisher and his wife, Ann, managed an apartment complex in Phoenix for Marguerite Bailey, a 71-year-old woman. As part of their duties, the Fishers collected the rent from the other tenants and delivered the money to Mrs. Bailey each Saturday. On September 12, 1981, Fisher and his wife decided to kill Mrs. Bailey for the money she carried in addition to the rent money. When Mrs. Bailey arrived shortly after noon to collect the rent, Fisher told his wife to go into the bathroom. Fisher then took a claw hammer and struck Mrs. Bailey over the head three times, splintering the skull and driving the fragments into the cortex of the brain. Fisher wrapped the victim's bloody head in a plastic shower curtain. He and his wife then left the apartment to dispose of Mrs. Bailey's car and purchase a car. Upon their return, they packed all their possessions. Fisher then bound Mrs. Bailey's arms and legs, wrapped her in a blanket, and dumped her body in an alley some distance away. Fisher and his wife were arrested five days later in Iowa. Mrs. Fisher pled guilty to hindering prosecution, a class 5 felony, and she received a 2.5 year sentence.

Start of Trial: April 20, 1982.
Verdict: April 29, 1982
Sentencing: July 12, 1982

•••

Fisher, David Lee	Virginia	M	W
Fisher, Robert	Pennsylvania	M	B
Fisher, James	Oklahoma	M	B
Fitzgerald, Edward	Virginia	M	W
Fitzpatrick, Bernard	Montana	M	W
Fix, Andrew	Missouri	M	W
Flamer, William	Delaware	M	B
Fleenor, D.H.	Indiana	M	W
Fleming, Son	**Georgia**	**M**	**B**

•••

SON FLEMING

FACTS

Fleming and two others were convicted on charges related to the Feb. 11, 1976 murder of Ray City, Georgia police chief Ed Giddens. Also convicted were Henry Willis, III, who was executed May 18, 1989, and Larry Fleming ,

Death Row Inmates

who was sentenced to life in prison. Son Fleming's appeals have been based in part upon defense claims that he is retarded. Giddens was abducted and shot to death after he stopped a car matching the description of one used in a robbery.

●●

Flores, Mario	Illinois	M	H	
Floyd, James	Florida	M	B	
Floyd, Tommy	Alabama	M	B	
Fontenot, Karl	Oklahoma	M	W	
Ford, Priscilla	Nevada	F	B	
Ford, Glenn	Louisiana	M	B	
Ford, Melbert Ray	Georgia	M	W	
Ford, James Arthur	Georgia	M	B	
Ford, Alvin	Florida	M	B	
Ford, Clay Anthony	Arkansas	M	B	
Ford, Pernell	Alabama	M	B	
Fortenberry, Tommy Jerry	Alabama	M	W	
Foster, Richard Donald	Texas	M	W	
Foster, Charles	Oklahoma	M	B	
Foster, Emmitt	Missouri	M	B	
Foster, James Henry	Mississippi	M	B	
Foster, LaFonda Fay	Kentucky	F	W	
Foster, James	Illinois	M	B	
Foster, Timothy	Georgia	M	B	
Foster, Charles Kenneth	Florida	M	W	1
Fowler, Mark	Oklahoma	M	W	
Fox, Billy	Oklahoma	M	W	
Francis, Bobby	Florida	M	B	
Francois, Marvin	Florida	M	B	5-29-85
Frank, Theodore	California	M	W	
Franklin, Donald Gene	Texas	M	B	11-3-88
Franklin, George	Ohio	M	U	
Franklin, William	Illinois	M	B	
Frazier, Wayne	Ohio	M	B	
Frazier, Leonard	Georgia	M	W	
Frazier, Richard	Alabama	M	W	
Free, James	Illinois	M	W	
Freeman, John	Florida	M	W	
Freeman, Fred	California	M	W	
Freeman, Darryl	Alabama	M	B	
Fretwell, Bobby Ray	Arkansas	M	W	
Frey, Roderick	Pennsylvania	M	W	
Frierson, Lavell	California	M	B	
Fronckiewicz, Mark	Texas	M	W	
Fudge, Keith	California	M	B	
Fuente, Hector	Florida	M	W	
Fuentes, Jose	California	M	H	

Death Row Inmates

Fugitt, John Thomas	Georgia	M	W	
Fullwood, Michael Lee	North Carolina	M	B	
Fulminante, Orestes	**Arizona**	**M**	**H**	

••

ORESTE FULMINANTE

Race: Caucasian

Date of Birth: July 2, 1941

FACTS

Fulminante was married to Mary Hunt. On September 13, 1982, Mary was in the hospital, and her ll-year-old daughter, Jeneane, was home with Fulminante. Fulminante bought an extra barrel for his .357 Don Wesson revolver at a gun shop in Mesa. He took Jeneane on his motorcycle to a secluded area of the desert. He choked her, forced her to beg for her life, and then shot her two times in the head. He hid the weapon, returned home, and washed his clothes. The next morning, he called the Mesa Police Department to report that Jeneane was missing. In 1983, Fulminante was convicted of possession of a firearm by a felon. While in prison, he told another inmate, Anthony Sarivola, that he killed his stepdaughter because she was always coming between him and his wife.

Start of Trial: December 2, 1985
Verdict: December 19, 1985
Sentencing: February 11, 1986

•••

Funchess, David	Florida	M	B	4-22-86
Gacho, Robert	Illinois	M	W	1
Gacy, John Wayne	Illinois	M	W	
Gaddis, Bobby Gene	Georgia	M	W	1
Gall, Eugene	Kentucky	M	W	
Gallego, Gerald	Nevada	M	W	
Gallego, Gerald	California	M	W	3
Games, James	Indiana	M	W	
Garceau, Robert	California	M	W	
Garcia, Henry	Florida	M	H	
Garcia, Enrique	Florida	M	H	
Gardner, Ronnie Lee	Utah	M	W	
Gardner, Billy Conn	Texas	M	W	
Gardner, David	Texas	M	W	
Gardner, John	North Carolina	M	W	
Gardner, Mark	Arkansas	M	W	
Garrett, Daniel	**Texas**	**M**		

•••

DANIEL GARRETT

Death Row Inmates

FACTS
Daniel Garrett was convicted with Karla Faye Tucker, 29, also imprisoned on Texas' death row, of participating in the 1983 pickax killings of Jerry Lynn Dean, 26, and Deborah Ruth Thornton, 32.

Garrett, Johnny F.	**Texas**	**M**	**W**	**2**

JOHNNY FRANK GARRETT

FACTS
Johnny Frank Garrett was convicted on Sept 1, 1982 of the rape, stabbing and strangulation of 76 year old Sister Tadea Benz at St. Francis Convent in Amarillo, Tex.

.Garrison, Richard	California	M	W	1
Gary, Carlton	Georgia	M	B	
Gaskins, Donald	South Carolina	M	W	
Gates, Johnny Lee	Georgia	M	B	
Gates, Oscar	California	M	B	
Gathers, Demetrious	South Carolina	M	B	1
Gay, Kenneth	California	M	B	
Gentry, Kenneth	Texas	M	W	
Gerlaugh, Darrick	**Arizona**	**M**	**N**	

DARRICK LEONARD GERLAUGH

Race: American Indian

Date of Birth: June 17, 1960

FACTS
On January 24, 1980, Gerlaugh, Joseph Encinas and Matthew Leisure decided to hitchhike from Chandler to Phoenix and rob whoever offered them a ride. Their victim turned out to be Scott Schwartz. Schwartz had a leg injury, wore a leg brace and used crutches. At a deserted location on the outskirts of Mesa, the group attacked Schwartz. Gerlaugh had Encinas and Leisure hold Schwartz on the road while he drove the car over him several times. Gerlaugh positioned the left rear tire on Schwartz' body and revved the engine so the spinning wheel would kill him. When the victim still seemed to be alive, Gerlaugh and Leisure stabbed him 30 to 40 times in the head, neck and shoulders with a screwdriver. The killers hid Schwartz' body in a nearby field and took $36.00 from him and left in his car. Gerlaugh and Encinas were convicted of the murder following a joint trial. Encinas received a life sentence. [See State v. Encinas, 132 Ariz. 493, 647 P.2d 624 (1982)]. Leisure pled guilty to first degree murder and also received a life sentence.

Start of Trial: December 15, 1980

Verdict: December 19, 1980
Sentencing: February 11, 1981

●●

Gerson-Fuller, Ronald	California	M	W	
Ghent, David	California	M	A	
Giarratano, Joseph	Virginia	M	W	
Gibbs, David Earl	Texas	M	W	
Gibson, Sherman	Illinois	M	B	
Gibson, Thomas Henry	Idaho	M	W	
Gilbert, Larry	South Carolina	M	B	
Giles, Arthur	Alabama	M	B	1
Gillard, John	Ohio	M	W	
Gilliam, Burley	Florida	M	W	
Gilliard, Robert	Mississippi	M	B	
Gillies, Jesse	**Arizona**	**M**	**W**	

●●

JESSE JAMES GILLIES

Race: Caucasian

Date of Birth: October 18, 1960

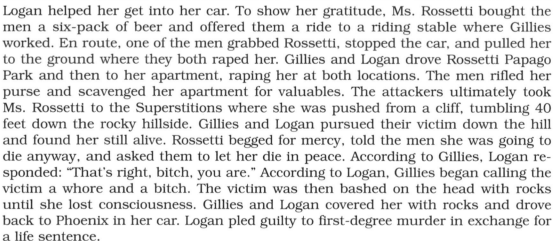

FACTS

On January 29, 1981, Suzanne Rossetti locked herself out of her car at a Phoenix convenience store. Gillies and Mike Logan helped her get into her car. To show her gratitude, Ms. Rossetti bought the men a six-pack of beer and offered them a ride to a riding stable where Gillies worked. En route, one of the men grabbed Rossetti, stopped the car, and pulled her to the ground where they both raped her. Gillies and Logan drove Rossetti Papago Park and then to her apartment, raping her at both locations. The men rifled her purse and scavenged her apartment for valuables. The attackers ultimately took Ms. Rossetti to the Superstitions where she was pushed from a cliff, tumbling 40 feet down the rocky hillside. Gillies and Logan pursued their victim down the hill and found her still alive. Rossetti begged for mercy, told the men she was going to die anyway, and asked them to let her die in peace. According to Gillies, Logan responded: "That's right, bitch, you are." According to Logan, Gillies began calling the victim a whore and a bitch. The victim was then bashed on the head with rocks until she lost consciousness. Gillies and Logan covered her with rocks and drove back to Phoenix in her car. Logan pled guilty to first-degree murder in exchange for a life sentence.

Start of Trial: August 20, 1981
Verdict: August 27, 1981
Sentencing: September 28, 1981
Resentencing: June 30, 1983

●●

| Gilmore, Gary | Utah | M | W | 1-17-77 |

Death Row Inmates

Gilmore, George	Missouri	M	W	

....

GEORGE GILMORE

FACTS

Gilmore was sentenced to die for the killing in 1979 of Mary Louella Waters, 83. Waters slaying was one of four in which Gilmore has been convicted and sentenced to die.

....

Gilreath, Fred	Georgia	M	W	
Gladden, Willie	North Carolina	M	B	1
Glass, Jimmy	Louisiana	M	W	6-12-87
Gleaton, J.D.	South Carolina	M	B	
Glenn, John	Ohio	M	B	
Glock, Robert D.	Florida	M	W	
Goad, William W. Jr.	Tennessee	M	W	
Godbolt, Jerry	Alabama	M	B	
Gonzalez, Martin	California	M	H	
Gonzalez, Jesse	California	M	H	
Goode, Arthur	Flordia	M	W	4-3-84
Goodman, Michael	Texas	M	B	
Goodwin, Alvin	Texas	M	W	
Gorby, Thomas	Pennsylvania	M	W	
Gordon, Patrick	California	M	W	
Gore, David	Florida	M	W	
Gorham, David	Florida	M	B	
Gosch, Lesley Lee	Texas	M	W	
Gosier, Harry	Illinois	M	B	
Goss, Cornelius	Texas	M	B	
Graham, Gary	Texas	M	B	2
Graham, Harrison	Pennsylvania	M	B	
Graham, Michael	Louisiana	M	W	
Grandison, Anthony	Maryland	M	B	
Grant, Rosalie	Ohio	F	B	
Grant, Richard	California	M	W	
Granviel, Kenneth	Texas	M	B	
Gray, Jimmy Lee	Massachusetts	M	W	9-2-83
Gray, Ronald	Federal	M	B	
Gray, Coleman Wayne	Virginia	M	B	
Grayson, Darrell	Alabama	M	B	
Green, G.W.	Texas	M	W	
Green, Anthony	South Carolina	M	B	
Green, William	Pennsylvania	M	B	
Green, Michael	Oklahoma	M	W	
Green, Elizabeth	Ohio	F	B	
Green, Alton Garner	North Carolina	M	W	

Green, Harvey Lee	North Carolina	M	B	
Green Rosevelt	Georgia	M	B	1-9-85
Green, Alphonso	Florida	M	B	
Greenawalt, Randy	Arizona	M	W	
Greene, Gary	North Carolina	M	W	
Greer, Paul	Ohio	M	B	
Gretzler, Douglas	**Arizona**	**M**	**W**	

••

DOUGLAS EDWARD GRETZLER

Race: Caucasian

Date of Birth: May 21, 1951

FACTS
On November 3, 1973, Gretzler and Willie Luther Steelman escorted Michael Sandberg at gunpoint from the parking lot of his condominium complex into his home in Tucson, where his wife, Patricia, was studying. They bound and gagged the Sandbergs. When night fell, Gretzler shot Michael Sandberg, who was bound and lying on the bed. He then shot Patricia Sandberg in the head, as she lay bound on the living room couch. Steelman fired another shot into her body. Gretzler and Steelman then took the Sandbergs' credit cards, checks, a camera and their car, and left for California. In California, the police apprehended Gretzler and Steelman, ending a crime spree that resulted in the deaths of at least 9 people. Steelman was also convicted of first-degree murder and sentenced to death. He died in prison in 1987.

Start of Trial: October 14, 1975
Verdict: November 5, 1975
Sentencing: November 15, 1976
Resentencing: October 23, 1981

••

Gribble, Timothy	Texas	M	W
Griffin, Jeffery	Texas	M	B
Griffin, Rodney	Pennsylvania	M	B
Griffin, Reginald	Missouri	M	B
Griffin, Milton	Missouri	M	B
Griffin, Larry	Missouri	M	B
Griffin, Gary	Mississippi	M	B
Griffin, Henry	Illinois	M	B
Griffin, Frank	Florida	M	B
Griffin, Kenneth	Florida	M	B
Griffin, Donald	California	M	W
Groover, Tommy	Florida	M	W
Groseclose, William	Tennessee	M	W
Grossman, Martin Edward	Florida	M	W
Grubbs, Ricky Lee	Missouri	M	W
Guerra, Ricardo	Texas	M	H

Death Row Inmates

Guest, Anthony	Illinois	M	B	
Guinan, Frank	Missouri	M	W	
Gunsby, Donald	Florida	M	B	
Gunther, James Lee	Texas	M	W	
Gusek, Randy	Oregon	M	W	
Guzman, Gary	California	M	W	
Haag, Randy	Pennsylvania	M	W	
Haberstroh, Richard	Nevada	M	W	
Hachett, Richard	Pennsylvania	M	W	
Hafdahl, Randall Wayne	Texas	M	W	
Hain, Scott Allan	Oklahoma	M	W	2
Hakim, Yaqub	Florida	M	B	
Hale, Alvie	Oklahoma	M	W	3
Haley, Kevin	California	M	B	
Haliburton, Jerry	Florida	M	B	
Hall, Donald	Pennsylvania	M	B	
Hall, Anthony	Illinois	M	B	
Hall, Willie James	Georgia	M	B	
Hall, Freddie Lee	Florida	M	B	1
Hallford, Phillip	Alabama	M	W	
Hallman, Darrell	Florida	M	W	
Halvorsen, Leif	Kentucky	M	W	
Halvorsen, Arthur	California	M	W	
Hamblen, James W.	Florida	M	W	
Hamilton, Thewell	Florida	M	W	
Hamilton, Michael	California	M	W	
Hamilton, Billy Ray	California	M	W	
Hamilton, Bernard Lee	California	M	B	
Hamilton, Tommy	Alabama	M	W	
Hamm, Doyle Lee	Alabama	M	W	
Hammond, Karl	Texas	M	B	
Hance, William Henry	Georgia	M	B	
Handy, William	North Carolina	M	B	
Haney, Judie	Alabama	F	W	
Hansem, Tracy	Mississippi	M	W	
Harbason, Edward	Tennessee	M	B	
Hardcastle, Donald	Pennsylvania	M	B	
Harding, Donald	**Arizona**	**M**	**W**	

••

DONALD EUGENE HARDING

Race: Caucasian

Date of Birth: March 1, 1949

FACTS
Late in the day of January 24, 1980, or early in the morning of January 25, 1980, Harding, probably posing as a security

guard, entered the Phoenix motel room of Allan Gage. Harding bound the victims hands and feet with adhesive tape and stuffed a gag in his mouth. He then took the victim's wallet and identification, stole his car, and drove to Tucson. Mr. Gage was left lying face down on the floor of the motel room, where he died from asphyxiation. Harding used the same security guard ruse to kill and rob two men in a Tucson motel. Harding was arrested in Flagstaff on January 26, 1980, and was in possession of Mr. Gage's wallet and identification. Gage's car had been left at the scene of the Tucson murders.

Start of Trial: October 19, 1982
Verdict: October 21, 1982
Sentencing: November 22, 1982

●●●

Hardison, Richard	Nevada	M	B	
Hardwick, John Gary	Florida	M	W	
Hardwick, Kenneth	Florida	M	W	
Hardy, Kenneth	Georgia	M	W	1
Hardy, James	California	M	W	
Hargrave, Lenson	Florida	M	W	1
Harich, Roy	Florida	M	W	
Harjo, Jerald	Oklahoma	M	N	
Harper, Steven	Nebraska	M	W	
Harper, Eddie Lee	Kentucky	M	W	
Harrell, Ed	Alabama	M	B	
Harries, Ronald	Tennessee	M	W	
Harris, Benjamin	**Washington**	**M**	**B**	

●●●

BENJAMIN HARRIS

FACTS.
Harris, said by his attorneys to be insane, was sentenced to die for the 1984 contract killing of Jimmie Lee Turner, who was shot to death outside his home. Harris, according to testimony of a psychologist, believes his conviction to be the result of a conspiracy involving the Ku Klux Klan and Green River killer, a serial murderer who has been sought for years by law enforcement officials in the Pacific Northwest.

●●●

Harris, Kenneth	Texas	M	B	
Harris, Danny Ray	Texas	M	B	
Harris, Curtis Paul	Texas	M	B	2
Harris, Edward	Tennessee	M	W	
Harris, Jackie	Maryland	M	B	1
Harris, James	Indiana	M	B	
Harris, Terry	Illinois	M	B	
Harris, James	Illinois	M	B	
Harris, Theodore	Florida	M	B	

Death Row Inmates

Harris, Von M.	California	M	B	1
Harris, Robert	California	M	W	
Harris, Johnny	Alabama	M	B	1
Harrison, Aden	Georgia	M	B	
Hart, Joseph	California	M	W	
Hartman, Eddie	Tennessee	M	W	
Harvey, Nathaniel	New Jersey	M	B	
Harvey, Harold	Florida	M	W	
Haskett, Randy	California	M	B	
Hatch, Steven	Oklahoma	M	W	
Hatcher, Ricky	Georgia	M	W	
Havard, Patrick Curtis	Texas	M	W	
Hawkins, Samuel	Texas	M	B	
Hawkins, Don Wilson	Oklahoma	M	W	
Hawkins, Earl	Illinois	M	B	
Hawthorne, Gene Willford	Texas	M	W	
Hawthorne, Anderson	California	M	B	
Hayes, Roger Dale	Oklahoma	M	W	
Hayes, Clarence	Illinois	M	B	
Hayes, Royal	California	M	W	
Hayes, Blufford	California	M	B	
Hayes, T.J.	Arkansas	M	B	
Hays, Thomas "Sonny"	Oklahoma	M	W	
Hays, Henry	**Alabama**	**M**	**W**	

●●

HENRY HAYS

FACTS.

Henry Hays, a former Ku Klux Klansman, was sentenced in 1983 to die in Alabama's electric chair for the 1981 kidnapping and murder of Michael Donald. Donald, a black, had been abducted from a downtown Mobile, Ala. street, forced into a car at gunpoint and taken to a wooded area where he was stabbed and beaten. After he was dead, Hays and an accomplice put Donald's body in the trunk of a car. Hays then cut Donald's throat, and the two tied a noose around his neck and brought him back to Mobile, where he was hanged from a tree.

●●

Heath, Larry	Alabama	M	W	3
Heatwole, George	North Carolina	M	W	
Hedgepeth, Roland	North Carolina	M	W	
Hegwood, Bernell	Florida	M	B	2
Heiney, Robert	Florida	M	W	
Heinish, Wayne	Ohio	M	W	
Heishman, Harvey	California	M	W	
Henderson, Charles	Ohio	M	W	
Henderson, Jerome	Ohio	M	B	
Henderson, Thomas	New Mexico	M	N	

Henderson, Demetrius	Illinois	M	B	
Henderson, Thomas	Florida	M	W	
Henderson, Wilbur	Arkansas	M	W	
Henderson, Jerry	Alabama	M	W	
Henderson, Curtis Lee	Alabama	M	B	
Henderson, Joe	Alabama	M	B	
Hendricks, Edgar	California	M	B	
Henley, Steve	Tennessee	M	W	
Hennis, Timothy	North Carolina	M	W	
Henry, Josoph	Pennsylvania	M	B	
Henry, Robert Lavern	Florida	M	B	
Henry, John	Florida	M	B	
Henry, Graham	**Arizona**	**M**	**W**	

●●

GRAHAM SAUNDERS HENRY

Race: Caucasian

Date of Birth: July 24, 1946

FACTS
On June 6, 1986, at approximately 3:00 p.m., Henry and Vernon Foote kidnapped Roy Estes from his Las Vegas apartment. The two men forced Estes into his truck and drove off with him. Estes, an elderly man, was partially paralyzed and used a walker. Henry and Foote took Estes to a desert area approximately 40 miles north of Kingman, where they cut his throat and stabbed him in the heart. After hiding Estes' body behind a bush, Henry and Foote drove back to Highway 93. At approximately 5:00 p.m., police officers stopped Henry, who was driving the wrong way on the highway. Henry gave the police a false name and was arrested for drunk driving. On June 8, 1986, after learning Henry's true name and that Estes was missing, the police questioned Henry about Estes' whereabouts. Henry immediately blamed Foote for killing Estes and led police to the body. In a separate trial, Foote was convicted of robbery and theft, but the jury could not reach a verdict on the murder charge. Foote later pleaded guilty to attempted first-degree murder.

Start of Trial: November 24, 1987
Verdict: December 9, 1987
Sentencing: March 16, 1988

●●

Hensley, Robert	Arizona	M	W	
Hernandez, Ramon	Texas	M	H	1-30-87
Hernandez, Rogelio	Texas	M	H	
Hernandez, Rudolfo Baiza	Texas	M	H	
Hernandez, Francis	California	M	H	
Herrera, Leonel	Texas	M	H	
Herring, Ted	Florida	M	B	
Hicks, David	Texas	M	B	

Hicks, John	Ohio	M	B	
Hicks, Robert Karl	Georgia	M	W	
Hiednik, Gary	Pennsylvania	M	W	
High, Jose	**Georgia**	**M**	**B**	**2**

JOSE HIGH

FACTS

Jose Martinez High, then 17, and two others, Judson Ruffin and Nathan Brown, kidnapped 11-year-old Bonnie Bullock and his stepfather, Henry Lee Phillips, in July 1976. According to trial testimony, the two were driven to a dirt road, with Phillips locked in the trunk of the car and the boy forced to ride with High and his two companions, who taunted him, telling him he was going to die and asking him if he was ready. Phillips, who lived to testify, said he and his stepson were forced to lie on the ground, then were shot with a pistol and a sawed-off shotgun. High, Ruffin and Brown were all sentenced to die for the murder.

Hightower, Bobby Ray	North Carolina	M	B	
Hightower, Jacinto	New Jersey	M	B	
Hightower, John	Georgia	M	B	
Hildwin, Paul	Florida	M	W	
Hill, Dorian	Ohio	M	B	
Hill, Danny Lee	Ohio	M	B	
Hill, James E.	Nevada	M	B	
Hill, Alvin	Mississippi	M	B	1
Hill, Floyd	Georgia	M	B	
Hill, George A.	Florida	M	B	
Hill, Clarence	Florida	M	B	
Hill, Shawn	California	M	B	
Hill, Michael	California	M	B	
Hill, Steven Douglas	Arkansas	M	W	
Hill, Darrell	Arkansas	M	W	
Hill, Walter	Alabama	M	B	
Hinchey, John	**Arizona**	**M**	**W**	

JOHN ALBERT HINCHEY

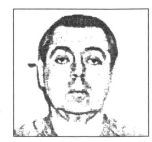

Race: Caucasian

Date of Birth: May 10, 1933

FACTS

On October 29, 1985, Hinchey and his common-law wife of 12 years, Marlyn Bechtel, got into an argument about a domestic matter. After Marlyn had gone into the living room to sleep, Hinchey came in with a gun he had purchased that day, and shot Marlyn four times. He then ran to the bedroom where Marlyn's 17-year-old daughter, Tammy, was sleeping. Tammy's infant son, Nicholas, was sleeping beside Tammy. Hinchey kicked in the door and shot Tammy in the face. Hinchey found out that Marlyn had run outside, and was going down the street. He caught her and hit her over the head with the gun until he broke the gun. Then he picked up a rock and hit her. When he returned to the house, he heard Tammy moaning. He hit her in the face with a glass bottle until it shattered. He then grabbed a butcher knife from the kitchen and stabbed her several times, leaving the blade protruding from her stomach. Tammy died, Nicholas was unhurt, and Marlyn survived. Hinchey originally pled guilty to avoid the death penalty, but the trial court set aside his plea at his request.

Start of Trial: October 14, 1987
Verdicts: October 28, 1987
Sentencing: December 8, 1987

Hines, Anthony	Tennessee	M	W	1
Hines, Gary	California	M	W	
Hinton, Anthony Ray	Alabama	M	B	
Hitchcock, James Ernest	Florida	M	W	
Hitchings, Keith	California	M	W	
Hochstein, Peter	Nebraska	M	W	
Hodge, Benny Lee	Kentucky	M	W	
Hoffman, Barry	Florida	M	W	
Hogan, Kenneth	Oklahoma	M	W	
Hogan, Michael Ray	Nevada	M	B	
Hogue, Jerry	Texas	M	W	
Hoke, Ronald Lee	Virginia	M	W	
Holden, Russell	North Carolina	M	B	
Holiday, Dallas	Georgia	M	B	
Holladay, Glenn	**Alabama**	**M**	**W**	

GLENN HOLLADAY

FACTS
Glenn Holladay was convicted on June 26, 1987 of the Aug. 25, 1986 killings of his ex-wife, Rebecca Ledbetter Holladay, 31; her boyfriend, William David Robinson, 25; and a neighbor, Larry D. Thomas, Jr., 16. His death sentence was upheld in May 1989 by the Alabama Supreme Court.

Holland, James	Utah	M	W
Holland, David Lee	Texas	M	W
Holland, William	Pennsylvania	M	W
Holland, Gerald	Mississippi	M	W
Holloway, Emmett	Texas	M	W
Holloway, Allen	Ohio	M	W

Holloway, Duayne	California	M	B	
Holman, Tafford	Illinois	M	B	
Holmes, James W	Arkansas	M	W	
Holoway, Arnold	Pennsylvania	M	B	
Holtan, Richard	Nebraska	M	W	1
Holton, Rudolph	Florida	M	B	
Hooker, John	Oklahoma	M	B	
Hooks, Danny	Ohio	M	W	
Hooks, Joseph	Alabama	M	W	
Hooper, Murray	Illinois	M	B	
Hooper, Harold	Florida	M	W	
Hooper, Murray	**Arizona**	**M**	**B**	**3**

•••

MURRAY HOOPER

Race: Black

Date of Birth: November 22, 1945

FACTS
During the late months of 1980, Robert Cruz decided to have William Patrick Redmond murdered. Mr. Redmond owned a printing business in partnership with Ron Lukezic, and Cruz's ultimate goal was to take over the printing business. To carry out the murder, Cruz hired William Bracy and Murray Hooper from Chicago and Edward Lonzo McCall, a former Phoenix police officer. On the evening of December 31, 1980, Bracy, Hooper, and McCall went to the Redmond home in Phoenix. Mr. Redmond, his wife Marilyn, and his mother-in-law Helen Phelps were at home preparing for a New Year's Eve party. The three men entered the house at gunpoint and forced the victims into the master bedroom. After taking jewelry and money, the killers bound and gagged the victims and made them lie face down on the bed. They then shot each victim in the head and also slashed Mr. Redmond's throat. Mr. Redmond and Mrs. Phelps died from their wounds, but Mrs. Redmond survived. Cruz and McCall were convicted of the murders following a joint trial. Cruz' conviction was reversed on appeal, but he was again convicted after two mistrials. Mrs. Lukezic was convicted in a separate trial, but, after obtaining a new trial, she was acquitted of all charges.

Start of Trial: November 4, 1982
Verdicts: December 24, 1982
Sentencing: February 11, 1983

•••

Hope, Edgar	Illinois	M	B
Hopkinson, Mark	Wyoming	M	W
Horsley, Edward	Alabama	M	B
Horton, Jimmy	Georgia	M	B
Horton, James	California	M	B
Hough, Kevin	Indiana	M	W
House, Paul Gregory	Tennessee	M	W

Death Row Inmates

House, Derrick	Illinois	M	B	
Housel, Tracey Lee	Georgia	M	W	
Houston, Richard	Tennessee	M	B	
Hovey, Richard	California	M		
Howard, Ronnie	**South Carolina**	**M**	**B**	

••

RONNIE HOWARD

FACTS

In June 1989, the U.S. Supreme Court rejected an appeal by Howard, a black, based on a claim that prosecutors wrongly excluded eight potential jurors from his trial because they were black. Howard and an accomplice were convicted in the August 1985 murder of Chinh Lee, a Vietnamese woman who authorities said had died of suffocation after a plastic bag had been tied around her head. Howard and another accomplice had been earlier convicted of the similar suffocation murder of another woman. In that case, Howard and his accomplice both received life sentences.

••

Howard, Samuel	Nevada	M	B	
Howard, Stanley	Illinois	M	B	
Howard, Albert C.	California	M	B	
Howard, Gary	California	M	W	
Howell, Michael	Oklahoma	M	W	
Hubbard, J.B.	Alabama	M	W	
Hudson, David Lee	Ohio	M	W	
Hudson, Timothy	Florida	M	B	
Huertas, Ediberto	Ohio	M	H	
Huff, Everett R.	North Carolina	M	W	
Huff, James	Florida	M	W	
Huffington, John	Maryland	M	W	
Huffman, Richard	Indiana	M	W	
Huffstetler, David	North Carolina	M	W	
Hughes, Billy George	Texas	M	W	
Hughes, Kevin	Pennsylvania	M	B	2
Hulsey, Dewayne	Arkansas	M	W	
Humphrey, Jackie	Oklahoma	M	W	
Hunt, Henry Lee	North Carolina	M	N	
Hunt, James	New Jersey	M	B	
Hunt, Flint	Maryland	M	B	
Hunter, Thomas	Oklahoma	M	W	
Hunter, Michael	California	M	W	
Hutchins, James	North Carolina	M	W	3-16-84
Hutton, Percy	Ohio	M	B	1
Ingram, Nicholas	Georgia	M	W	
Irick, Billy Ray	Tennessee	M	W	
Irvine, Michael	Florida	M	W	

Irving, John Buford	Mississippi	M	B	
Isaacs, Carl	Georgia	M	W	
Jackson, Tommy Ray	Texas	M	B	3
Jackson, Simon	Oklahoma	M	B	
Jackson, Andre	Ohio	M	B	
Jackson, Kevin	New Jersey	M	B	
Jackson, Donald	Indiana	M	W	
Jackson, Lawrence	Illinois	M	B	
Jackson, Clinton L.	Florida	M	B	
Jackson, Etheria	Florida	M	B	
Jackson, Douglas	Florida	M	B	
Jackson, Clarence	Florida	M	B	
Jackson, Nathaniel	Florida	M	B	
Jackson, Andrea H.	Florida	F	B	
Jackson, Carl	Florida	M	B	
Jackson, Ronald	Florida	M	B	1
Jackson, Michael	California	M	B	
Jackson, Earl	California	M	B	
Jacobs, Bruce	Texas	M	W	
Jacobs, Jesse DeWayne	Texas	M	W	
Jacobs, Eligaah	Florida	M	N	1
James, Terrence	Oklahoma	M	N	3
James, Antonio	Louisiana	M	B	
James, Davidson	Florida	M	B	
James, Steven	**Arizona**	**M**	**W**	

••

STEVEN CRAIG JAMES

Race: Caucasian

Date of Birth: May 24, 1958

FACTS

On November 16, 1981, Juan Maya picked up 14-year-old James Norton and made homosexual advances towards him. Norton rebuffed Maya, but suggested that he might find a more hospitable reception in a trailer belonging to Steven James. When Maya followed Norton into the trailer, James, Lawrence Libberton, and Norton took turns beating him. The three then forced Maya into the backseat of his own car and drove toward Salome, where James' parents owned some property with an abandoned mine shaft on it. En route, a police officer stopped them but Libberton threatened to kill Maya if he attempted to draw the officer's attention. After arriving at the Salome property around dawn, James ordered Maya to step up to the mine shaft. As Maya pleaded for his life, James fired directly at him from a distance of less than 5 feet. Maya charged James and tried to get the gun, so Libberton and Norton began striking Maya with large rocks and a board. After Maya fell to the ground, they fired point blank at him three more times. Nothing came out of the pistol because the barrel was fouled with debris. They then dragged Maya to the mine shaft and threw him in, dropping rocks and railroad ties on top of him. Norton pled to several charges

Death Row Inmates

as a juvenile and testified against Libberton and James.

Start of Trial: September 16, 1982
Verdict: October 4, 1982
Sentencing: November 23, 1982

●●●

Jamison, Derrick	Ohio	M	B	
Jarrell, David	Georgia	M	W	1
Jarrells, Jonathen	Georgia	M	W	
Jasper, Alfred	Pennsylvania	M	B	
Jeffers, Jimmy	Arizona	M	W	1
Jefferson, Lawrence	Georgia	M	B	
Jefferson, Albert	Alabama	M	B	
Jeffries, Patrick	Washington	M	W	
Jells, Reginald	Ohio	M	B	
Jenecka, Allen	Texas	M	W	
Jenkins, Leonard	Ohio	M	B	
Jenkins, Daniel	California	M	B	
Jennings, Bryan	Florida	M	W	
Jennings, Wilbur	California	M	B	
Jennings, Michael	California	M	W	
Jermyn, Frederic	Pennsylvania	M	W	
Jernigan, Joseph	Texas	M	W	
Jester, Willie Lee	Ohio	M	B	
Jimenez, Victor	Nevada	M	W	
Jimenez, Jesus	**Arizona**	**M**	**H**	**2**

●●●

JESUS JIMENEZ

Race: Hispanic

Date of Birth: September 7, 1969

FACTS

On November 30, 1986, Jimenez called 5-year-old Marisol Diaz and invited her over to his house. Jimenez claimed that voices told him to kill the girl, so he started to strangle her. After the girl was unconscious, Jimenez hid the girl under a bed when he heard someone knocking at the door. The little girl's brother and sister were at the door and asked about Marisol. Jimenez told them he had not seen her. He then heard the girl begin to cry, so he quickly got the children to go away. He returned Marisol and strangled her. He also stabbed her in the breasts, vagina, and rectum. He left the knife protruding from her mouth and throat. Jimenez cleaned up the house, placed the body in a garbage bag, and hid it in a trunk of an old car. He told police he had not seen the girl, and helped in the neighborhood search.

Start of Trial: September 23, 1987
Verdict: October 7, 1987
Sentencing: January 22, 1988

●●●

Death Row Inmates

Jimerson, Verneal	Illinois	M	B	
Johns, Stephen	Missouri	M	W	
Johnson, Gary	Texas	M	W	
Johnson, Edward Earl	Massachuetts	M	B	5-20-87
Johnson, Elliott	Texas	M	B	6-24-87
Johnson, Eddie	Texas	M	B	
Johnson, Dorsie	Texas	M	B	
Johnson, Curtis	Texas	M	B	
Johnson, Carl	Texas	M	B	
Johnson, Erskine Leroy	Tennessee	M	B	
Johnson, Donnie Edward	Tennessee	M	W	
Johnson, Walter	Tennessee	M	W	
Johnson, Cecil	Tennessee	M	B	1
Johnson, Richard	South Carolina	M	W	
Johnson, Robert Grady	Oklahoma	M	W	
Johnson, Malcolm	Oklahoma	M	B	
Johnson, Gary	Ohio	M	B	
Johnson, Walter	New Jersey	M	W	
Johnson, Samuel	Mississippi	M	B	
Johnson, Gregory Scott	Indiana	M	W	
Johnson, Mark	Illinois	M	B	
Johnson, Andrew	Illinois	M	B	
Johnson, Brian	Illinois	M	B	
Johnson, Milton	Illinois	M	B	
Johnson, Paul Beasley	Florida	M	W	
Johnson, Terrell	Florida	M	W	
Johnson, Larry Joe	Florida	M	W	
Johnson, Marvin	Florida	M	W	
Johnson, Laverne	California	M	B	
Johnson, Willie D.	California	M	B	
Johnson, James	California	M	B	
Johnson, Joe	California	M	B	1
Johnson, Anthony Keith	Alabama	M	W	
Johnston, David E.	Florida	M	W	
Joiner, Orien	Texas	M	W	
Jones, Willie Leroy	Virginia	M	B	
Jones, Arthur Lee	Alabama	M	B	3-21-86
Jones, Michael Steven	Texas	M	B	
Jones, Richard	Texas	M	W	
Jones, James Lee	Tennessee	M	B	
Jones, Donald Allen	South Carolina	M	B	
Jones, Damon	Pennsylvania	M	B	
Jones, Thomas	Pennsylvania	M	B	
Jones, James	Pennsylvania	M	B	
Jones, D.L.	Oklahoma	M	W	
Jones, William Q.	North Carolina	M	B	
Jones, William	Missouri	M	W	
Jones, Marvin	Missouri	M	W	

Death Row Inmates

Jones, Gregory M.	Mississippi	M	B	
Jones, Gregory	Maryland	M	B	1
Jones, Andrew Lee	Louisiana	M	B	
Jones, William	Illinois	M	B	
Jones, Andre	Illinois	M	B	
Jones, Brandon	Georgia	M	B	1
Jones, Randall Scott	Florida	M	W	
Jones, Leo	Florida	M	B	
Jones, Ronnie Lee	Florida	M	B	
Jones, Leslie	Florida	M	B	1
Jones, Jeffry	California	M	B	
Jones, Earl	California	M	B	
Jones, Troy	California	M	B	
Jones, Aaron	Alabama	M	B	
Jordan, Clarence	Texas	M	W	
Jordan, Richard	Mississippi	M	W	1
Joubert, John	Nebraska	M	W	
Juarez Rosales, Mariane	Texas	M	H	
Judge, Roger	Pennsylvania	M	B	
Judy, Steven	Indiana	M	W	3-9-81
Julius, Arthur	Alabama	M	B	
Justus, Buddy	Virginia	M	W	
Justus, Buddy	Georgia	M	W	3
Justus, Buddy	Florida	M	W	3
Karis, James	California	M	H	
Kaurish, Jay	California	M	W	
Keen, Michael Scott	Florida	M	W	
Keenan, Maurice	California	M	W	
Kelley, William	Florida	M	W	
Kelly, Carl E.	Texas	M	B	
Kelly, Horace	California	M	B	
Kemp, Emanuel	Texas	M	B	
Kenley, Kenneth	Missouri	M	W	
Kennedy, Stuart	Indiana	M	W	
Kennedy, Edward Dean	Florida	M	B	
Kennedy, Victor	Alabama	M	B	
Kidd, Leonard	Illinois	M	B	
Kight, Charles	Florida	M	W	
Kilgore, Bruce	Missouri	M	B	
Kills On Top, Vern	Montana	M	N	
Kills On Top, Lester	Montana	M	N	
Kimble, Eric	California	M	B	
Kindler, Joseph	Pennsylvania	M	W	
King, Leon Rutherford	Texas	M	B	
King, Terry	Tennessee	M	W	
King, Thomas	Tennessee	M	B	
King, Mack Arthur	Mississippi	M	B	
King, Derrick	Illinois	M	B	

King, Amos Lee	Florida	M	B	
Kinnamon, Raymond	Texas	M	W	
Kinsman, Ronald	Georgia	M	W	
Kipp, Martin	California	M	N	
Kirkpatrick, Frederick	Louisiana	M	W	
Kirkpatrick, William	California	M	B	
Kitchens, William	Texas	M	W	
Knighton, Ernest	Louisiana	M	B	10-30-84
Knox, James Roy	Texas	M	W	
Koedatich, James	New Jersey	M	W	1
Kokal, Gregory	Florida	M	W	
Kokoraleis, Andrew	Illinois	M	W	
Koon, Paul	South Carolina	M	W	1
Koon, Raymond	Florida	M	W	
Kordenbrock, Paul	Kentucky	M	W	
Kornahrens, Fred	South Carolina	M	W	
Kubat, Robert	Illinois	M	W	1
Kuenzel, William	Alabama	M	W	
Kunkle, Troy	Texas	M	W	
Kyles, Curtis	Louisiana	M	B	
LaFever, Lloyd	Oklahoma	M	W	
LaGrand, Walter	**Arizona**	**M**	**W**	

••

WALTER BURNHART LaGRAND

Race: Mixed

Date of Birth: January 26, 1962

FACTS
Shortly after 8:00 on the morning of January 7, 1982, Walter LaGrand and his brother, Karl, entered the Valley National Bank in Marana. Armed with a toy pistol, Karl tried to force Ken Hartsock, the 63-year-old branch manager, to open the vault. Hartsock couldn't open the vault because he had only half of the combination. The brothers then forced Hartsock and Dawn Lopez, a bank clerk, into Hartsock's office and bound them. After threatening Hartsock with a letter opener, the brothers began beating him. Hartsock died from 24 stab wounds. Karl and Walter tried to kill Lopez by stabbing her six times, then fled the bank.

Start of Trial: January 31, 1984
Verdict: February 17, 1984
Sentencing: December 14, 1984

••

LaGrand, Karl	**Arizona**	**M**	**W**	

••

KARL HINZE LaGRAND

Race: Mixed

Date of Birth: October 20, 1963

FACTS

Shortly after 8:00 on the morning of January 7, 1982, Karl LaGrand and his brother, Walter, entered the Valley National Bank in Marana. Armed with a toy pistol, Karl tried to force Ken Hartsock, the 63-year-old branch manager, to open the vault. Hartsock couldn't open the vault because he had only half of the combination. The brothers then forced Hartsock and Dawn Lopez, a bank clerk, into Hartsock's office and bound them. After threatening Hartsock with a letter opener, the brothers began beating him. Hartsock died from 24 stab wounds. Karl and Walter tried to kill Lopez by stabbing her six times, then fled the bank.

Start of Trial: January 31, 1984
Verdict: February 17, 1984
Sentencing: December 14, 1984

●●

Lackey, Clarence	Texas	M	W	
Ladner, Jeffrey	Mississippi	M	W	
Lafferty, Ron	Utah	M	W	
Laird, Richard	**Pennsylvania**	**M**	**W**	

●●

RICHARD LAIRD

FACTS.

Laird, 25, and an accomplice, Frank Chester, 21, were sentenced to die for the murder of Anthony Milano, a 26-year-old gay they picked up in a bar in December of 1987. Chester, who Laird said framed him and who he called a psychopath and a liar, admitted shoving Milano to the ground, but said it was Laird who cut Milano's throat repeatedly with a box-cutting knife. According to trial testimony, the two left the bar with Milano in his car, forced him to drive them to a location where they could buy drugs, then attacked and murdered him because he was gay.

●●

Lamb, John Michael	Texas	M	W	
Lamb, Wilburn	Florida	M	W	2
Lambert, James	Pennsylvania	M	B	
Lambert, Robert	Oklahoma	M	W	
Lambright, Joe	Arizona	M	W	
Lambrix, Cary	Florida	M	W	
Landry, Raymond	Texas	M	B	12-13-88

Landrum, Lawrence	Ohio	M	W	
Lane, Harold	Texas	M	W	
Laney, Thomas Gerald	Tennessee	M	W	
Lang, Kenneth	California	M	W	
Lanier, Johnny	Mississippi	M	B	1
Lanier, Arthur Ray	Mississippi	M	B	
Lankford, Mark	Idaho	M	W	
Lankford, Brian	Idaho	M	W	
Lara, Mario	Florida	M	H	1
Larette, Anthony	Missouri	M	W	
Lark, Robert	Pennsylvania	M	B	
Lashley, Frederick	Missouri	M	B	2
Lauti, Aua	Texas	M	A	
Lawrence, Jeffrey	Ohio	M	W	
Laws, Wayne Alan	North Carolina	M	W	
Laws, Leonard	Missouri	M	W	
Lawson, Jerry	Ohio	M	W	
Lawson, David	North Carolina	M	W	
Leatherwood, Alfred	Mississippi	M	B	
Leavitt, Richard	Idaho	M	W	
Lecroy, Cleo	Florida	M	W	2
Lee, Percy	Pennsylvania	M	B	
Lee, Tracy	Louisiana	M	B	
Lee, Larry	Georgia	M	W	
Lee, Jessie	Georgia	M	B	
Legare, Andrew	Georgia	M	W	1
Leger, William	Illinois	M	W	
Lego, Donald	Illinois	M	W	
Leisure, David	Missouri	M	W	
Lesko, John	Pennsylvania	M	W	
Lewis, Andre	Texas	M	B	
Lewis, David Lee	Texas	M	W	
Lewis, Reginald	Pennsylvania	M	B	
Lewis, Lawrence	Florida	M	W	
Lewis, Robert	California	M	B	
Libberton, Lawrence	**Arizona**	**M**	**W**	

••

LAWRENCE KEITH LIBBERTON

Race: Caucasian

Date of Birth: February 26, 1961

FACTS

On November 16, 1981, Juan Maya picked up 14-year-old James Norton and made homosexual advances towards him. Norton rebuffed Maya, but suggested that he might find a more hospitable reception in a trailer belonging to Steven James. When Maya followed Norton into the trailer, James, Lawrence Libberton, and Norton took turns beating him. The three then forced Maya into the backseat of his own car and drove toward Salome, where James parents owned some property with an abandoned mine shaft on it. En route, a police officer stopped them but Libberton threatened to kill Maya if he attempted to draw the officer's attention. After arriving at the Salome property around dawn, James ordered Maya to step up to the mine shaft. As Maya pleaded for his life, James fired directly at him from a distance of less than 5 feet. Maya charged James and tried to get the gun, so Libberton and Norton began striking Maya with large rocks and a board. After Maya fell to the ground, they fired point blank at him three more times. Nothing came out of the pistol because the barrel was fouled with debris. They then dragged Maya to the mine shaft and threw him in, dropping rocks and railroad ties on top of him. Norton pled to several charges as a juvenile and testified against Libberton and James.

Start of Trial: June 23, 1982
Verdict: June 30, 1982
Sentencing: October 25, 1982

●●

Lightbourne, Ian	Florida	M	B	
Liles, Mark	Oklahoma	M	W	
Lincecum, Kevin	Texas	M	B	
Lindsey, Tyronne	Louisiana	M	B	
Lindsey, Michael	Alabama	M	B	
Lingar, Stanley	Missouri	M	W	
Lipham, William	Georgia	M	W	
Little, William Hamilton	Texas	M	W	
Livaditis, Steven	California	M	W	
Livingston, Charles	Texas	M	B	
Lloyd, Oscar	North Carolina	M	B	
Lockett, Carl	Mississippi	M	B	
Lockhart, Michael	Texas	M	W	
Logan, Ronald	Pennsylvania	M	B	
Lonchar, Larry Grant	Georgia	M	W	
Long, David Martin	Texas	M	W	
Long, Michael Edward	Oklahoma	M	W	
Long, Ronald	New Jersey	M	B	
Long, Robert	**Florida**	**M**	**W**	1

●●

ROBERT LONG

FACTS

Robert Joe Long, 35, a former x-ray technician, was arrested in November 1984 and confessed to the May, 1984 murder of Michelle Denise Simms, 22, and nine other killings. Simms' body was found bound with rope and nearly decapitated from a throat slashing. In that case, Long pleaded guilty to first degree murder, kidnapping and sexual battery, and was sentenced to be electrocuted. In June 1988, however, Florida's Supreme Court reversed the sentence, requiring that a new sentencing hearing be held.

●●

Lopez, Manual	Nevada	M	H
Lopez, Eduardo	Florida	M	H
Lopez, Samuel	**Arizona**	**M**	**H**

••

SAMUEL VILLEGAS LOPEZ

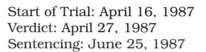

Race: Mexican-American

Date of Birth: June 30, 1962

FACTS

On October 29, 1986, Lopez broke into the home of 59-year-old Estafana Holmes. He raped her, beat her, and then murdered her. Her body was found nude from the waist down, with her pajama bottoms tied around her eyes. A lace scarf was crammed tightly into her mouth. She had been stabbed 23 times, and her throat was cut.

Start of Trial: April 16, 1987
Verdict: April 27, 1987
Sentencing: June 25, 1987

••

Lord, Brian Keith	Washington	M	W	
Lorraine, Charles	Ohio	M	W	
Losada, Davis	Texas	M	H	
Lott, Gregory	Ohio	M	B	
Lowenfield, Leslie	Louisiana	F	B	4-13-88
Lowery, Terry	Indiana	M	W	
Lowery, James	Indiana	M	W	
Loyd, Alvin	Louisiana	M	W	
Lucas, Henry Lee	Texas	M	W	
Lucas, Cecil	South Carolina	M	W	
Lucas, John	Illinois	M	W	
Lucas, Harold	Florida	M	W	
Lucas, Larry	California	M	W	
Lucero, Philip	California	M	H	1
Lucky, Darnell	California	M	B	
Luke, Johnny	Alabama	M	B	
Lusk, Bobby	Florida	M	W	1
Ly, Cam	Pennsylvania	M	A	
Lynch, Gregory	North Carolina	M	B	
Lynn, Frederick	Alabama	M	B	2
Macias, Frederico	Texas	M	H	
Mack, Larry	Illinois	M	B	
Mackabee, Frank	Mississippi	M	B	
Mackall, Tony	Virginia	M	B	
Madden, Robert	Texas	M	W	
Madej, Gregory	Illinois	M	W	

Death Row Inmates

Magwood, Billy Joe	Alabama	M	B	
Magwood, Kenneth	Alabama	M	B	
Mahaffey, Reginald	Illinois	M	B	
Mahaffey, Jerry	Illinois	M	B	
Maharaj, Krishna	Florida	M	A	
Mak, Kwan	Washington	M	A	
Mallett, Jerome	Missouri	M	B	1
Malone, Kelvin	Missouri	M	B	3
Malone, Kelvin	California	M	B	
Mann, Fletcher	Texas	M	W	
Mann, Anthony	Oklahoma	M	W	
Mann, Larry	Florida	M	W	1
Mapes, David	Ohio	M	B	
Marek, John R.	Florida	M	W	
Marlow, James	**Arizona**	**M**	**W**	

●●●

JAMES WILLIAM MARLOW

Race: Caucasian

Date of Birth: July 29, 1943

FACTS

On August 26, 1985, Marlow and Roger Cannon met Joseph John Mazzocco at a Las Vegas Casino. Mazzocco informed the pair that he just won a "6 spot" on a Keno ticket. Marlow plotted to get Mazzocco drunk and then rob him. After stopping at several bars, they decided to go either to a brothel or a friend's place near Hoover Dam. Several miles past the dam, Marlow stopped the car, bound Mazzocco's hands and feet with shoelaces, and pushed him down an embankment. He then struck Mazzocco with a large rock, and stole an automatic bank card from him. Cannon pled guilty to attempted aggravated robbery, and was sentenced to 4 years in prison. Cannon testified against Marlow.

Start of Trial: November 24, 1986
Verdict: December 3, 1986
Sentencing: February 27, 1987

●●●

Marlowe, Hugh	Kentucky	M	W
Marquez, Mario	Texas	M	H
Marquez, Howard	Oklahoma	M	N
Marquez, Gonzalo	California	M	H
Marshall, Jerome	Pennsylvania	M	B
Marshall, Robert	**New Jersey**	**M**	**W**

●●●

ROBERT MARSHALL

FACTS.

Marshall, convicted of the 1986 murder of his wife, Maria, killed her to collect on a sizeable insurance policy so he and his then lover, Sarann Kraushaar could live together, according to trial testimony. Kraushaar told the trial jury that Marshall had discussed with her his plans to kill his wife.

●●

Marshall, Sam	California	M	B
Marshall, Ryan	California	M	W
Marshall, George	California	M	B
Martin, Ernest	Ohio	M	B
Martin, Daryl	Louisiana	M	B
Martin, Nollie	Florida	M	W
Martin, James	Alabama	M	W
Martinez, Gilberto	Oklahoma	M	H
Martinez-Villareal, Ramon	**Arizona**	**M**	**H**

●●

RAMON MARTINEZ-VILLAREAL

Race: Hispanic

Date of Birth: February 12, 1946

FACTS

On the weekend of October 9-11, 1982, Martinez-Villareal and an accomplice burglarized the Tumacacori home of Sarah Bailey, taking rifles and ammunition. On their way back to Mexico with the stolen goods, Martinez and his accomplice came upon James Thomas McGrew and Fernando Estrada-Babichi, who were grading a Salerno Ranch road with a tractor. Martinez and his accomplice decided to rob the two men of their money and pickup truck, and waited overnight for them to return. When McGrew and Estrada returned on October 14, Martinez killed and robbed them with the rifles stolen from the Bailey residence.

TRIAL COURT PROCEEDINGS

Presiding Judge: Roberto C. Montiel
Prosecutors: Robert Bruce Stirling, II and Michael Alfred
Defense Attorney: William Rothstein

Start of Trial: April 19, 1983
Verdict: April 27, 1983
Sentencing: May 20, 1983

●●

Mason, Oscar	Florida	M	B	
Mason, David	California	M	W	
Mason, Morris	Virginia	M	B	6-25-85
Mata, Ramon	Texas	M	H	
Mata, Luis	**Arizona**	**M**	**H**	

Death Row Inmates

•••

LUIS MORINE MATA

Race: Mexican-American

Date of Birth: July 10, 1951

FACTS
On the evening of March 10, 1977, Mata and his brother, Alonzo, were at their Phoenix apartment with Debra Lopez. When Ms. Lopez got up to leave, Luis Mata stopped her and told her they were going to rape her. The brothers began beating her with a rifle and their fists, and each raped her. They then drove the unconscious victim away from the apartment and Luis killed her by cutting her throat with a knife, nearly decapitating her in the process. Alonzo Mata was convicted for the murder of Ms. Lopez, but received a life sentence.

Start of Trial: October 4, 1977
Verdict: October 17, 1977
Sentencing: December 9, 1977
Resentencing: December 8, 1978

•••

| Mathenia, Charles Lee | Missouri | M | W |
| **Mathers, Jimmy Lee** | **Arizona** | **M** | **W** |

•••

JIMMY LEE MATHERS

Race: Caucasian

Date of Birth: November 27, 1946

FACTS
Fred Robinson and Susan Hill lived together for 11 years. Beginning in 1983, Susan made a number of efforts to leave Robinson, but he always forced her to return. On June 8, 1987, Robinson believed that Susan was staying in Yuma with her parents, Ralph and Sterleen Hill. Robinson persuaded his friends, Mathers and Theodore Washington, to go to Yuma with him, telling them that they were going to rip off a drug dealer. The three men loaded Robinson's car with weapons and drove to Yuma. They arrived at the Hills' home around midnight. Mathers and Washington entered the house, forced Mr. and Mrs. Hill to lie down on their bedroom floor and tied them up. The men demanded money and Washington went through the Hills' belongings. Mathers then fired his shotgun into the backs of the Hills. Sterleen Hill died from her wounds but Ralph Hill survived.

Start of Trial: December 1, 1987
Verdict: December 15, 1987
Sentencing: January 13, 1988

•••

Martin, David	Louisiana	M	W	1-4-85
Mathis, James	Georgia	M	B	1
Matson, John, Jr.	Texas	M	B	
Matson, Michael	Tennessee	M	W	
Matthews, Earl	South Carolina	M	B	
Matthews, David	Kentucky	M	W	
Mattson, Michael	California	M	B	
Maurer, Donald	Ohio	M	W	
Maxwell, Fred	Pennsylvania	M	B	
Maxwell, Andrew	Illinois	M	B	
Maxwell, Chester	Florida	M	B	
May, Justin Lee	Texas	M	W	
Mayfield, Dennis	California	M	B	
Mayfield, Demetrie	California	M	B	
Mayhue, Fred	Pennsylvania	M	W	
Maynard, Anson	North Carolina	M	N	
Mayo, Randy	Texas	M	W	
Mays, Nobel	Texas	M	W	
Mazzen, John	Nevada	M	W	
McBride, Michael	Texas	M	W	
McCall, Edward	**Arizona**	**M**	**W**	

●●●

EDWARD LONZO McCALL

Race: Caucasian

Date of Birth: October 4, 1941

FACTS

In December, 1980, McCall, a former Phoenix police officer, was hired by Robert Charles Cruz to murder William Patrick Redmond. McCall was to receive $10,000 for his work, and Cruz intended to take over a printing business owned by Mr. Redmond and Ron Lukezic. On the evening of December 31, 1980, McCall and two other hired killers, William Bracy and Murray Hooper, went to the Redmond home in Phoenix. Mr. Redmond, his wife Marilyn, and his mother-in-law Helen Phelps were at home preparing for a New Year's Eve party. The three men entered the house at gunpoint and forced the victims into the master bedroom. After taking jewelry and money, the killers bound and gagged the victims and made them lie face down on the bed. They then shot each victim in the head and also slashed Mr. Redmond's throat. Mr. Redmond and Mrs. Phelps died from their wounds, but Mrs. Redmond survived. Cruz and McCall were convicted of the murders following a joint trial. Cruz' conviction was reversed on appeal; he was convicted again after two mistrials. Joyce Lukezic (the wife of Ron Lukezic) was convicted in a separate trial, but, after obtaining a new trial, she was acquitted of all charges. Bracy and Hooper were also convicted following a joint trial.

Start of Trial: November 9, 1981
Verdicts: December 10, 1981
Sentencing: January 11, 1982 —Resentencing: January 30, 1986

●●●

McCarver, Ernest	North Carolina	M	W	
McClain, Robert	California	M	W	
McCord, J.B.	Tennessee	M	W	
McCormick, Michael	Tennessee	M	W	
McCorquodale, Timothy	Georgia	M	W	9-21-87
McCoy, Stephen	Texas	M	W	
McCrae, James	Florida	M	B	
McCullom, Phillip	Indiana	M	B	
McDonald, Sam	Missouri	M	B	
McDonnell, Michael	Oregon	M	W	
McDougald, Anthony	New Jersey	M	B	
McDougall, Mike	North Carolina	M	W	
McDowell, Charles	California	M	W	
McFadden, Jerry	Texas	M	W	
McGahee, Earl	Alabama	M	B	
McGee, Jewel R.	Texas	M	B	
McGowen, Roger Wayne	Texas	M	B	
McKague, Kenneth	Nevada	M	W	
McKay, David Wayne	Texas	M	W	
McKay, William	Tennessee	M	B	
McKenna, Patrick	Nevada	M	W	
McKenzie, Duncan	Montana	M	W	
McKinney, Randy	Idaho	M	W	
McKoy, Dock	North Carolina	M	B	
McLaughlin, Elton	North Carolina	M	B	
McMillan, Richard	Missouri	M	W	
McMillan, Walter	Alabama	M	B	
McMurtrey, Jasper	**Arizona**	**M**	**W**	

••

JASPER NEWTON McMURTREY

Race: Caucasian

Date of Birth: October 29, 1951

FACTS
On August 10, 1979, McMurtrey became involved in a fight at the Ranch House Bar in Tucson. McMurtrey was a biker and the Ranch House was a biker hangout. Three men wanted a piece of McMurtrey and invited him outside. McMurtrey claimed he did not want any trouble so he armed himself for self-defense. He claimed that one of the victims pointed a gun at him so he opened fire, killing Barry Collins and Albert Hughes, and wounding the third man.

Start of Trial: July 1, 1981
Verdicts: July 13, 1981
Sentencing: August 28, 1981
Resentencing: November 17, 1983

Death Row Inmates

April 30, 1985 (second resentencing)
●●●

McNair, Nathaniel	Pennsylvania	M	B	
McNeil, Leroy	North Carolina	M	B	
McNish, David	Tennessee	M	W	
McPeters, Ronald	California	M	B	
McQueen, Harold	Kentucky	M	W	
McWilliams, James	Alabama	M	B	
Meanes, James R.	Texas	M	B	
Medina, Pedro	Florida	M	B	
Medina, Teofilo	California	M	H	
Medrano, Angel	Arizona	M	H	
Meeks, Douglas	Florida	M	B	
Melendez, Juan Roberto	Florida	M	H	
Melson, Hugh	Tennessee	M	W	
Melton, James	California	M	B	
Memro, Harold	California	M	W	
Mendoza, Manuel	California	M	H	
Mendyk, Todd	Florida	M	W	
Mercer, George Tiny	Missouri	M	W	1-6-89
Messer, James	Georgia	M	W	7-28-88
Messiah, Keith	Louisiana	M	B	
Meyer, Jeffrey	North Carolina	M	W	
Michael, John	Florida	M	W	1
Mickey, Douglas	California	M	W	
Mickle, Denny	California	M	B	
Middleton, Frank	South Carolina	M	B	
Middleton, William	Florida	M	W	1
Mikell, William	Pennsylvania	M	B	
Mikenas, Mark	Florida	M	W	1
Miller, Donald A.	Texas	M	W	
Miller, David	Tennessee	M	W	
Miller, Robert Lee	Oklahoma	M	B	
Miller, Michael	Georgia	M	B	
Miller, Donald	California	M	B	
Miller, Eddie Lee	Arkansas	M	B	
Miller-El, Thomas Joe	Texas	M	B	
Mills, James E.	Ohio	M	B	
Mills, Ralph	Maryland	M	W	1
Mills, John	Florida	M	B	
Mills, Gregory	Florida	M	B	
Milner, Lynn	California	M	B	1
Milton, Charles	Texas	M	B	6-25-85
Mincey, Terry	Georgia	M	W	
Mincey, Bryan	California	M	W	
Miniel, Peter	Texas	M	H	
Minnick, Robert	Mississippi	M	W	

Death Row Inmates

Minnick, William	Indiana	M	W	
Miranda, Reyes	Oregon	M	H	
Miranda, Roberto	Nevada	M	H	
Miranda, Adam	California	M	H	
Mitcham, Stephan	California	M	B	
Mitchell, Billy	Georgia	M	B	9-1-87
Mitchell, Gerald Lee	Texas	M	B	
Mitchell, Andrew L.	Texas	M	B	
Mitchell, Willie	Florida	M	B	
Modden, Willie Max	Texas	M	B	
Moen, Ronald H.	Oregon	M	W	
Monroe, Casey Jack	North Carolina	M	B	
Monroe, Ronald	Louisiana	M	B	
Montez, Marco	Oregon	M	H	
Montgomery, William	Ohio	M	B	
Montgomery, Ulece	Illinois	M	B	
Montiel, Richard	California	M	H	
Montoya, Irineo	Texas	M	H	
Montoya, Ramon	Texas	M	H	
Moon, Larry Eugene	Georgia	M	W	
Mooney, Nelson W.	Texas	M	W	
Moore, Alvin	Louisiana	M	B	6-9-87
Moore, Bobby James	Texas	M	B	
Moore, Tyrone	Pennsylvania	M	B	
Moore, Dewey	Oklahoma	M	W	
Moore, Scott Lee	Oklahoma	M	W	
Moore, George	North Carolina	M	B	1
Moore, Samuel Leon	New Jersey	M	B	
Moore, Randolph	Nevada	M	W	1
Moore, Carey	Nebraska	M	W	1
Moore, Brian Keith	Kentucky	M	W	
Moore, Richard	Indiana	M	B	
Moore, Carzell	Georgia	M	B	1
Moore, William Neal	Georgia	M	B	1
Moore, Charles	California	M	B	
Moormann, Robert Henry	**Arizona**	**M**	**W**	

• •

ROBERT HENRY MOORMANN

Race: Caucasian

Date of Birth: June 4, 1968

FACTS
While serving a sentence of 9 years to life at the Arizona State Prison in Florence, Moormann was given a 72-hour compassionate furlough to visit with his mother. The two stayed at the Blue Mist Motel in Florence. On January 13, 1984, Moormann bound and gagged his mother

and then strangled and stabbed her. Moormann chopped the body into many parts and disposed of them in dumpsters throughout Florence.

Start of Trial: March 26, 1985
Verdict: April 4, 1985
Sentencing: May 7, 1985

••

Morales, Salvador	Pennsylvania	M	H	
Morales, Alfred	Ohio	M	N	
Morales, Michael	California	M	H	
Moran, Willard	Pennsylvania	M	W	
Moran, Richard	Nevada	M	W	
Moreland, James	Texas	M	W	
Moreland, Samuel	Ohio	M	B	
Moreno, Elisio	Texas	M	H	
Moreno, Jose	Texas	M	H	
Morin, Stephen Peter	Texas	M	W	3-13-85
Morgan, Derrick	Illinois	M	B	
Morgan, Samuel	Illinois	M	B	
Morgan, Alfonso	Georgia	M	B	1
Morgan, Floyd	Florida	M	W	1
Morris, Timothy	Tennessee	M	W	
Morris, Kelvin	Pennsylvania	M	B	
Morris, Bruce	California	M	W	
Morris Jr., George	Florida	M	B	
Morrison, Earnest	**Georgia**	**M**	**W**	

•••

EARNEST MORRISON

FACTS

Morrison was convicted of the 1987 robbery, rape and strangulation of 54-year-old Mary Edna Griffin, who was related to Morrison by marriage. Morrison, who was staying with Griffin and her husband at the time of the killing, had escaped just four days earlier from a Georgia detention center where he was being held on charges involving the rape and robbery of another woman. At the time of the trial, Morrison asked the trial judge to impose the death sentence, calling it the right punishment.

•••

Morrison, Jesse	Alabama	M	B	
Moser, Leon	Pennsylvania	M	W	
Motley, Jeffrey	Texas	M	W	
Muehleman, Jeffrey A.	Florida	M	W	
Muhammad, Askari	Florida	M	B	1
Mulligan, Joseph	Georgia	M	B	5-15-87
Mulligan, Ronnie Gayle	Nevada	M	W	
Muniz, Pedro Cruz	Texas	M	H	

Death Row Inmates

Munson, Adolf	Oklahoma	M	B
Murphy, James	Federal	M	B
Murphy, Craig	Pennsylvania	M	B
Murphy, Joseph	Ohio	M	W
Murray, Robert "Tony"	Missouri	M	B
Murry, Paul	Alabama	M	B
Murtishaw, David	California	M	W
Musgrove, Donnis	Alabama	M	W
Musgrove, Phillip	Alabama	M	W
Myers, Venson	California	M	B
Napier, Carl	Texas	M	W
Narvaiz, Leopoldo	Texas	M	H
Nash, Viva Leroy	**Arizona**	**M**	**W**

••

VIVA LEROY NASH

Race: Caucasian

Date of Birth: September 10, 1915

FACTS

While serving two consecutive life sentences for murder and robbery in Utah, Nash escaped. Three weeks later on November 3, 1982, he entered a coin shop in north Phoenix, demanded money from an employee, Greggory West, and then shot Mr. West three times with a .357 Colt trooper. Another employee, Susan McCullough, was in the line of fire but was not hit. As Nash fled, the proprietor of a nearby shop pointed a gun at him and told him to stop. Nash grabbed the weapon and the two men struggled over it. Police officers soon arrived and arrested Nash.

Start of Trial: May 25, 1983 (submission)
Verdict: May 25, 1983
Sentencing: June 27, 1983

••

Nave, Emmett	Missouri	M	N	
Neal, Howard	Mississippi	M	W	
Neal, John	Illinois	M	W	
Neelley, Judith	Alabama	F	W	
Neely, Charles	California	M	W	
Neill, Jay Wesley	Oklahoma	M	W	
Nelson, Marlin	Texas	M	W	
Nelson, Gary	Georgia	M	B	
Nelson, David	Alabama	M	W	
Nestead, Stephen	Oregon	M	W	
Nethery, Stephen	Texas	M	W	
Neushafer, Jimmy	Nevada	M	W	
Nevius, Thomas	Nevada	M	B	
Newland, Robert	Georgia	M	W	
Newlon, Rayfield	Missouri	M	B	1

Death Row Inmates

Newstead, Norman Lee	Oklahoma	M	W	
Newton, Frances	**Texas**	**F**	**B**	

••

FRANCES NEWTON

FACTS
Newton, at 24 the youngest woman on Texas' death row, was convicted of murdering her 23-year-old husband, seven-year-old son and 21-month-old daughter for insurance proceeds on April 7, 1987.

••

Nguyen, Tuan	Oklahoma	M	A	
Nibert, Billy Ray	Florida	M	W	
Nichols, Joseph B.	Texas	M	B	
Nicks, Harry	Alabama	M	B	
Nicolaus, Robert Henry	California	M	W	
Nitz, Richard	Illinois	M	W	
Nixon, John	Mississippi	M	W	
Nixon, Joe Elton	Florida	M	B	
Nobles, Jonathan	Texas	M	W	
Noguera, William	California	M	H	
Noland, John	North Carolina	M	W	
Nolte, Michael	Oklahoma	M	W	
Norris, Michael	Texas	M	B	
Nowitzke, Frederick	Florida	M	W	
Nuckols, Kenneth	Oklahoma	M	W	
Oats, Sonny Boy	Florida	M	B	
Odle, Thomas	Illinois	M	W	
Odle, James	California	M	W	
Ogelsby, Walter	New Jersey	M	B	
Olausen, John	Nevada	M	W	
Olinger, Perry	Illinois	M	W	
Oliver, John Wesley	North Carolina	M	B	
Orange, Leroy	Illinois	M	B	
Orndorff, Michael	Arkansas	M	W	1
Ortiz, Ignacio	Arizona	M	H	
Osband, Lance	California	M	B	
Otey, Harold	Nebraska	M	B	
Ottwell, Clarence	Missouri	M	W	
Owen, Duane	Florida	M	W	
Owens, Gaile	Tennessee	F	W	4
Owens, Alvin	South Carolina	M	W	
Owens, Robin	Illinois	M	B	
Oxford, Richard	Missouri	M	W	
O'Bryan, Ronald	Texas	M	W	3-31-84
O'Callaghan, John	**Florida**	**M**	**W**	

Death Row Inmates

••

JOHN O'CALLAGHAN

FACTS

In April 1989, Florida's supreme court ordered a new sentencing hearing for O'Callaghan. The court ruled that the trial judge erred in failing to instruct jurors that they could have considered as a mitigating factor the lighter sentence and immunity given to others involved in the Aug. 20, 1980 slaying of Gerald Vick. Vick was beaten, shot twice in the head and left in a ditch by O'Callaghan and others in a dispute over an $8,000 gambling debt.

••

Name	State			
O'Dell, Joseph	Virginia	M	W	
O'Guinn, Kenneth W.	Tennessee	M	W	
O'Neal, Robert	Missouri	M	W	
O'Neil, John	Colorado	M	W	
O'Rourke, Michael	Arkansas	M	W	
O'Shea, Ronald	Pennsylvania	M	W	
Padilla, Daniel	Nevada	M	W	
Page, Jerry	Georgia	M	W	1
Palmer, Charles	Nebraska	M	W	
Palmes, Timothy	Florida	M	W	11-8-84
Paradis, Donald	Idaho	M	W	
Pardo, Manuel	Florida	M	H	
Parker, Henry	Oklahoma	M	W	
Parker, Byron	Georgia	M	W	
Parker, Robert Lacey	Florida	M	W	1
Parker, J.B.	Florida	M	B	
Parker, Norman	Florida	M	B	
Parker, William Frank	Arkansas	M	W	
Parks, Robin Leroy	Oklahoma	M	B	
Parkus, Steven J.	Missouri	M	W	
Pasch, John	Illinois	M	W	
Paster, James	Texas	M	W	
Patillo, Keith	Georgia	M	W	
Patten, Robert	Florida	M	W	1
Patterson, Raymond	South Carolina	M	B	
Payne, Joseph	Virginia	M	W	
Payne, Edward	Texas	M	B	
Payne, Pervis	Tennessee	M	B	
Payne, Randy Joe	North Carolina	M	W	
Payton, William	California	M	W	
Paz, Federico	Idaho	M	H	
Pecoraro, John	Illinois	M	W	
Peede, Robert	Florida	M	W	
Peek, David	Georgia	M	B	
Pelligrini, David	Nevada	M	W	
Pennington, Frank	New Jersey	M	W	

Penry, Johnny Paul	Texas	M	W	
Pensinger, Brett	California	M	W	
Pentecost, David	Florida	M	W	
Peoples, John	Alabama	M	W	
Perdgen, Wes	Nevada	M	W	
Perez, Manual J.	Texas	M	H	
Perez, Domingo	Illinois	M	H	
Perillo, Pamela	**Texas**	**F**	**W**	

PAMELA PERILLO

FACTS

Perillo, 30, a former Houston barmaid, was convicted of participating in the robbery-killing of 26 year old Bob Skeens of Houma, La.

Perry, Arthur	New Jersey	M	B	
Perry, Michael Owen	Louisiana	M	W	
Perry, Eugene	Arkansas	M	W	
Petary, Donald	Missouri	M	W	
Peterkin, Otis	Pennsylvania	M	B	
Peterson, Derrick	Virginia	M	B	
Petrocelli, Tracy	Nevada	M	W	
Phillips, Clifford X.	Texas	M	B	
Phillips, John Paul	Illinois	M	W	
Phillips, Harry	Florida	M	B	
Phillips, Richard	California	M	W	1
Pickens, Charles	Arkansas	M	B	
Pierce, Anthony Leroy	Texas	M	B	
Pinch, Michael	North Carolina	M	W	
Pinholster, Scott	California	M	W	
Pinkerton, Jay	Texas	M	W	5-15-86
Pinkney, Bobby Joe	Mississippi	M	B	
Pitsonbarger, Jimmy	Illinois	M	W	
Pitts, Darryl Lee	New Jersey	M	W	
Pizzuto, Gerald	Idaho	M	W	
Plath, John	South Carolina	M	W	
Plemmons, Jerry	South Carolina	M	W	1
Poe, David	Tennessee	M	W	
Poggi, Joseph	California	M	H	
Poindexter, Dewaine	Ohio	M	B	
Poland, Michael	**Arizona**	**M**	**W**	

MICHAEL KENT POLAND

Race: Caucasian

Date of Birth: June 11, 1940

FACTS

On the morning of May 24, 1977, two Purolator guards, Russell Dempsey and Cecil Newkirk, left Phoenix in an armored van on their scheduled run to banks in Prescott, Sedona and Flagstaff. At the Bumblebee Road exit on Interstate-17, the van was stopped by the Polands, who were disguised as highway patrolmen and were driving a car with an emergency light bar on the top. The Polands took the guards captive, removed close to $300,000 in cash from the van, and left the scene. Around 6:00 a.m. on May 25, 1977, authorities found the abandoned Purolator van near the Bumblebee Road exit. That same morning, Michael Poland rented a boat at the Lake Mead marina. He then piloted the boat to a little-used landing where he met his brother. The Polands put the guards into canvas bags, took them across the lake and dumped them into the water. Three weeks later, the bodies surfaced in a cove on the Nevada side of the lake.

The Polands were convicted in federal court on robbery and kidnapping charges arising from these events. Their trial in state court on the murder charges followed.

Start of Trial: October 23, 1979 (first trial)
October 18, 1982 (second trial)
Verdicts: November 24, 1979 (first trial)
November 18, 1982 (second trial)
Sentencing: April 9, 1980 (first trial)
February 3, 1983 (second trial)

●●

Poland, Patrick   Arizona   M   W

●●

PATRICK GENE POLAND

Race: Caucasian

Date of Birth: March 8, 1950

FACTS

On the morning of May 24, 1977, two Purolator guards, Russell Dempsey and Cecil Newkirk, left Phoenix in an armored van on their scheduled run to banks in Prescott, Sedona and Flagstaff. At the Bumblebee Road exit on Interstate-17, the van was stopped by the Polands, who were disguised as highway patrolmen and were driving a car with an emergency light bar on the top. The Polands took the guards captive, removed close to $300,000 in cash from the van, and left the scene. Around 6:00 a.m. on May 25, 1977, authorities found the abandoned Purolator van near the Bumblebee Road exit. That same morning, Michael Poland rented a boat at the Lake Mead marina. He then piloted the boat to a little-used landing some 14 miles away where he met his brother. The Polands put the guards into canvas bags, took them across the lake and dumped them into the water. Three weeks later, the bodies surfaced in a cove on the Nevada side of the lake. The Polands were convicted in federal court on robbery and kidnapping charges arising from these events. Their trial in state court on the murder charges followed.

Start of Trial: October 23, 1979 (first trial)
October 18, 1982 (second trial)
Verdicts: November 24, 1979 (first trial)
November 18, 1982 (second trial)
Sentencing: April 9, 1980 (first trial)
February 3, 1983 (second trial)

Pollard, Roosevelt	Missouri	M	B	
Ponticelli, Anthony	Florida	M	W	
Pope, Carlton	Virginia	M	B	
Pope, Jimmie	North Carolina	M	W	
Pope, John David	Georgia	M	W	1
Pope, Thomas Dewey	Florida	M	W	
Porter, Ernest	Pennsylvania	M	B	
Porter, Roger	Oklahoma	M	W	
Porter, William Howard	North Carolina	M	N	
Porter, Anthony	Illinois	M	B	
Porter, Henry Martinez	Texas	M	H	7-9-85
Porter, George	Florida	M	W	
Porter, Raleigh	Florida	M	W	
Porterfield, Sidney	Tennessee	M	B	
Post, Ronald	Ohio	M	W	
Potts, Larry	Indiana	M	B	
Potts, Jack	Georgia	M	W	
Powell, David Lee	Texas	M	W	
Powell, Tony	Ohio	M	B	
Poyner, Syvasky	Virginia	M	B	
Pratt, Jesse	Oregon	M	W	
Prejean, Dalton	**Louisiana**	**M**	**B**	**2**

DALTON PREJEAN

FACTS

Prejean was 17 and on parole when he shot and killed Louisiana state trooper Donald Cleveland on July 2, 1977 after Cleveland had stopped him for driving with a malfunctioning taillight. Three years earlier, Prejean had killed a cab driver during a robbery. He had been free on parole from that conviction for six months when he killed Cleveland.

Presnell, Virgil	Georgia	M	W
Preston, Elroy	Missouri	M	B
Preston, Robert A.	Florida	M	W
Price, Ricky Lee	North Carolina	M	W
Price, Curtis	California	M	W

Death Row Inmates

Pride, Timothy	California	M	B	
Pridgen, Charles	Florida	M	W	1
Prince, Larry	**Arizona**	**M**	**W**	

●●

LARRY JOE PRINCE

RACE: Caucasian

Date of Birth: August 4, 1963

FACTS

Robert Dana Richards was Prince's cocaine supplier and claimed that Prince owed him $1,100. On October 12, 1984, shortly after being released from jail on an assault charge, Prince called Richards and arranged a meeting. When Richards drove up in his car, Prince was waiting for him with a KG99 gun. Prince put the barrel of the weapon into Richards' mouth and fired a single, fatal shot. He then took Richards' jewelry, emptied his wallet, and used his keys to enter Richards' apartment. Prince searched the apartment for money and cocaine but found none. He did take more of Richards' jewelry.

Start of Trial: March 17, 1986
Verdict: April 4, 1986
Sentencing: May 15, 1986

●●

Proctor, Roger	Pennsylvania	M	B	
Proctor, William	California	M	W	
Provenzano, Thomas	Florida	M	W	
Pruett, David Mark	Virginia	M	W	
Pruett, Marion	Arkansas	M	W	
Pruitt, Mark Anthony	Georgia	M	W	
Pugh, Willie	Illinois	M	B	
Puiatti, Carl	Florida	M	W	
Pursell, Alan	Pennsylvania	M	W	
Purtell, Robert Michael	Texas	M	W	
Putman, William	Georgia	M	W	
Pyles, Johnny	Texas	M	W	
Quesinberry, Michael	North Carolina	M	W	
Quick, Harold	North Carolina	M	B	
Quince, Kenneth	Florida	M	B	
Rabbani, Syed	Texas	M	A	
Ragsdale, Edward	Florida	M	W	
Raley, David	California	M	W	
Rambaugh, Charles	Texas	M	W	9-11-85
Ramirez, Carlos	Texas	M	H	
Ramirez, Anthony Richard	California	M	H	
Ramos, Marcelino	California	M	H	
Ransom, Kenneth Ray	Texas	M	B	

Death Row Inmates

Raulerson, James	Florida	M	W	1-30-85
Rault, Sterling	Louisiana	M	W	8-24-87
Reaves, William	Florida	M	B	
Rector, Charles	Texas	M	B	
Rector, Ricky	Arkansas	M	B	
Redd, Frank	Illinois	M	B	
Redd, Bobb	Georgia	M	W	
Reddix, Willie	Mississippi	M	B	
Reed, Jonathan	Texas	M	W	
Reed, Grover	Florida	M	W	
Reese, Donald	Missouri	M	W	
Reeves, Randolph	Nebraska	M	N	
Reilly, Michael	Florida	M	W	
Reilly, Mark	California	M	W	
Remeta, Daniel	Florida	M	N	
Remeta, Daniel	Arkansas	M	N	3
Resnover, Gregory	Indiana	M	B	
Rest, Theodore	California	M	W	
Revilla, Daniel	Oklahoma	M	W	
Rhoades, Paul	Idaho	M	W	
Rhodes, William	Florida	M	W	
Rhodes, Richard	Florida	M	W	
Rice, David Lewis	Washington	M	W	
Rice, Tony	Texas	M	W	
Rich, Darrell	California	M	W	
Richards, Michael	Texas	M	B	
Richardson, Damon	Texas	M	B	
Richardson, James	Texas	M	B	
Richardson, Miguel A.	Texas	M	B	
Richardson, Floyd	Illinois	M	B	
Richardson, Herbert	Alabama	M	B	
Richey, Kenneth	Ohio	M	W	
Richley, Daryl	Arkansas	M	W	1
Richmond, Willie Lee	**Arizona**	**M**	**B**	

••

WILLIE LEE RICHMOND

RACE: Black

Date of Birth: March 21, 1948

FACTS

On August 25, 1973, Richmond and two female accomplices took Bernard Crummett to a spot on the outskirts of Tucson. Crummett believed that one of the women was going to commit an act of prostitution with him, but Richmond and the two women intended to rob Crummett. At the scene, Richmond knocked Crummett to the ground with his fists, then hit him over the head with some rocks. One of the women took Crummett's wallet. Then either Richmond or one of the girls twice drove the car over Crummett, killing him.

Start of Trial: January 15, 1974
Verdict: January 22, 1974
Sentencing: February 25, 1974
Resentencing: March 13, 1980

Rickman, Ronald	Tennessee	M	W	
Riddle, Ernest	South Carolina	M	W	
Riechmann, Dieter	Florida	M	W	
Riggins, David	Nevada	M	W	
Riles, Raymond	Texas	M	B	
Riley, Michael Lynn	Texas	M	B	
Riley, Wardell	Florida	M	B	1
Riley, James	Delaware	M	B	
Ritter, Wayne	Alabama	M	W	8-28-87
Rivera, Angel	Texas	M	H	
Rivera, Samuel	Florida	M	H	
Rivera, Michael	Florida	M	H	
Rivers, Warren	Texas	M	B	
Roach, James Terry	South Carolina	M	W	1-10-86
Rook, John	North Carolina	M	W	9-19-86
Rosa, Jessa Desa	Texas	M	H	5-15-85
Robbins, Phillip	North Carolina	M	B	
Robbins, Malcolm	California	M	W	
Roberson, Brian	Texas	M	B	
Roberts, Sammy	South Carolina	M	W	
Roberts, Michael	Oklahoma	M	B	
Roberts, Roy	Missouri	M	W	
Roberts, Victor	Georgia	M	B	
Roberts, Rickey	Florida	M	B	
Roberts, Larry	California	M	B	
Robertson, Andrew	California	M	B	
Robinson, William	Texas	M	B	
Robinson, Dwight	North Carolina	M	B	
Robinson, Eddie	North Carolina	M	B	
Robinson, Johnny L.	Florida	M	B	1
Robinson, Fred	**Arizona**	**M**	**B**	

FRED ROBINSON

Race: Black
Date of Birth: May 3, 1941

FACTS
Robinson and Susan Hill lived together for 11 years. Beginning in 1983, Susan made a number of efforts to leave

Robinson, but he always forced her to return. On June 8, 1987, Robinson believed that Susan was staying in Yuma with her parents, Ralph and Sterleen Hill. Robinson persuaded his friends, Mathers and Theodore Washington, to go to Yuma with him, telling them that they were going to rip off a drug dealer. The three men loaded Robinson's car with weapons and drove to Yuma. They arrived at the Hills' home around midnight. Mathers and Washington entered the house, forced Mr. and Mrs. Hill to lie down on their bedroom floor and tied them up. The men demanded money and Washington went through the Hills' belongings. Mathers then fired his shotgun into the backs of the Hills. Sterleen Hill died from her wounds but Ralph Hill survived.

Start of Trial: December 1, 1987
Verdict: December 15, 1987
Sentencing: January 13, 1988

●●●

Robison, Larry	Texas	M	W
Robison, Olan Randle	Oklahoma	M	W
Rockwell, Ronald	**Arizona**	**M**	**W**

●●●

RONALD EDWIN ROCKWELL

Race: Caucasian

Date of Birth: June 12, 1956

FACTS

On March 25, 1978, Rockwell entered the Bingo Truck Stop in Kingman, Arizona. He removed cash from the register and led the night attendant, Lynn Allen Anderson, into a hallway area which opened into a bathroom. While Anderson knelt in the bathroom doorway, Rockwell shot him through the back of the head. Anderson was flown to a nearby hospital where he died a few hours later. Rockwell boasted about the slaying to several people and he indicated that others were involved.

Start of Trial: November 4, 1985
Verdict: November 7, 1985
Sentencing: January 9, 1986

●●●

Rodden, James	Missouri	M	W	
Rodriguez, Frank	Colorado	M	H	
Rodriguez, Jose	California	M	H	
Rodriguez, Luis	California	M	H	1
Roe, John Glenn	Ohio	M	W	
Rogers, Patrick	Texas	M	B	
Rogers, Mark	**Nevada**	**M**	**W**	

Death Row Inmates

•••

MARK ROGERS

FACTS.
Rogers, 32, was sentenced to death in 1981 for the December 1980 murders of an elderly couple and their adult daughter in a mining camp outside Lovelock, Nevada. Rogers, an aspiring actor known also as "Teepee Fox," was convicted of repeatedly stabbing and shooting Emery and Mary Strode, a couple in their 70s, and their 41-year-old daughter, Meriam Strode Treadwell.

•••

Rogers, Wayne	Illinois	M	W	1
Rogers, James	Georgia	M	W	
Rogers, Jerry Layne	Florida	M	W	
Rogers, David	California	M	W	
Rogers, David	Alabama	M	W	
Rojas, Martin	Ohio	M	B	
Rojem, Richard	Oklahoma	M	W	
Rolan, Florencio	Pennsylvania	M	H	
Rollins, Saharris	Pennsylvania	M	B	
Romano, John	Oklahoma	M	W	
Romanosky, John	**Arizona**	**M**	**W**	

•••

JOHN ROMANOSKY

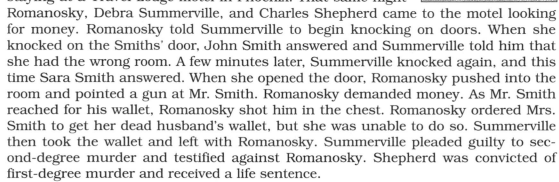

Race: Caucasian

Date of Birth: March 19, 1950

FACTS
On the night of May 17, 1986, John and Sara Smith were staying at a Travel Lodge motel in Phoenix. That same night Romanosky, Debra Summerville, and Charles Shepherd came to the motel looking for money. Romanosky told Summerville to begin knocking on doors. When she knocked on the Smiths' door, John Smith answered and Summerville told him that she had the wrong room. A few minutes later, Summerville knocked again, and this time Sara Smith answered. When she opened the door, Romanosky pushed into the room and pointed a gun at Mr. Smith. Romanosky demanded money. As Mr. Smith reached for his wallet, Romanosky shot him in the chest. Romanosky ordered Mrs. Smith to get her dead husband's wallet, but she was unable to do so. Summerville then took the wallet and left with Romanosky. Summerville pleaded guilty to second-degree murder and testified against Romanosky. Shepherd was convicted of first-degree murder and received a life sentence.

Start of Trial: March 10, 1987
Verdict: March 26, 1987
Sentencing: May 26, 1987

•••

Death Row Inmates

Romero, Jesus	Texas	M	H
Romine, Larry	Georgia	M	W
Rompilla, Ronald	Pennsylvania	M	W
Rondon, Reynaldo	Indiana	M	H
Rosales, Mariano Juarez	Texas	M	H
Roscoe, Kevin	**Arizona**	**M**	**W**

●●

KEVIN SCOTT ROSCOE

Race: Caucasian

Date of Birth: July 14, 1962

FACTS
On May 13, 1982, Roscoe kidnapped 7-year-old Laura Dunn from the area behind her house in Gilbert and drove her to the San Tan Mountains. There he took off her clothing, tied her hands behind her back with her socks, stuffed her panties into her mouth, put a ligature around her neck and strangled her. Her body was found the next day. Seminal fluid was found in her mouth and vagina and her vaginal area was injured. A week later Roscoe sold his car. A small amount of blood was found on the backseat, and carpet fibers from inside the car matched two pieces of fiber found next to Laura's body. A scent-discriminating dog found Laura's scent in Roscoe's car and also found Roscoe's scent on Laura's clothing and her bicycle found at the kidnapping scene.

Start of Trial: January 5, 1983
Verdict: January 26, 1983
Sentencing: February 25, 1983

●●

Rose, Teddy	New Jersey	M	W	1
Rose, James	Florida	M	W	
Rose, Milo A.	Florida	M	W	
Ross, Bobby Lynn	Oklahoma	M	B	
Ross, James Keith	North Carolina	M	W	
Ross, Eddie Lee	Georgia	M	B	
Ross, Michael	Connecticut	M	W	
Ross, Craig	California	M	B	
Rossi, Richard	**Arizona**	**M**	**W**	

●●

RICHARD MICHAEL ROSSI

Race: Caucasian

Date of Birth: October 30, 1947

FACTS
Around 12:30 p.m. on August 29, 1983, Rossi went to the Scottsdale home of

Harold August, supposedly to sell a typewriter. Instead, he shot Mr. August three times. After the first two shots, Mr. August said, "You've got my money and you've shot me, what more do you want?" Rossi then shot August in the mouth, killing him. A neighbor, Sherrill Nutter, heard the shots and walked into the August home. Rossi hit her over the head with a blackjack and shot her twice in the chest. Rossi used exploding bullets on both victims, but Mrs. Nutter survived.

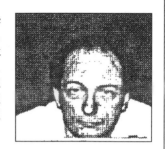

Start of Trial: April 10, 1984
Verdict: April 19, 1984
Sentencing: June 25, 1984
Resentencing: January 22, 1986
June 23, 1988 (second resentencing)

Roubeaux, James	Oklahoma	M	N	
Rougeau, Paul	Texas	M	W	
Roundtree, Robert	Florida	M	B	
Rouster, Gregory	Indiana	M	B	
Routly, Daniel	Florida	M	W	
Rowland, Guy Kevin	California	M	W	
Ruffin, Mack	Florida	M	B	1
Ruiz, Luis	Illinois	M	H	
Ruiz, Alejandro	California	M	N	
Ruiz, Paul	Arkansas	M	H	
Running Eagle, Sean	Arizona	M	N	
Rupe, Mitchell	Washington	M	W	
Rush, Larry	Pennsylvania	M	U	
Rushing, David	Louisiana	M	W	
Russell, Clifton Charles	Texas	M	W	
Russell, James	Texas	M	B	
Rust, John	Nebraska	M	W	
Rutherford, Arthur	Florida	M	W	
Rutledge, Mitchell	Alabama	M	B	1
Ryan, Michael	Nebraska	M	W	
Salazar, Maximo	Oklahoma	M	N	
Salazar, Manuel	Illinois	M	H	
Salazar, Alfonso	**Arizona**	**M**	**H**	

ALFONSO RAYMOND SALAZAR

Race: Hispanic

Date of Birth: August 25, 1963

FACTS
On July 25, 1986, Salazar and Michael Davis pulled the wrought iron bars from a window and entered the Tucson

home of Sarah Kaplan. Ms. Kaplan was 83 years old, weighed less than 90 pounds, was 5 feet tall, and wore a patch on one eye. Salazar and Davis beat her and strangled her with the telephone cord. Fingerprints belonging to both men were found at the scene. One of Salazar's prints was in blood. In a separate trial, Davis was convicted and sentenced to death.

Start of Trial: December 2, 1987
Verdict: December 14, 1987
Sentencing: February 9, 1988

••

Samayoa, Richard	California	M	A	
Sample, Michael	Tennessee	M	B	
Sanchez, Hector	Illinois	M	H	
Sanchez, Rigoberto	Florida	M	H	
Sanchez, Teddy	California	M	H	
Sanders, Stanley	North Carolina	M	B	
Sanders, Clindell	Missouri	M	B	
Sanders, David Lee	Kentucky	M	W	
Sanders, Reginald	Delaware	M	B	
Sanders, Ricardo	California	M	B	
Sanders, Ronald	California	M	W	
Sanderson, Ricky Lee	North Carolina	M	W	
Sandoval, Alfred	California	M	H	
Santana, Carlos	Texas	M	H	
Santiago, Salvadore	Pennsylvania	M	H	
Satterwhite, John	Texas	M	B	1
Sattiewhite, Vernon	Texas	M	B	
Savage, Roy	New Jersey	M	B	
Sawyer, Robert	**Louisiana**	**M**	**W**	

••

ROBERT SAWYER

FACTS.
Sawyer was convicted in 1980 of torturing and raping Frances Arwood and then burning her to death. Arwood, 23, was killed in September 1979 while baby sitting at the home of Cynthia Shano, a friend who lived with Sawyer. Shano and Sawyer had gone out the evening before the murder and Shano testified she saw Sawyer and an accomplice torture and kill Arwood the following morning. Shano said Arwood was beaten, kicked and dunked in scalding water until she was unconscious. Sawyer then poured lighter fluid on Arwood's body and set her afire, according to Shano.

••

Sawyers, John	Texas	M	W
Schad, Edward	**Arizona**	**M**	**W**

••

EDWARD HAROLD SCHAD

Race: Caucasian

Date of Birth: July 27, 1942

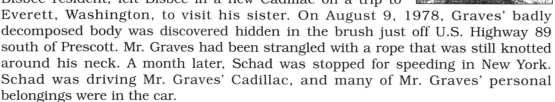

FACTS
On August 1, 1978, Lorimer "Leroy" Graves, a 74-year-old Bisbee resident, left Bisbee in a new Cadillac on a trip to Everett, Washington, to visit his sister. On August 9, 1978, Graves' badly decomposed body was discovered hidden in the brush just off U.S. Highway 89 south of Prescott. Mr. Graves had been strangled with a rope that was still knotted around his neck. A month later, Schad was stopped for speeding in New York. Schad was driving Mr. Graves' Cadillac, and many of Mr. Graves' personal belongings were in the car.

Start of Trial: September 26, 1979 (first trial)
June 18, 1985 (second trial)
Verdict: October 5, 1979 (first trial)
June 27, 1985 (second trial)
Sentencing: December 27, 1979 (first trial)
August 29, 1985 (second sentencing)

Schafer, Arthur	Florida	M	W	1
Schiro, Thomas	Indiana	M	W	
Schlup, Lloyd	Missouri	M	W	
Schneider, Eric	Missouri	M	W	
Schnick, James	Missouri	M	W	
Scire, Anthony	Louisiana	M	W	
Scott, Jay D.	Ohio	M	B	
Scott, Larry	Illinois	M	B	
Scott, Bradley	Florida	M	W	
Scott, Abron	Florida	M	B	
Scott, Paul	Florida	M	W	
Scull, Jesus	Florida	M	H	1
Sechrest, Ricky	Nevada	M	W	
Seiber, Lee	Ohio	M	W	
Selby, Dale Pierra	Utah	M	B	8-28-87
Sellers, Sean	Oklahoma	M	W	2
Selvage, John Henry	Texas	M	B	
Serna, John	**Arizona**	**M**	**H**	

JOHN SERNA

Race: Mexican-American
Date of Birth: November 17, 1959

FACTS
Serna was an inmate at the Perryville prison. On June 21, 1985, Patrick Chavarria

was transferred from the Florence prison to Perryville. When Serna learned Chavarria was at Perryville, he decided to kill him. Serna obtained a length of steel pipe and cornered Chavarria in the laundry room of the San Juan Unit. Serna broke Chavarria's kneecap and beat him over the head, killing him.

Start of Trial: January 19, 1987 (deadlocked jury)
April 27, 1987
Verdict: May 19, 1987
Sentencing: June 26, 1987

•••

Session, James	Texas	M	B	
Seuffer, James	Illinois	M	W	
Shcackart, Ronald	**Arizona**	**M**	**W**	

•••

RONALD SCHACKART

Race: Caucasian

Date of Birth: December 2, 1989

FACTS

Schackart and Charla Regan had known each other since high school and they continued to be friends at the University of Arizona. On March 8, 1984, Schackart told Regan he needed a place to stay since his parents had kicked him out of their house. He also told her he needed to talk to her about his wife's filing rape charges against him. They went to a Tucson Holiday Inn where Schackart raped Charla at gunpoint, hit her in the face with the gun, strangled her to death and stuffed a large sock into her mouth. He later reported the killing to the police and claimed he had not intended to kill Charla.

Start of Trial: March 12, 1985
Verdict: March 16, 1985
Sentencing: May 3, 1985

•••

Sharp, Michael	Texas	M	W	
Shaw, Joseph Carl	South Carolina	M	W	1-11-85
Shaw, Robert	Missouri	M	B	
Sheldon, Jeffrey	California	M	W	
Shell, Robert Lee	Mississippi	M	B	
Shriner, Carl	Florida	M	W	6-20-84
Shurn, Daryll	Missouri	M	B	
Shurn, Keith	Illinois	M	B	
Sidebottom, Robert T.	Missouri	M	W	
Siebert, Daniel Lee	Alabama	M	W	

Death Row Inmates

Silagy, Charles	Illinois	M	W	
Silva, Mauricio	California	M	H	
Silva, Benjamin	California	M	A	
Simmons, Beoria	Kentucky	M	B	
Simmons, Ronald	Arkansas	M	W	
Simmons, Thomas	Arkansas	M	W	
Simms, Darryl	Illinois	M	B	
Simon, Richard	Tennessee	M	B	
Simonsen, David	Oregon	M	W	
Simpson, Pierre Dyon	North Carolina	M	B	1
Sims, Terry	Florida	M	W	
Sims, Mitchell	California	M	W	
Singleton, Fred	South Carolina	M	B	
Singleton, Cornelius	Alabama	M	B	
Sireci, Henry	Florida	M	W	1
Siripongs, Jaturun	California	M	A	
Sivak, Lacey	Idaho	M	W	
Sixto, Felipe	California	M	H	
Skaggs, David	Kentucky	M	W	
Skelton, John	Texas	M	W	
Skillern, Doyle	Texas	M	W	1-16-85
Skipper, Gilbert	Georgia	M	W	1
Slagel, Billy	Ohio	M	N	
Slawter, James	Kentucky	M	B	
Sloan, Jeffrey	Missouri	M	W	
Smalley, Leonard	Florida	M	W	
Smith, Sammie Louis	Texas	M	W	
Smith, James E.	Texas	M	B	
Smith, Jack Harvey	Texas	M	W	
Smith, Ricky	Tennessee	M	B	
Smith, Andy Laverne	South Carolina	M	B	
Smith, Jay C.	Pennsylvania	M	W	
Smith, James	Pennsylvania	M	B	
Smith, Charles F.	Oregon	M	W	
Smith, Richard	Oklahoma	M	W	
Smith, Henry	Oklahoma	M	W	
Smith, Phillip	Oklahoma	M	W	
Smith, Lois Nadine	Oklahoma	F	W	
Smith, William Henry	Ohio	M	B	
Smith, Roger	North Carolina	M	B	
Smith, Rowland	North Carolina	M	W	
Smith, Terry William	North Carolina	M	W	
Smith, Kermit	North Carolina	M	W	
Smith, John Eldon	Georgia	M	W	12-15-83
Smith, Michael	Virginia	M	B	7-31-86
Smith, Larry	Texas	M	B	8-22-86
Smith, Ronald	Montana	M	W	
Smith, Samuel D.	Missouri	M	B	

Smith, Gerald	Missouri	M	W	
Smith, Willie Albert	Mississippi	M	B	
Smith, Norvell	Louisiana	M	B	
Smith, Clarence	Louisiana	M	W	
Smith, David	Kentucky	M	W	
Smith, Charles	Indiana	M	B	
Smith, Tommie	Indiana	M	B	
Smith, David	Illinois	M	W	
Smith, Steven	Illinois	M	B	
Smith, William	Georgia	M	B	1
Smith, Frank L.	Florida	M	B	
Smith, Frank	Florida	M	B	
Smith, Jimmy Lee	Florida	M	W	
Smith, Bernard	**Arizona**	**M**	**B**	

••

BERNARD SMITH

Race: Black

Date of Birth: October 3, 1953

FACTS

Shortly after midnight on August 22, 1983, Smith entered the Low Cost Market in Yuma, went to cash register No. 5 and requested Kool cigarettes, paying with a $5 bill. When the transaction was rung up and the cash drawer opened, Smith pointed a pistol at Charles Pray, the 57-year-old cashier, and demanded the money. When Pray turned and called out the name of a fellow employee, Smith raised the pistol and fired one .22 caliber bullet through the base of Pray's head, severing the spinal cord. Smith walked around the counter and removed the paper money from the cash register and left. Two women outside the store watched Smith walk to his car, followed him from the parking lot, and called the police with his license number. Smith was arrested within minutes of the shooting.

Start of Trial: January 10, 1984
Verdict: January 19, 1984
Sentencing: February 17, 1984

••

Smith, Roger Lynn	**Arizona**	**M**	**W**

••

ROGER LYNN SMITH

Race: Caucasian

Date of Birth: October 26, 1959

FACTS

On June 6, 1981, Smith, along with Alfredo and Antonio Abila, decided to rob

Farmer's Liquor Store in Phoenix. While the Abila brothers waited outside in the car, Smith entered the store carrying a sawed-off shotgun. Smith pointed the weapon at the clerk, Herman Helfand, and demanded money. Helfand opened the cash register and stepped back. Smith took approximately $150 from the register and then shot Helfand once in the head. The Abila brothers pled guilty to armed robbery and were sentenced to prison.

Start of Trial: March 15, 1982
Verdict: March 22, 1982
Sentencing: April 20, 1982
Resentencing: December 2, 1983

●●

| **Smith, Robert** | **Arizona** | **M** | **W** |

●●

ROBERT DOUGLAS SMITH

Race: Caucasian

Date of Birth: December 8, 1948

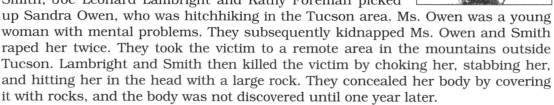

FACTS
Sometime between March 11, 1980, and March 14, 1980, Smith, Joe Leonard Lambright and Kathy Foreman picked up Sandra Owen, who was hitchhiking in the Tucson area. Ms. Owen was a young woman with mental problems. They subsequently kidnapped Ms. Owen and Smith raped her twice. They took the victim to a remote area in the mountains outside Tucson. Lambright and Smith then killed the victim by choking her, stabbing her, and hitting her in the head with a large rock. They concealed her body by covering it with rocks, and the body was not discovered until one year later.
Lambright and Smith were tried in a joint trial before two separate juries. Ms. Foreman testified against them in exchange for a grant of immunity.

Start of Trial: March 23, 1982
Verdict: March 30, 1982
Sentencing: May 27, 1982

●●

| **Smith, Joe** | **Arizona** | **M** | **W** |

●●

JOSEPH CLARENCE SMITH, JR.

Race: Caucasian

Date of Birth: June 15, 1949

FACTS

Shortly before midnight on December 30, 1975, 18-year-old Sandy Spencer finished work at a fast food restaurant and began hitchhiking home. Smith picked her up and drove her to a desert location north and west of Phoenix. There he bound her, forced dirt into her mouth and nostrils, and taped her mouth closed. Ms. Spencer died of asphyxiation, but to satisfy himself that she was actually dead, Smith stabbed her numerous times and embedded a 2-inch long sewing needle in her breast. Ms. Spencer's nude body was found on January 1, 1976. In late January of 1976, Smith picked up another hitchhiker, 14-year-old Neva Lee. Smith took the girl to another desert location and killed her by forcing dirt into her mouth and nostrils and taping her mouth closed. Ms. Lee also died of asphyxiation, was stabbed several times, and had been jabbed in the breasts with needles. Her nude body was discovered on February 2, 1976. Smith was first tried and convicted for the murder of Neva Lee. Several days into the trial for the murder of Sandy Spencer, Smith entered a plea of guilty to the charge.

Start of Trial: May 24, 1977 (Neva Lee)
June 28, 1977 (Sandy Spencer)
Verdict: June 17, 1977 (Neva Lee)
Guilty Plea: July 7, 1977 (Sandy Spencer)
Sentencing: August 31, 1977 (both murders)
Resentencing: November 7, 1979 (both murders)

Smith, James Wyman	Alabama	M	W	
Sneed, Willie	Pennsylvania	M	B	
Sneed, David	Ohio	M	B	
Snell, Richard Wayne	Arkansas	M	W	
Snow, John	Nevada	M	B	
Sochor, Dennis	Florida	M	W	
Soffar, Max	Texas	M	W	
Songer, Carl	Florida	M	W	
Sonnier, Elmo	Louisiana	M	W	4-5-84
Solomon, Van Roosevelt	Georgia	M	B	2-20-85
Soria, Juan	Texas	M	H	
Sosa, Pedro S.	Texas	M	H	
Soult, Charles	Pennsylvania	M	W	
South, Robert	South Carolina	M	W	
South, George	Florida	M	W	
Sowell, Billie	Ohio	M	B	
Spann, Sterling	South Carolina	M	B	
Sparks, Willy	Tennessee	M	B	
Spaziano, Joseph	Florida	M	W	
Spence, David Wayne	Texas	M	W	
Spence, Morris	Pennsylvania	M	B	
Spencer, Timothy	Virginia	M	B	
Spencer, James	Georgia	M	B	
Spencer, Leonard	**Florida**	**M**	**B**	

LEONARD SPENCER

FACTS

The Florida supreme court has erased Spencer's first degree murder conviction, holding that the jury selection process in Palm Beach County, where Spencer was tried is racially biased. Spencer, a black, had been convicted of participating in two murders in West Palm Beach in 1986. Spencer will be retried for a June 1986 crime spree that included the murders of two men.

••

Spenkelink, John	Florida	M	W	2-25-79
Spirko, John George	Ohio	M	W	
Spisak, Frank	Ohio	M	W	
Spivey, Ronald	Georgia	M	W	
Spranger, William	Indiana	M	W	
Spreitzer, Edward	W			
Spruill, Jonnie Lee	North Carolina	M	B	
Squires, William	Florida	M	W	
St. Pierre, Robert	Illinois	M	W	
Stafford, Roger	Oklahoma	M	W	
Stamper, Charles	Virginia	M	B	
Stanford, Kevin	**Kentucky**	**M**	**B**	**2**

••

KEVIN STANFORD

FACTS.

Kevin Stanford was sentenced to die in Kentucky's electric chair for the 1981 abduction and murder of Baerbel Poore, a 20 year old gas station attendant. Stanford, who is now 25, was 17 at the time of the crime, and is one of two whose cases were at the heart of the recent U.S. Supreme Court ruling permitting the execution of killers as young as 16. Stanford and two others robbed the gas station of $143.07 in cash, 300 cartons of cigarettes and two gallons of gasoline, Then, according to police reports, Stanford and another teenager sexually abused and terrorized Poore before Stanford gave her a last cigarette, then shot her twice in the head.

••

Stankewitz, Douglas	California	M	N	
Stanley, Evon	Georgia	M	B	7-13-84
Stanley, Gerald	California	M	W	
Stanley, Milo	**Arizona**	**M**	**W**	

••

MILO STANLEY

Race: Caucasian

Date of Birth: March 11, 1963

FACTS

On the evening of June 19, 1986, Stanley and his wife, Susan, were arguing about his drinking problem. He drove Susan, his 5-year-old daughter, Seleste, and his 1-year-old son, Chad, to a remote area outside Cottonwood. Stanley and Susan continued to argue as they sat in the car. Stanley ended the argument by shooting Susan three times in the head. He then shot Seleste once in the top of the head, pressing the muzzle of the gun into the skin. Stanley did not shoot Chad because the boy was too young to tell what he had seen. After dumping Susan's and Seleste's bodies off the side of the road, Stanley went home and put Chad to bed. Several hours later, he called the police and told them that Susan and Seleste were missing. The police began a wide-ranging search that ended late the following day when Stanley confessed. Stanley received the death penalty for the murder of Seleste, and a life sentence for the murder of Susan.

Start of Trial: June 24, 1987
Verdict: July 10, 1987
Sentencing: September 25, 1987

●●●

Stano, Gerald	Florida	M	W	
Stansbury, Robert	California	M	W	
Starr, Gary	Pennsylvania	M	W	
Starr, David Lee	Arkansas	M	B	
Starvaggi, Joseph	Texas	M	W	9-10-87
Steele, Roland	Pennsylvania	M	B	
Steffen, David	Ohio	M	W	
Steidl, Gordon	Illinois	M	W	
Steinhorst, Walter	Florida	M	W	
Stephens, Alpha Otis	Georgia	M	B	12-12-84
Stephens, William	Georgia	M	B	1
Sterling, Gary	Texas	M	B	
Sterling, Terry Nash	Texas	M	N	
Stevens, Dallas Ray	Oregon	M	W	
Stevens, Dwayne	Nevada	M	W	
Stevens, Thomas	Georgia	M	W	
Stevens, Rufus	Florida	M	W	
Stewart, Darryl E.	Texas	M	B	
Stewart, Raymond	Illinois	M	B	
Stewart, Walter	Illinois	M	B	
Stewart, Kenneth	Florida	M	W	
Stewart, Roy	Florida	M	W	
Stiles, Russell	Oklahoma	M	W	
Stocker, David	Texas	M	W	
Stockton, Dennis	Virginia	M	W	1
Stokes, Ralph	Pennsylvania	M	B	
Stokes, Winford	Missouri	M	B	
Stokes, Jerry	Florida	M	B	

Death Row Inmates

Stone, Raymond	Florida	M	W	1
Stouffer, Bigler	Oklahoma	M	W	
Stout, Larry Alan	Virginia	M	B	
Stout, Billy Gene	Oklahoma	M	W	
Straight, Ronald	Florida	M	H	5-20-86
Streetman, Robert	Texas	M	W	1-7-88
Strickland, Tyrone	Illinois	M	B	
Stringer, James R.	Mississippi	M	W	
Strong, James	Pennsylvania	M	W	
Strouth, Donald	Tennessee	M	N	
Stuart, Eugene	Idaho	M	W	
Stumpf, John	Ohio	M	W	
Suarez, Ernesto	Florida	M	H	
Sullivan, John	Louisiana	M	W	
Sullivan, Robert	Floridia	M	W	11-30-83
Sully, Anthony Jack	California	M	W	
Summerlin, Warren	Arizona	M	W	
Sutton, Nicholas	Tennessee	M	W	
Swafford, Roy	Florida	M	W	
Sweet, Glennon	Missouri	M	W	
Swindler, John	Arkansas	M	W	
Szabo, John	Illinois	M	W	
Szuchon, Joseph	Pennsylvania	M	W	
Tafero, Jesse	Florida	M	W	
Tarver, Bobby	Alabama	M	B	
Tarver, Robert Lee	Alabama	M	B	
Tassin, Robert	Louisiana	M	W	
Tate, Kenneth	Oklahoma	M	W	
Taylor, Darryl	Tennessee	M	W	
Taylor, John	Louisiana	M	B	2-29-84
Taylor, Richard C.	Tennessee	M	W	
Taylor, Norris	North Carolina	M	B	
Taylor, Victor	Kentucky	M	B	
Taylor, Freddie Lee	California	M	B	
Teague, Delbert Boyd	Texas	M	W	
Teague, Raymond	Tennessee	M	W	
Tedford, Donald	Pennsylvania	M	W	
Teel, Bouldin	Tennessee	M	W	
Teffeteller, Robert	Florida	M	W	
Tennard, Robert	Texas	M	B	
Terrell, Drew	Illinois	M	B	
Terry, John David	Tennessee	M	W	1
Terry, Benjamin	Pennsylvania	M	B	
Thacker, Lois	Indiana	F	W	
Thigpen, Donald	Alabama	M	B	
Thomas, Daniel	Floridia	M	B	4-15-86
Thomas, Joseph L.	Federal	M	U	
Thomas, Kenneth Wayne	Texas	M	B	

Death Row Inmates

Thomas, Danny Dean	Texas	M	N	
Thomas, Leroy	Pennsylvania	M	B	
Thomas, Brian	Pennsylvania	M	B	
Thomas, Darrell	Oklahoma	M	W	
Thomas, James Edward	North Carolina	M	B	
Thomas, Donald	Maryland	M	B	
Thomas, Alfred	Kentucky	M	W	
Thomas, Walter	Illinois	M	B	
Thomas, Willie	Illinois	M	B	
Thomas, Edward	Florida	M	W	
Thomas, Donrell	California	M	B	
Thomas, Ralph	California	M	B	
Thomas, Kenneth Glenn	Alabama	M	W	
Thomas, Wallace	Alabama	M	B	
Thomas, Patricia	Alabama	F	B	
Thompkins, Willie	Illinois	M	B	
Thompson, John R.	Texas	M	W	7-8-87
Thompson, Gregory	Tennessee	M	B	
Thompson, William	**Nevada**	**M**	**W**	

••

WILLIAM THOMPSON

FACTS

Thompsons, 46 , when he was convicted in 1984 of killing a
28-year-old transient, had spent 23 years in reform schools
or prisons in Texas, New York and Florida.Thompson has insisted that that he will forego appeals, and wishes to be executed for the killing of Randy Waldron at Waldron's campsite

on the banks of the Truckee River in Reno, Nevada. At the time of that killing,
Thompson was wanted for the murder of two California brothers.

••

Thompson, John	Louisiana	M	B	
Thompson, William	Kentucky	M	W	
Thompson, Joey	Florida	M	W	
Thompson, Charlie	Florida	M	B	
Thompson, Raymond	Florida	M	W	
Thompson, William	Florida	M	W	1
Thompson, Thomas Martin	California	M	W	
Thompson, Robert	California	M	W	
Thompson, Steven Allen	Alabama	M	W	
Thompson, Michael Eugene	Alabama	M	W	
Thorson, Roger	Mississippi	M	W	
Tibbs, Derek	Oklahoma	M	W	
Tichnell, Richard	Maryland	M	W	1
Tilley, William	Pennsylvania	M	W	
Tillman, Elroy	Utah	M	B	

| Tillman, Gary | Florida | M | B | 1 |
| **Tison, Ricky** | **Arizona** | **M** | **W** | |

•••

RICKY WAYNE TISON

Race: Caucasian

Date of Birth: December 7, 1958

FACTS

Ricky Tison, together with his brothers Ray and Donnie, helped break Randy Greenawalt and their father, Gary Tison, out of the Arizona State Prison on July 30, 1978. During the night of July 31-August 1, 1978, the group kidnapped and shotgunned to death John and Donnelda Lyons, their infant son Christopher, and their teenaged niece, Theresa Tyson, in a desert area near Quartzsite. They then drove north, changing cars several times, and apparently murdered a newlywed couple, James and Margene Judge, in Colorado, though they were never tried for those killings. The gang then turned south again and were recaptured on August 11, 1978, after a gun-battle at a roadblock in Pinal County that left Donnie Tison dead. Gary Tison was found dead in the desert several days later.

Start of Trial: Feburary 20, 1979
Verdict: February 27, 1979
Sentencing: March 29, 1979
Resentencing: November 20, 1987

•••

| **Tison, Raymond** | **Arizona** | **M** | **W** | |

•••

RAYMOND CURTIS TISON

Race: Caucasian

Date of Birth: October 31, 1959

FACTS

Raymond Tison, together with his brothers Ricky and Donnie, helped break Randy Greenawalt and their father,  Gary Tison, out of the Arizona State Prison on July 30, 1978. During the night of July 31-August 1, 1978, the group kidnapped and shotgunned to death John and Donnelda Lyons, their infant son Christopher, and their teenaged niece, Theresa Tyson, in a desert area near Quartzsite. They then drove north, changing cars several times, and apparently murdered a newlywed couple, James and Margene Judge, in Colorado, though they were never tried for those killings. The gang then turned south again and were recaptured on August 11, 1978, after a gun-battle at a roadblock in Pinal County that left Donnie Tison dead. Gary Tison was found dead in the desert several days later.

Death Row Inmates

Start of Trial: Feburary 28, 1979
Verdict: March 6, 1979
Sentencing: March 29, 1979
Resentencing: November 20, 1987

•••

Titone, Dino	Illinois	M	W	
Tokman, George	Mississippi	M	W	1
Tompkins, Phillip D.	Texas	M	B	
Tompkins, Wayne	Florida	M	W	
Torrence, Michael	South Carolina	M	W	
Torres-Arboledo, Oscar	Florida	M	B	
Townes, Richard	Virginia	M	B	
Townsend, Johnny	Indiana	M	B	
Travaglia, Michael	Pennsylvania	M	W	
Trawick, Gary	Florida	M	B	1
Trevino, Jose Mario	Texas	M	H	
Trice, Eddie	Oklahoma	M	B	
Trimble, James	Maryland	M	W	2
Trotter, Melvin	Florida	M	B	
Truesdale, Louis	South Carolina	M	B	
Tucker, Karla Fay	**Texas**	**F**	**W**	

•••

KARLA FAY TUCKER

FACTS.

Karla Fay Tucker, 29, was convicted in 1983 of participating in the pickax killings of Jerry Lynn Dean, 26, and Deborah Ruth Thornton, 32. A co-defendant in the trial, Daniel Garrett, is also on Texas' death row.

•••

Tucker, Michael	Oregon	M	W	
Tucker, Richard	Georgia	M	B	5-19-87
Tucker, William Boyd	Georgia	M	W	5-28-87
Tuggle, Lem	Virginia	M	W	
Tuilaepa, Paul	California	M	A	
Turner, Willie Lloyd	Virginia	M	B	
Turner, Jessel	Texas	M	W	
Turner, Joseph Paul	Texas	M	W	
Turner, Claude	North Carolina	M	W	
Turner, Kevin	Mississippi	M	B	
Turner, Robert	Illinois	M	W	
Turner, William	Florida	M	B	
Turner, Richard	California	M	W	
Turner, Melvin	California	M	B	
Turner, Thaddeus Louis	California	M	B	
Twenter, Virginia	Missouri	F	W	

Death Row Inmates

Tye, Jimmy	Illinois	M	B	
Tyler, Arthur	Ohio	M	B	
Underwood, Herbert	Indiana	M	W	
Upton, Jackie Wayne	Texas	M	W	
Valdez, Alberto	Texas	M	H	
Valerio, John	Nevada	M	H	
Valle, Manuel	Florida	M	H	
Van Cleave, Greg	Indiana	M	B	
Van Denton, Earl	Arkansas	M	W	
Van Hook, Robert	Ohio	M	W	
Van Poyck, William	Florida	M	W	
Van Woudenberg, Sammy	Oklahoma	M	N	
Vanderbilt, Jimmy	**Texas**	**M**	**W**	**1**

••

JIMMY VANDERBILT

FACTS.
Jimmy Vanderbilt, a former Amarillo, Tex. police officer is among the more senior of Texas death row inmates. Vanderbilt was convicted of the April 1975 killing of 16-year-old Katina Moyer whose body was found on a rural road with a single gunshot would to the head.

••

Vega, Martin	Texas	M	H	
Vandiver, William	Indiana	M	W	10-16-85
Ventura, Peter	Florida	M	W	
Vickers, Robert	**Arizona**	**M**	**W**	

••

ROBERT WAYNE VICKERS

Race: Caucasian

Date of Birth: April 29, 1958

FACTS
On March 4, 1982, Vickers was an inmate on death row at the Arizona State Prison in Florence. At around 6:30 p.m., Vickers was out of his cell, allegedly doing clean-up chores. Instead, he went to the cell of Buster Holsinger, another death row inmate. Vickers was upset over an earlier remark Holsinger had made about Vickers' niece. Vickers doused Holsinger and his cell with some Vitalis he had been saving and then threw burning toilet paper on Holsinger, setting him ablaze. Holsinger died as a result of tracheobronchial burns suffered in the resulting flash fire.

Verdict: September 29, 1982
October 25, 1985 (second trial)
Sentencing: October 18, 1982
April 24, 1986 (second trial)

••

Death Row Inmates

Victor, William	South Carolina	M	W
Victor, Clarence	Nebraska	M	B
Vigneault, Donald L.	Texas	M	W
Villafuerte, Jose	**Arizona**	**M**	**H**

• •

JOSE ROBERTO VILLAFUERTE

Race: Hispanic

Date of Birth: December 2, 1952

FACTS

On February 22, 1983, Villafuerte was arrested near Ash Fork in connection with a disturbance. He was in possession of a car belonging to Amelia Scoville. Phoenix police officers were contacted and they went to Villafuerte's trailer to look for Scoville. They found her body, clad only in a blouse, bra, and panties, on a bed. Her hands were tied behind her back and a strip of bedding bound one of her ankles to her hands. Scoville's head was wrapped in a sheet, a bedspread, and long thermal underwear, all of which were blood-stained. A ball made of a tightly wrapped strip of bedsheet was found in her throat. Lab tests showed the presence of seminal fluid in her vagina. Scoville had died as a result of gagging.

Start of Trial: July 11, 1983
Verdict: July 18, 1983
Sentencing: September 9, 1983

• •

Viscotti, John	California	M	W
Vuong, Hai Hai	Texas	M	A
Wacaser, Nila	Missouri	F	W
Waddy, Warren	Ohio	M	B
Wade, Johnny	Georgia	M	W
Wade, Melvin	**California**	**M**	**B**

• •

MELVIN WADE

FACTS

Melvin Wade, 33, was sentenced to die for the 1981 torture murder of his 10 year old stepdaughter. Evidence indicated that over a 20 hour period, he beat the child with his fists and a board broken from a sofa, put her in a duffle bag, choked her with a dog leash and punched and stomped on her stomach, while drinking a bottle of wine and shouting that he was an archangel and would kill the child because she was a devil.

• •

Wader, Michael	California	M	W
Wagner, Jeffrey Scott	Oregon	M	W

Waldrop, Billy	Alabama	M	W
Walker, Gary Alan	Oklahoma	M	W
Walker, Charles	Illinois	M	W
Walker, Richard	Georgia	M	B
Walker, Marvin	California	M	B
Walker, Altione	Alabama	F	W
Wallace, William	Pennsylvania	M	B
Wallace, Donald	Indiana	M	W
Wallace, James	**Arizona**	**M**	**W**

••

JAMES WALLACE

Race: Caucasian

Date of Birth: April 28, 1950

FACTS
Wallace lived with Susan Insalaco and her two children, 16-year-old Anna and 12-year-old Gabe. On the night of January 31, 1984, Susan and Wallace had an argument and Wallace planned to leave the next day. However, when Anna returned from school that day, Wallace killed her by striking her repeatedly with a baseball bat until it broke and then pushing the broken end of the bat through her throat. He then placed her in the bathroom and cleaned up. Wallace decided he needed a better killing instrument, so he went to a shed where he obtained a steel pipe wrench. When Gabe arrived home, Wallace killed him by striking him with the pipe wrench. When Susan arrived home a few hours later he killed her with the same wrench. The next day Wallace called the police and confessed. He refused a trial and pleaded guilty to first-degree murder.

Plea: March 1, 1985
Sentencing: May 15, 1985
Resentencing: August 25, 1987

••

Walls, Robert	Missouri	M	W
Walls, Christopher	Kentucky	M	W
Walls, Frank	Florida	M	W
Walton, Tyrone	Oregon	M	B
Walton, Jason Dirk	Florida	M	W
Walton, Jeffrey	**Arizona**	**M**	**W**

••

JEFFREY ALAN WALTON

Race: Caucasian

Date of Birth: January 29, 1966

FACTS

On March 2, 1986, Walton, Sharold Ramsey, and Robert Hoover, waited outside a bar in Tucson for someone to rob. When Thomas Dale Powell left the bar, Hoover alerted Walton that he was coming. Walton pointed a pistol at Powell and ordered him to lie down and empty his pockets. The trio then forced Powell into Powell's car and drove out to the desert area west of Tucson. Powell was tied up, taken away, and shot in the head by Walton. The shot blinded Powell but did not kill him. When Powell regained consciousness, he floundered in the desert for approximately 1 week before he died from exposure and pneumonia. Ramsey pled guilty to a lesser offense and testified for the state. Hoover was convicted and received a life sentence.

Start of Trial: December 2, 1986
Verdict: December 16, 1986
Sentencing: January 27, 1987

● ●

Ward, Thomas Lee	Louisiana	M	B	
Ward, Jerry	Illinois	M	B	
Warren, Woodrow	California	M	B	1
Warren, Robert	California	M	B	1
Wash, Jeffery David	California	M	W	
Washington, Robert Wayne	Florida	M	B	7-13-84
Washington, Earl Jr.	Virginia	M	B	
Washington, Terry	Texas	M	B	
Washington, Willie	**Texas**	**M**	**B**	

● ●

WILLIE WASHINGTON

FACTS.

Willie Washington was sentenced to death in 1986 for killing Kiflemariam Tareh, 27, an Ethiopian political refugee who was working at a grocery store when Washington robbed it of about $100 in 1985. Tareh died of a gunshot wound to the head. Another Ethiopian employee was shot in the face, but lived to testify at the trial, in which prosecutors exposed a list of previous crimes by Washington, including burglary and rape.

● ●

Washington, John Paul	Oklahoma	M	B
Washington, Theodore	**Arizona**	**M**	**B**

● ●

THEODORE WASHINGTON

Race: Black

Date of Birth- June 7, 1960

FACTS

Fred Robinson and Susan Hill lived together for 11 years. Beginning in 1983, Susan made a number of efforts to leave Robinson, but he always forced her to return. On June 8, 1987, Robinson believed that Susan was staying in Yuma with her parents, Ralph and Sterleen Hill. Robinson persuaded his friends, Jimmy Mathers and Theodore Washington, to go to Yuma with him, telling them that they were going to rip off a drug dealer. The three men loaded Robinson's car with weapons and drove to Yuma. They arrived at the Hills' home around midnight. Mathers and Washington entered the house, forced Mr. and Mrs. Hill to lie down on their bedroom floor and tied them up. The men demanded money and Washington went through the Hills' belongings. Mathers then fired his shotgun into the backs of the Hills. Sterleen Hill died from her wounds but Ralph Hill survived.

Start of Trial: December 1, 1987
Verdict: December 15, 1987
Sentencing: January 13, 1988

●●●

Waterhouse, Robert	Florida	M	W	1
Waters, Eurus	Georgia	M	W	
Watkins, Ronald	Virginia	M	B	
Watkins, Johnny	Virginia	M	B	
Watkins, Darryl	Alabama	M	B	
Watson, Herbert	Pennsylvania	M	B	
Watson, Kevin	Ohio	M	B	
Watson, Willie	Louisiana	M	W	7-24-87
Way, Fred	Florida	M	W	
Waye, Alton	Virginia	M	B	
Weaver, William	Missouri	M	B	
Weaver, Ward Francis	California	M	W	
Webb, Freddie	Texas	M	B	
Webb, Dennis	California	M	W	
Webster, Larry	California	M	N	
Weeks, Varnell	Alabama	M	B	
Welcome, Herbert	Louisiana	M	B	
Weldon, Dana	South Carolina	M	B	1
Wells, Luther	Missouri	M	B	
Wesley, Ronald	Alabama	M	B	
West, Robert W.	Texas	M	W	
West, Steven	Tennessee	M	W	
West, Floyd	South Carolina	M	W	
West, Othie Lee	Mississippi	M	B	
West, Paul	Illinois	M	B	
West, Thomas	**Arizona**	**M**	**W**	

●●●

THOMAS PAUL WEST

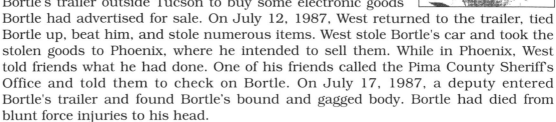

Race: Caucasian

Date of Birth: April 28, 1959

FACTS
On June 26, 1987, West and some friends went to Don Bortle's trailer outside Tucson to buy some electronic goods Bortle had advertised for sale. On July 12, 1987, West returned to the trailer, tied Bortle up, beat him, and stole numerous items. West stole Bortle's car and took the stolen goods to Phoenix, where he intended to sell them. While in Phoenix, West told friends what he had done. One of his friends called the Pima County Sheriff's Office and told them to check on Bortle. On July 17, 1987, a deputy entered Bortle's trailer and found Bortle's bound and gagged body. Bortle had died from blunt force injuries to his head.

Start of Trial: March 8, 1988
Verdict: March 17, 1988
Sentencing: August 1, 1988

•••

| **Westley, Anthony Ray** | **Texas** | **M** | **B** | |

•••

ANTHONY RAY WESTLY

FACTS.
Anthony Ray Westly, 25, was sentenced to die in 1986 for killing Chester Frank Hall, 38, during a 1984 robbery of Hall's bait shop. A second gunman in the robbery was killed and a third wounded.

•••

Wharton, Robert	Pennsylvania	M	B	
Wharton, George	California	M	B	
Wheat, Kenneth	Mississippi	M	W	1
Whisenhant, Thomas	Alabama	M	W	
White, Excell	Texas	M	W	
White, Larry Wayne	Texas	M	W	
White, Billy Wayne	Texas	M	B	
White, Derrick	Maryland	M	B	
White, Larry	Kentucky	M	B	1
White, Gene "Karu"	Kentucky	M	W	
White, Jerry	Florida	M	B	
White, William	Florida	M	W	
White, Michael	**Arizona**	**M**	**W**	

•••

MICHAEL R. WHITE

Death Row Inmates

Race: Caucasian

Date of Birth: October 10, 1951

FACTS

White and Susan Minter were lovers. Minter was also having a relationship with David Johnson, a miner from Bagdad. Minter and White decided to kill Johnson to collect on his life insurance policy, so in November of 1987, Minter married Johnson. She then had herself and her children named beneficiaries on the policy. On December 12, 1987, White waited outside Johnson's home for Johnson to return from work. Using a potato as a silencer, White shot Johnson with a .357 Magnum in the face and the back. Minter, who was inside the home, locked the doors and refused to let Johnson in as he called for help. Johnson died later that night. Minter was tried separately and convicted of first-degree murder. She received a life sentence.

Start of Trial: June 29, 1988
Verdict: July 14, 1988
Sentencing: August 8, 1988

White, Beauford	Florida	M	B	8-28-87
Whitehead, John	Illinois	M	W	
Whitley, Richard	Virginia	M	W	7-6-87
Whitmore, Jonas Hotan	Arkansas	M	W	
Whitney, Ray	Pennsylvania	M	B	
Whitt, Charles	California	M	W	
Wickham, Jerry	Florida	M	W	
Wickline, William	Ohio	M	W	
Wilcher, Bobby	Mississippi	M	W	
Wicker, Chester	Texas	M	W	8-26-86
Wilcoxson, Bobby	Tennessee	M	W	
Wiles, Mark Wayne	Ohio	M	W	
Wiley, William	Mississippi	M	B	
Wilhoit, Gregory	Oklahoma	M	W	
Wilkens, James Jay	Texas	M	W	
Wilkerson, Richard	Texas	M	B	
Wilkins, Heath	**Missouri**	**M**	**W**	**2**

HEATH WILKINS

FACTS

Heath Wilkins was sentenced to die for murdering Nancy Allen, a liquor store clerk, during a 1985 robbery. Allen, a 26-year-old mother of two, first was stabbed in the chest and back, then, as she pleaded for mercy, was stabbed four times in the throat by Wilkins. Wilkins, who was 16 when he killed Allen, was one of those whose cases were involved in the recent U.S. Supreme Court ruling permitting execution of killers as young as 16.

Death Row Inmates

Wille, John Francis	Louisiana	M	W	
Williams, Anthony	Texas	M	B	5-28-87
Williams, Terry	Virginia	M	B	
Williams, Robert Wayne	Louisiana	M	B	12-14-83
Williams, Toby Lynn	Texas	M	B	
Williams, Arthur Lee	Texas	M	B	
Williams, Walter Key	Texas	M	B	
Williams, Willie Ray	Texas	M	B	
Williams, Calvin Joseph	Texas	M	B	
Williams, James C.	Texas	M	B	
Williams, Terrance	Pennsylvania	M	B	
Williams, Craig	Pennsylvania	M	B	
Williams, Kenneth	Pennsylvania	M	W	
Williams, Ronald	Pennsylvania	M	B	
Williams, Melvin	Oklahoma	M	N	
Williams, Donald	Ohio	M	B	
Williams, Lewis	Ohio	M	B	
Williams, Douglas	North Carolina	M	B	
Williams, Larry Darnel	North Carolina	M	B	
Williams, Cary	Nevada	M	B	
Williams, Robert	Nebraska	M	B	
Williams, Doyle	Missouri	M	W	
Williams, Jesse	Mississippi	M	W	
Williams, Dobie	Louisiana	M	B	
Williams, Darnell	Indiana	M	B	
Williams, Larry	Indiana	M	W	1
Williams, Dennis	Illinois	M	B	
Williams, Bennie	Illinois	M	B	
Williams, Hernando	Illinois	M	B	
Williams, Alexander	**Georgia**	**M**	**B**	**2**

••

ALEXANDER WILLIAMS

FACTS

Williams was 17 when he kidnaped, raped and murdered 16-year-old Aleta Carol Bunch in March 1986. Bunch, a high school junior and part-time model, was shot four times in the head and once in the chest.

••

Williams, Harold	Georgia	M	W
Williams, Andrew	Florida	M	B
Williams, Freddie Lee	Florida	M	B
Williams, Darren C.	California	M	B
Williams, Barry	California	M	B
Williams, Michael	California	M	W

Williams, Kenneth	California	M	B	
Williams, Stanley	California	M	B	
Williams, Keith	California	M	W	
Williams, Ronald Turney	**Arizona**	**M**	**W**	**3**

••

RONALD TURNEY WILLIAMS

Race: Caucasian

Date of Birth: April 4, 1943

FACTS
On the morning of March 12, 1981, Ronald Williams kicked in the front door of a home in Scottsdale and began to burglarize it. A short time later a neighbor, John V. Bunchek, went to the home to investigate. He confronted Williams and Williams killed Bunchek by shooting him in the chest. Williams fled and was apprehended 3 months later in New York City.

Start of Trial: November 28, 1983
Verdict: February 10, 1984
Sentencing: April 23, 1984

••

Williams, Roy	Alabama	M	W	1
Williamson, Robert	Oklahoma	M	W	
Williamson, Johnny	Florida	M	W	
Willie, Robert Lee	Louisiana	M	W	12-28-84
Willis, Ernest Ray	Texas	M	W	
Willis, James Earl	North Carolina	M	W	
Willis, Henry	Georgia	M	B	
Willis, Mose	California	M	B	
Willoughby, Mitchell	Kentucky	M	W	
Wills, Bobby Joe	Texas	M	B	2
Wilson, Zachary	Pennsylvania	M	B	
Wilson, Michael	North Carolina	M	W	
Wilson, Edward	Nevada	M	W	
Wilson, David Earl	Louisiana	M	B	
Wilson, Gregory	Kentucky	M	B	
Wilson, Willie	Georgia	M	B	
Wilson, Robert	California	M	W	
Wilson, Shepp	Alabama	M	B	
Wingo, Jimmy	Louisana	M	W	6-16-87
Wise, Joe	Virginia	M	B	
Wisehart, Mark	Indiana	M	W	
Witt, Johnny Paul	Floridia	M	W	3-6-85
Woodruff, David	Oklahoma	M	W	
Woods, Billy Joe	Texas	M	W	
Woods, David	Indiana	M	W	

Woods, Ronald	Florida	M	B	1
Woodward, Claude	Oklahoma	M	W	
Woodward, Paul	Mississippi	M	W	
Woolls, Randy	Texas	M	W	8-20-86
Woomer, Ronald	**South Carolina**	**M**	**W**	

RONALD WOOMER

FACTS.
Ronald "Rusty" Woomer was sentenced to die for the Feb. 19, 1979 murder of Della Louise Sellers. Sellers was killed during an eight hour crime spree that included three armed robberies, four murders, two rapes, a suicide by Woomer's accomplice, and a shotgun assault that cost a woman the bottom third of her face.

| **Woratzeck, William** | **Arizona** | **M** | **W** | **1** |

WILLIAM LYLE WORATZECK

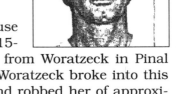

Race: Caucasian

Date of Birth: September 11, 1945

FACTS
Linda Louise Leslie was a 36-year-old woman who, because of Huntington's Chorea, had the mental capacity of a 15-year-old. She lived in a small sleeping room she rented from Woratzeck in Pinal County. On March 6, 1980, at approximately 2:30 a.m., Woratzeck broke into this room, strangled, stabbed and beat the victim to death, and robbed her of approximately $107. He then set the shed on fire.

Start of Trial: September 10, 1980
Verdict: September 15, 1980
Sentencing: November 10, 1980

Workman, Phillip	Tennessee	M	W
Workman, Wendell	Oklahoma	M	W
Wright, Charles	Tennessee	M	B
Wright, Patrick	Illinois	M	W
Wright, Mack Ray	Florida	M	B
Wright, Joel	Florida	M	W
Wright, Bronte	California	M	B
Wright, Freddie	Alabama	M	B
Wyle, James	Texas	M	B
Wynne, Carl	North Carolina	M	W

Yarris, Nicholas	Pennsylvania	M	W	
Yates, Dale Robert	South Carolina	M	W	
Ybarra, Robert	Nevada	M	H	
Young, John	Georgia	M	B	3-20-85
Young, Joseph	Pennsylvania	M	B	
Young, Moses	Missouri	M	B	
Young, William	Illinois	M	B	1
Young, David	Florida	M	B	
Zagorski, Edmund	Tennessee	M	W	
Zaragosa, Ruben	**Arizona**	**M**	**H**	

••

RUBEN C. ZARAGOZA

Race: Mexican-American

Date of Birth: March 2, 1946

FACTS
On May 26, 1981, Zaragoza encountered Winifred Duggan in downtown Phoenix. Mrs. Duggan was an elderly woman with very limited mental capabilities due to a lobotomy that she had undergone years before. Zaragoza apparently sexually assaulted her before bludgeoning her in the head with a wine bottle. He then left her in an alley to bleed to death.

Start of Trial: September 22, 1981
Verdict: September 28, 1981
Sentencing: October 26, 1981

••

Zeigler, William	Florida	M	W	1
Zeitvogel, Richard	Missouri	M	W	
Zerquera, Jorge	Florida	M	H	
Zettlemoyer, Keith	Pennsylvania	M	W	
Zola, James E.	New Jersey	M	W	1
Zuern, William	Ohio	M	W	
Zuniga, Bernardino	North Carolina	M	H	